Cocktail Investing

Cocktail Investing

Distilling Everyday Noise into Clear Investment Signals for Better Returns

Christopher J. Versace
Lenore Elle Hawkins

WILEY

Published by John Wiley & Sons, Inc., Hoboken, New Jersey.
Published simultaneously in Canada.

For general information on our other products and services or for technical support, please contact our Customer Care Department within the United States at (800) 762–2974, outside the United States at (317) 572–3993 or fax (317) 572–4002.

Wiley publishes in a variety of print and electronic formats and by print-on-demand. Some material included with standard print versions of this book may not be included in e-books or in print-on-demand. If this book refers to media such as a CD or DVD that is not included in the version you purchased, you may download this material at http://booksupport.wiley.com. For more information about Wiley products, visit www.wiley.com.

Library of Congress Cataloging-in-Publication Data is available:

ISBN 9781119003946 (Hardcover)
ISBN 9781119004103 (ePDF)
ISBN 9781119004059 (ePub)

Cover Design: Michael J. Freeland
Cover Images: glass © iStock.com/cc-stock; olive © iStock.com/AndrewJohnson

10 9 8 7 6 5 4 3 2 1

I'd like to dedicate this book to my family and friends that have been so helpful and supportive on my journey, as well as to all the fledgling investors that are just getting started on their investing path.

— Chris

To Marco, Cat, Emmy, Kimberly, Bill, Sara, Tom, Sheila, Jordan, Sharron, Karen, Jaime, and Mom for helping me laugh, maintaining my sanity, and pouring the occasional vino when it was needed most. Not only do you all inspire me to aim higher every day, but your love makes the joys of life all the sweeter and the struggles easier to bear.

— Lenore

Contents

Preface

A man must defend his home, his wife, his children and his martini.
— *Jackie Gleason*

Happiness is … finding two olives in your martini when you're hungry.
— *Johnny Carson*

My focus sharpened as I ascended the steps to the presentation platform. I may have some generous delusions about myself, but I am pretty clear that seeing me trip backside-over-tea-kettle in a skirt and stilettos when trying to mount the all-of-five steps up to the stage where the other panelists were sitting would not exactly give the audience the image of a highly competent woman I'd like to convey.

Hating to be the first to speak, I always try to sit farthest from the moderator in the hope that he or she will get to me later on and give me a chance to come up with something funny or memorable in response to what another panelist has stated with total conviction: my inner–Conference Katniss gets competitive. Damn it, though, some guy with a cocksure grin had taken the spot I covet. I grumbled internally and took the seat next to him. Nonchalant chit-chat ensued, as usual, between the panelists as we waited for the presentation hall to fill. In my Katniss-mind, this lull before the action is akin to that of the Roman gladiators prior to their entrance into the Coliseum. With my usual level of pre–public speaking adrenaline flowing, the reality that the average fitness level of those of us on stage was somewhere around that of *The Big Bang Theory*'s Sheldon Cooper was irrelevant.

Finally, the hall was sufficiently full and the moderator asked us to take our seats on stage. He grabbed his microphone and introduced us Investment Gladiators with a *Cliff's Notes* version of our respective resumes, giving each of us the opportunity to try and smile wisely to the crowd and offer appropriate glances of modesty ... as if we hadn't sent those bios in ourselves. A bit of throat clearing and water sipping followed. I haven't yet met a speaker at one of these things who isn't secretly at least a little nervous that when he or she first opens their mouth, their voice will come out sounding squeaky like a boy in the tumult of pre-pubescence.

The moderator thankfully began with the gentleman seated immediately to his left, who launched into a clearly well-practiced diatribe, painfully monotone, on his favorite asset class, with a series of statistics and proclamations, clearly intended to exact awe as to his technical prowess and engender confidence in his ability to read through all that analysis to find the "truth." All of us on that stage seek to be useful truth tellers, financial diviners in suits, toting iPads.

As the first panelist gets momentum going in his spiel, Mr. Seat Stealer to my left slid an innocuous sheet of paper with some rough scrawls on it toward me. I glanced down, as I nodded my head, hopefully sagely, along with the speaker's various points. The scratchy text read, "Has he taken a single breath yet?" I barely managed to suppress an entirely undignified giggle, face flushing a telltale pink as I was painfully aware of the some thousand or so individual investors watching us all on stage. Those in the audience giving us their time are each hoping that if they pay attention and focus hard enough, they'll learn "The Secret" that will give them the ability to invest safely and successfully—or at least learn a few "hot" stock tips that they can "ride to big profits." Who doesn't want that? They deserved my utmost attention and A-level effort, but I'm a sucker for an irreverent sense of humor, and speaker #1's droning was like a high-powered Unisom.

With brows furrowed in an attempt to appear as though I was taking thoughtful notes, I quickly jotted back, "My yawn is just a silent scream for coffee." SS stifles a laugh and writes back, "So I've been wondering what my dogs have named me." I responded with, "I have a suspicion that my inner child is never moving out." So began a friendship and eventually a partnership that has spanned years, continents, oceans, and eventually led to the writing of this book.

The truth about investing and the markets is that no one knows where the market is going to close today, this week, this month, or this year. No one. People can come up with all kinds of fancy models that arguably have some value, but the truth is it is a guess. It may be a well-thought-out guess, an educated guess, a mathematically beautiful and sound guess, but at the end of the day it is still a guess. When you run across anyone who tells you differently, be careful. Also, be careful of the talking heads on TV who speak with such confidence about the direction of the market or a particular company within a specific time frame. There are some talking heads that are more than helpful, offering up helpful insights and data points, but there are also those that gloss over details and focus on less than helpful and in some cases outdated indicators. Look below the headline and do a little research of your own. It isn't nearly as tough as it sounds, and we can show how fun it really can be! Also realize the more supporting data you have, the more clear the investing picture will be and the better off you are going to be.

The heart of *Cocktail Investing* recognizes the intersection of several powerful forces—economics, demographics, psychographics, technology, policy, and more we will discuss—that, when combined, give way to a powerful force that shifts the *what, where*, and *how* people and businesses go about their daily activities. Much like a tailwind that pushes a plane faster across the United States or the Atlantic Ocean, these shifting forces can propel a company's business or slow it down dramatically if it is ill-prepared to deal with the changes it faces, much like a headwind. The great thing about these trends is that they are often evident in things you observe every day and arise in conversations you have with friends over cocktails—you just need to recognize them.

We wrote this book to give you a lens through which you will be able to clearly see the actionable, observable, and recognizable trends that surround you every day to help you build a profitable portfolio for the long run. Unlike most every other book on investing, though, this book is written the way most people like to learn, with stories that you will find (we hope) not only informative but entertaining and relatable.

We will give you **a process that will allow you to successfully build and maintain a portfolio** and avoid the all-too-common errors caused by emotional investing. Thinking like a successful investor will become as routine as tying your shoes, and before you know it, you'll be walking through the mall making mental notes of the must-have items and the hot retailer, all without stepping foot inside a store.

We also wrote this book in such a way as to **allow you to quickly get to the heart of the material**, avoiding the majority of the related stories, although you're missing out on some serious entertainment, but we might be slightly biased here. If you want to read just the bones, avoid the areas in gray. Don't worry, we only have one shade of gray in this book. We've also written up chapter summaries that highlight the key points and finish every chapter with a Bottom Line section to call out key concepts.

We will talk about how to find specific investments, but we will not talk about theories on what combinations of investments you ought to have in your portfolio, as that is highly dependent on each individual's circumstance. That being said, here are a few **good rules of thumb** to keep in mind as you build an investment portfolio:

- Your portfolio should **never have more than 5 percent invested in one security** (e.g., a stock, bond, mutual fund, or ETF). You can give yourself a little more room if you are dealing with a widely diversified mutual fund or ETF, meaning one that holds a lot of individual securities. In practice, this usually means that you'll want to buy less than 5 percent of any one security; otherwise, if it goes up disproportionately relative to the rest of your portfolio, you'll need to sell some more quickly than would likely be prudent given the current tax code's treatment of long-term gains versus short-term gains.
- Before you start buying securities for your portfolio, decide **how much cash you need to keep on hand**. You should have at least three months' worth of your typical living expenses on hand in case of an emergency. If your primary source of income is unpredictable and/or volatile, you should have more. You've probably heard people

talk about need for liquidity, a term that is widely bandied about and often misunderstood. We'll talk more about what it means, how to figure out just how liquid a security may be, and why you care.

- Once you've identified a security you want to add into your portfolio, you need to decide **if you should buy then and there or hold off doing so. If it's time to buy that security, how should you do so, up to what price should you buy, at what price would you back up the truck and buy more, and later when the time is right, how should you sell it?** We'll cover how these decisions can be even more important than deciding what to buy.

- Finally, when it comes to your portfolio, **be cold-blooded**. Fall in love with your partner, a song, a good book, a gorgeous sunset, or luscious Bordeaux, but never, ever with one of your investment picks. We'll talk about ways to stay cool as a cucumber, even when the markets get wobbly.

So without further ado, let's talk about one of the most emotionally charged words in the world—*Money*.

Acknowledgments

From Chris: Sitting down to put fingers to keyboard and write the volume you have before you would not have been possible were it not for the education, learnings, and conversations that helped develop the thematic way I look at the world. As you might imagine, the list is far from short, but also like any list, there are several central figures worth noting. These include David Snyder, Dr. Phil Lane, and Dr. Ben Fine, who had an influential hand from the very beginning; friends and compatriots Keith Bliss, Mike Canevaro, Brian Vosburgh, and Chris Broussard; Dr. Bernard McSherry, who wrangled me into the classroom and afforded me the opportunity to stun graduate and undergraduate students alike with my desk walking; A.J. Rice, without whom my time on the radio and elsewhere with people such as John McCaslin, Matt Ray, Chris Salcedo, Melanie Morgan, and others would never have happened; and Stephanie Link, who welcomed me to The Street and allowed me to work with folks like Bob Lang, Kamal Khan, Paul Curcio, and many other wonderful people, including Jim Cramer, who has been nothing but encouraging and enthusiastic as my role at The Street has grown over the years.

From Lenore: This book would not have been possible without the insights gained from conversations with some of the most truly spectacular economic, investing, and scientific minds I've had the pleasure of getting to know. I'd specifically like to thank Raoul Pal, not only for sharing your brilliance, but for assuring me that I had something worthwhile to say in my moments of greatest frustration; Grant Williams for your uniquely humorous insights; Richard Rahn for everything as there is just too much to list; Dan Mitchell for showing me how to make even tax policy positively riveting to your audience; Tom Palmer for enlightening me in countless ways; David Abner for getting me started in this direction; Peter Whybrow for showing me how to make even the most complex understandable and entertaining; Ed Crane, you are an endless inspiration; Alessandro Dusi, what would I do without you? Michael Cannon, you've taught me to never give up. Finally, thank you to Eric Spinato for helping me evolve from those first truly cringe-worthy television appearances, which helped open the doors that led to the eventual writing of this book.

Chapter 1

Money

Cash, *bread, dough, greenbacks, loot, moola, scratch, wampum, soldi, dinero, l'argent, geld, penge, dinheiro* …

No matter what language, *money* is a simple word that, if you aren't careful, can cause you a lot of problems. If not you, then chances are, a family member or a close friend has struggled with it.

It's a word that can make people very uncomfortable. How many times have you been in a group when everyone gets that awkward no-eye-contact nervousness because someone (*gasp*) mentioned "money"?

1

Some abhor it as a dirty word; some worship it as the purpose of life. For one of your authors it means the latest Apple tech joy, climbing an adventure course, adding to his Under Armour "collection," or streaming the latest Marvel series or other must-watch program on Netflix or Amazon Prime as he rockets to New Jersey from just outside of Washington, D.C., while for your other it sure helps with her obsessions: travel, power tools (working on those Bob Vila skills), the latest new tech toy, stilettos, wine, and photography equipment (hoping her talent will eventually catch up with the equipment).

Some have a lot of it and some purposefully eschew it, but the bottom line—and that is what our book is all about—is we *all* need it.

Whether it's to put food on the table, buy the latest whiz-bang device, which neither one of us can resist, or clothes for that soon-to-be-tween who is growing like a cornstalk on steroids, or simply to buy a great bottle of wine to celebrate that it's Tuesday and life is good, let alone to save for your golden years or to pay down the debt that's already been rung up, money is required both for the necessities and for having options: the "need to haves" and "want to haves."

Without it, you may find yourself forced into a situation you would desperately like to avoid, like Bob.

Have you met Bob?

On an unusually chilly day in San Diego, Lenore was rushing into her local UPS store in Del Mar when she essentially body-slammed into a rather strikingly handsome (her description), silver-haired gentleman who was rushing out with equal ferocity, sporting a scowl that would have made even the Dalai Lama take a step back. A shroud of sadness and anger seemed to emanate from his very being.

She apologized profusely to him for her clumsiness, something for which she has had a great deal of practice, to which he responded with an eloquent, "*Harumph.*" Undaunted, Lenore was determined to get a smile out of this guy.

"After making you drop so many things, the least I could do is buy you a cup of coffee or tea?"

Silver-hair looked straight at Lenore like she was speaking Klingon, followed by a long, awkward silence. Her stubborn streak kicked in and she summoned up her best smile for him, trying to channel a Julia Roberts grin. He either decided he didn't have the energy to fight her or was so thrown he couldn't come up with something to help him escape and mumbled what sounded vaguely like "OK."

"Oh good! I could clearly use a few minutes to slow down. Thank you," she said, and off they walked to the Starbucks next door. More precisely, Lenore walked and Silver-hair, whose name turned out to be Bob, followed begrudgingly.

After an excruciatingly awkward five minutes of ordering and making feeble attempts at smalltalk while they waited for their white-and-green paper cups of warm magic to appear on the counter, they took a seat at a little table by the window. Lenore apologized again for running into him and told him how she was rushing around because she was flying back to Italy the following week, explaining how she ended up living a life on two continents after her father died, then getting a divorce and very much needing to escape the sadness of it all. Normally, Lenore never shares that level of personal detail with someone she has just met, but for some reason the gift of her Irish genes took over and her mouth took on a life of its own.

Eventually, after a torrential river of words flowed from her mouth, the need to take a breath kicked in. Wondering if perhaps she had overshared, Lenore took a long sip of piping hot pumpkin latte (seriously, Starbucks, why not offer it *all* year?).

Without warning, frustrated words started awkwardly tumbling out of Bob's mouth, and Lenore learned that his wife, Beth, had recently passed away. The cost of her medical care had destroyed much of their life's savings, which Bob had a hard time understanding, as he thought he had been so careful that he'd not even ventured near the stock market. On top of that, two of his three children were not even speaking to him because he had started dating his neighbor, Madeleine. Lenore got the distinct impression that Bob's wife hadn't particularly cared for Madeleine, which must have made for some painful family get-togethers.

As he continued to talk, Bob jumped back and forth between expressing frustration over his financial affairs, the anguish he felt now that he was having to move in with his daughter, Sophia, who'd recently gone through a divorce herself, the delight at having found a woman who could make him laugh despite all his troubles and sadness, and anger at his other children for resenting his new relationship. When he finished, he stared down at his cup, fidgeting nervously with its plastic lid.

Lenore could see he had the same, "Have I overshared?" look on his face, so she told him about how after her father's death, his side of the family had imploded with relationships permanently damaged at a time when she thought the family would have and should have been closer than ever.

Sensing his troubles, Lenore offered, "My firm does investment management for families, so maybe we could help you sort through your finances and figure out where to go from here. It would help me feel better about having nearly knocked you into that wall!"

They set a date and Bob suggested that perhaps Lenore could talk to his daughter, Sophia, who was struggling with pretty much everything as her divorce was finalizing. As they finished their respective beverages, Lenore suggested that Bob have Sophia call her, and they went their separate ways.

In our collective experience, we've seen that money can be a lot like love. It can be heaven, or it can be hell.

While we could ask you about money, odds are you would have a pretty good idea of just what that stuff in your wallet is and how it's used. Maybe not the history and legacy of it and you may not be fine-tuned on the inner workings of monetary policy, but when it comes to the functional use we're pretty sure you've figured it out. You did buy this book after all.

We think a much better question to ask you is, "Do you think you have enough money … enough saved … enough invested for what is to come? If you think you do, how do you know?"

Savings and Debt

Bob thought he'd been exceptionally responsible. He'd put funds away every month for most of his adult life and proudly avoided investing in the stock market, believing his friends who did were essentially gambling. He's not alone in that. In Italy, the older generations do not even refer to investing in stock and bonds with the proper translation, "*investire in borsa,*" but rather more often use the term, "*giocare in borsa,*" which literally means "gambling on the stock exchange."

Even if you think you have it covered, the harsh reality is that many of us, like Bob, simply may not be as prepared as we think. Even for those who have been saving for a long time and are ahead of the 31 percent of U.S. adults who have no savings or pension plan,[1] it may not be enough. According to Bankrate.com, even 46 percent of the highest-income households ($75,000+ per year) and 52 percent of college graduates lack enough savings to cover a $500 car repair or $1,000 emergency room visit.[2] Did you know the cost of raising a child through the age of 18 in either the United States or Canada is more than $240,000?!? In the United Kingdom, that number is $342,000.[3] A recent report by AMP and the National Centre for Social and Economic Modeling in Australia found that the cost of raising two children to the age of 21 in that country rose more than 50 percent between 2007 and 2013 is now about $720,000. No wonder people are having fewer and fewer kids in the Western world!

And it can be more, a lot more. Those are only the averages!

We'd point out that excludes the cost of college, let alone if they get into an Ivy League! According to the College Board, a "moderate" college budget for an in-state public college for the 2013–2014 academic year averaged $22,826, while a moderate budget at a private college averaged $44,750. Some quick math puts that four-year cost between $91,000 and $180,000, but that's just the education part—room, board, and other items are extra. That's a pretty penny if you only have one child; if you have two or more children, it could easily cost over $1 million to raise them into their early twenties.

Trust us, you are not alone in looking at that cost.

According to the Consumer Financial Protection Bureau (CFPB), more than 40 million Americans are working to repay more than $1.2 trillion in outstanding student loan debt, and we're sorry to say the conventional wisdom on this is wrong in the United States. What's the conventional wisdom, you ask? Well, the herd (we'll have more on who that is and why they tend to miss what's really going on later) view is that all these people struggling to pay off student loans are young people, primarily recent college graduates.

They're not.

A report by the New York Federal Reserve showed that in 2012, the last year for which there are records, 4.7 million people who owe money on student loans are between the ages of 50 and 59. Perhaps more of a surprise—2.2 million are age 60 and older!

Is it hard to fathom then that 40 percent of Americans past the age of 45 said they had thought "only a little" or "not at all" about financial planning for retirement? No—lest you think we are making it up, that was revealed in a 2014 Federal Reserve Board study.

According to the OECD (Organization for Economic Co-Operation and Development), the ratio of household debt to income in the Eurozone has gone from 77.2 percent in 2002 to 97 percent in 2013. In Italy, this ratio has risen from 37.7 percent to 65.8 percent in 2012; but that isn't nearly as bad as in Spain where debt has gone from 79.3 percent of household income to 122.9 percent by 2012. In the United States, in 2000 this same ratio was about 90 percent. It peaked at 133.6 percent in the fourth quarter of 2007 (no surprise, given all those crazy 0-percent-down mortgages being handed out left and right, coupled with the home equity credit lines that became ATMs for many) but has improved to now be about 108 percent by 2015.

For argument's sake, let's say that you've been a diligent person and you're socking some of your after-tax dollars every month as best you can, to chip away at that looming cost.

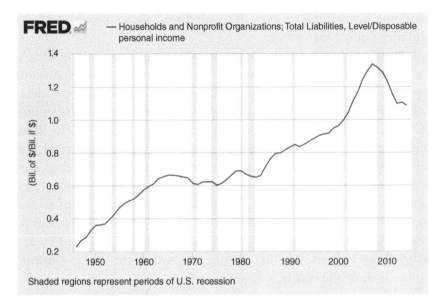

Figure 1.1 Total liabilities to disposable income* ratio for households and non-profit organizations

*Disposable personal income is total personal income less personal income taxes.

SOURCE: St. Louis Federal Reserve

If at this point you understand that you will need to invest to ensure you meet your financial goals, you can skip to Chapter 2; just be sure to check the summary located at the end of this chapter.

State of Savings in the United States

If you are a data lover like us and want to know more about just how startlingly dire the situation may become, read on. We really geek out on the stats in this next section.

Congratulations!

We say that because saving money is a good thing, despite what the elected officials in Washington, D.C., would have you believe in our consumer-driven economy. How often have you heard how we need to get consumers spending? It's as if the key to a successful economy is to spend every dime you make, and then borrow some more! As thrilled as we are that you are taking steps forward, the reality is if that's all you are doing, then you have a much tougher road ahead of you—and one you may not see the end of.

There are two other big concerns that most people face. One is being able to afford the level of care required as you get older. According to a Harris Poll, nearly three quarters (74 percent) of respondents said they worry about having enough money to retire and two-thirds (67 percent) of respondents said they worry about being able to afford unexpected healthcare costs.[4] Among those who are not yet retired, 7 in 10 worry about being able to pay for their healthcare costs when they retire. And worried is exactly what the findings of Age Wave, a think tank that specializes on aging, say you should do, because out-of-pocket healthcare costs in retirement may equal $318,800 if retirement lasts 30 years; $220,600 for 25 years; $146,400 for 20 years; $91,200 for 15 years; $50,900 for 10 years. And in case you were wondering, these estimates do not include the cost of long-term care.

And that brings us to the next big concern—the really big concern—having enough saved and invested to actually retire. Three-quarters of U.S. adults who are not yet retired say they worry about having enough money to retire, and 70 percent say planning for retirement is a key priority to them. One thing those still in the workforce are not planning to use is Social Security—only about a third say they have faith in Social Security being there when they retire. If you have such concerns, or even if you don't, we would suggest you point your web browser at USDebtClock.org to better understand the country's mounting debt and how much is attributed to entitlements such as Medicare, Medicaid, and Social Security. Perhaps Social Security will be around when you retire, but we would hate for you to be banking on that only to find out the program was significantly altered when it was your turn to collect.

Pundits say you will need 60 to 85 percent of your gross household income today to sustain the same lifestyle after you retire. A different perspective from Fidelity Investments says that, depending on factors such as your ability to save, your starting age to save, and retirement age, you'll need eight times your ending salary. Data from Sentier Research recently pegged average household income at $53,891; for reference, that is still 4.8 percent lower than it was at the start of the Great Recession in December 2007. If your ending salary was in that range, then at minimum you would need another $430,000 on top of the amount you would need to fund education needs and healthcare concerns. Odds are, however, that would not be enough given the impact of inflation, which saps the purchasing power of your saved dollars. If you are the sole bread-winner in the family, that means eight times your ending salary needs to be stretched even further—perhaps you need to be saving more than you think?

This is hardly an outrageous thought when you consider that these figures are the *averages*. Depending on your current lifestyle or the one you aspire to have, it could mean needing far more than that. For others who are earning below the median income, and per data from the Social Security Administration, roughly 50 percent of American wage earners fall into that camp, while 47 million receive food stamps and 47 million live in poverty, it means having to close an even bigger gap.

We've already mentioned inflation and how it cuts into purchasing power. Ask any retired person living on a fixed income how much beef they've been eating over the last year or two, given the more than 50 percent increase in beef prices! The same goes for the other parts of the protein complex: pork, chicken, dairy products, coffee, and more. As the standard of living improves across the globe, it means there will be more mouths looking for the same foods that you've enjoyed. Not a bad thing (do you really think others should *not* be allowed to enjoy chocolate or a nice cup of coffee in the morning?), but simple laws of supply and demand tell us that if global demand is climbing past a certain point, then supply is constrained and prices will rise. This is particularly true of the more complex proteins like beef. It takes a lot of feed to produce just one pound of beef versus the relatively smaller amounts required to produce one pound of fish.

Another easy factor to observe is that we are simply living longer lives.

If you don't see that when you are out and about in your daily lives—well we've got some data to share with you. According to a report from the Stanford Center on Longevity (SCL), in 1950 a 65-year-old man could expect to live to age 78, or an additional 13 years. By 2010, a man age 65 could expect to live to age 82, or 17 years longer. A woman age 65 in 1950 could expect to live another 15 years, to age 80, but by 2010 her life expectancy was 84.

The same report shows that the average length of retirement in 1950 was 8 years for men, increasing to 19 years by 2010. This is due to the combination of earlier retirement ages and longer life expectancies. (There are no comparable figures for women, since women didn't enter the paid workforce in substantial numbers until the 1970s.)

Another SCL report shows that the percentage of older employees in the workforce is back on the upswing. In 1950, 45 percent of men age 65 and older were still working. This percentage declined to about 15 percent by 1990, but increased slowly to about 22 percent by 2010. (It's worth noting that this figure encompasses all men over age 65, including men in their 80s and 90s. The percentages of men working in their late 60s and early 70s are much higher.)

Another important difference between then and now is that in 1950, retirement hadn't yet been glamorized by the media as the "golden years," an extended period of travel and recreation. Most retirees didn't retire to pursue their hobbies and interests—rather, they stopped working because they were unable to continue. After retirement, they lived simply and modestly in the communities where they had worked and lived all their lives. And it bears repeating, the average length of retirement today is far longer than it was several years ago. The rise in the standards of living has been a blessing, of course, but it also has been accompanied by a rise in expectations—expectations that require a lot more funds to fulfill than in years past.

According to the Administration on Aging (yes, there is such an institution, and it can be found at www.aoa.gov), by the end of 2009 (that latest year for which data are available), persons 65 years or older numbered 39.6 million, roughly 13 percent of the U.S. population, or one in every eight Americans. By 2030, the AOA estimates there will be about 72.1 million older persons, more than twice the number in 2000. Keep in mind, the current domestic population according to the U.S. Census is 319 million people and some simple math tells us that as the number of retirees more than doubles from the current 48 million, we will be facing a retirement crisis.

Living longer lives is not a new concept. When we trace back to 1900, we find the percentage of Americans 65+ has more than tripled (from 4.1 percent in 1900 to 12.9 percent by 2009). In looking at the data, it becomes clear that it's not just more people who are

65+, but the population cohort itself is living longer. In 2008, the 65–74 age group (20.8 million) was 9.5 times larger than in 1900, while the 75–84 group (13.1 million) was 17 times larger and the 85+ group (5.6 million) was 46 times larger. This really put the data into perspective for us: A child born in 2007 could expect to live 77.9 years, about 30 years longer than a child born in 1900.

As a result of increasing longevity and the decline in the average number of children people are having, the domestic population is skewing older. That pace began to accelerate even further in 2011, when the Baby Boomer generation (those born between January 1, 1946, and December 31, 1964) started turning 65. Beginning January 1, 2011, every single day more than 10,000 Baby Boomers will reach the age of 65. That is going to keep happening every single day for the next 19 years and will add roughly 70 million to the 65+ category.

But what if you're a few decades or more away from entering your Golden Years and are a member of Generation X?

If you were born between the early 1960s and the early 1980s, then you're probably between the ages of 33 and 53 years old. Even more likely, between 2007 and 2010, you saw a drop in your wealth coming out of the Great Recession. Perhaps you lost your job for a while or thought you were going to … maybe you were one of the lucky ones who didn't have those concerns, but if you did, it meant falling behind in your savings and investing efforts. Unlike those at or near the door of retirement, Gen-Xers as well as Millennials (if you were born between the early 1980s and early 2000s) have time on their side when it comes to saving and investing for their retirement and other life goals.

Despite the time factor that affords the power of compound investing, more Millennials have opted to choose cash as their favorite long-term investment than any other age group, according to a new Bankrate.com. Per that report, 39 percent of Millennials surveyed said cash was their preferred way to invest money they don't need for at least 10 years—that was three times the number who picked the stock market.

The eschewing of the stock market by Millennials is likely to prove a costly mistake and raises the question as to where and how you are building your nest egg. If you are a diligent saver and have been putting money in the bank, the returns you are getting given the low interest rate environment won't help you much. **Simply saving in a bank account is not going to get you where you need to be for an eventual retirement.** Over the last few years, the Federal Reserve's easy money polices and artificially low interest rates have left you earning next to nothing in your savings accounts or with CDs. The Fed has begun raising interest rates again, but even if we get back to average interest rates on savings accounts and CDs, they will barely put a dent in the amount you'll need over the course of your life.

The Rules Have Changed

Consider that if you put away $250 per month over a period of 30 years in a savings account, you will probably end up with something around $145,000. If you could only sock that much away each month for a period of 20 years, you would have more like $82,000. As you can imagine, if you only had 10 years of saving like that, you would have even far less.

How would you feel upon realizing that you didn't prepare sufficiently—and by that we mean save and invest properly and you had to alter your lifestyle when you finally retire? Think that's far-fetched? A survey conducted by The American Association of Retired People (AARP) found that 60 percent of New Yorkers over the age of 50 said they were likely to go somewhere else in retirement. The same survey found 40 percent worried about paying rent or mortgages, 56 percent were extremely or very worried about paying property taxes, 51 percent worried about utility bills and most were looking for improvements in healthcare, housing, transportation, and jobs for older residents.

The bottom line is you need to grow your savings in order to meet the money needs you will have. In our view, one of the best if not the best way to achieve this is through investing in the stock market, but we need to warn you that the rules of investing have changed.

Although 2013 was a banner year for the stock market with the S&P 500 up more than 32 percent and 2014 saw the index rise another 11.4 percent, a longer view shows that the 15-year total return as of October 31, 2015, for the S&P 500 was less than 3 percent (see Figure 1.2).

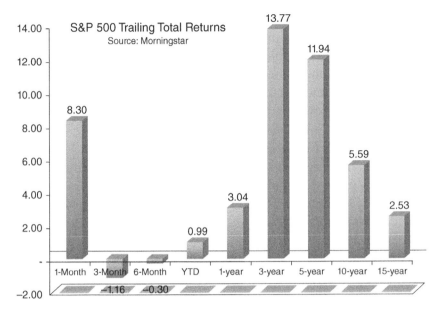

Figure 1.2   S&P 500 trailing total returns as of October 31, 2015
SOURCE: Morningstar

Whether you are a mutual fund manager, hedge fund fat cat, or Wall Street trader, buy-and-sleep investing is over. As we have said many a time, whether it is when giving presentations at the MoneyShow, or speaking to groups at various American Association of Individual Investor chapters or at other conferences, gone are the days when you could buy a stock, an exchange-traded fund (ETF), or mutual fund and, much like crockpot cooking, forget about it until you are ready.

You don't have to be an aggressive trader—frankly, few can do that successfully for any sustained period of time—but, rather, you must be a proactive investor, and that means regularly updating your investment thesis, knowing how to weed through the heaps and heaps of information out there, and when necessary, jettisoning a position that is no longer viable. That in turn means knowing where and when to reinvest.

Given today's fast-paced world of tweets, texts, and barely-scratching-the-surface news reporting inside an ever-increasing deluge of information, the average individual investor faces the ever-growing challenge of having to cut through the clutter and decipher what it means ... to understand how, where, and why they should be investing given the current environment and what lies ahead.

That means being able to read the economy like a professional investor, filtering out all the useless and misleading data, recognizing the investable signals, and identifying which company or companies stand to benefit. It also means identifying both cyclical and structural changes—like the Internet, mobility, social media, and other forces that have drastically altered business models. Think about Blockbuster Video, any record label, Borders bookstores, Circuit City, or Palm computing. They all faced a shift in their industries that they were not prepared for and where did it leave them, a footnote in business history. Psychographics (the *how*, *where*, and *on what* both people and companies are spending) and demographic trends (the evolving political landscape and significant regulatory implications) need to be understood in order to grow and protect your life's savings. This may sound overwhelming, but there is a way to stay focused on just those things that truly matter.

We mentioned several pain points earlier that have arisen from our living longer lives, but there are others such as the growing water crisis, the explosion in the depth and frequency of cyberattacks, severe swings in key input costs and commodities such as corn, wheat, coffee, beef, and other parts of the protein complex, and that's just getting started. As you'll see in Chapter 7, we love pain-point investing because it creates a situation that screams for a solution. An investor who is able to identify a company situated to fill that need can profit bigtime.

While any one of these factors can lead to a good investment, the intersection of these factors leads to waves of changes that companies must contend with—some will capitalize on them while others will be left behind.

The essence of *Cocktail Investing* recognizes the intersection of several powerful forces—economics, demographics, psychographics, technology, policy, and more—that, when combined, give way to a powerful force that shifts the *what*, *where* and *how* people and businesses are going about their daily activities. At the very core of these uber-catalysts, companies, be they business-to-business (B2B) or business-to-consumer (B2C), need to respond to the changing landscape and adapt their business models. If they don't, odds are they will shift from a once-thriving business to one that is struggling and likely to be left behind and replaced by others. Think of the transformation and rise in the share price at Apple post iPod, iTunes (its payment processing content engine), iPhone, and iPad compared to the fall of BlackBerry and its shares after the iPhone. One could argue these waves of transformation are affecting how and where future generations will be educated.

As we'll talk about in the coming pages, buy-and-sleep investing in the stock market won't help you, either. You need to have at least some of your assets in growth and that's true even after you retire.

No matter how you look at it, not only do you have to save but you have to be an active investor to get the most from your money and get the life you want, be it debt free or kicking back in the lifestyle you want in your golden years. In many ways, what we're saying is rather similar to what hockey legend Wayne Gretzky has said is one of the secrets of his success—knowing that he needed to be where the puck was going … he had to get ahead of it and all the other players that were simply following it. The same holds true for investors.

Inherent in that statement, which we suspect you subscribe to, is being able to decipher from all the noise that is out there and putting the pieces of the puzzle together to identify the companies that are best positioned for what lies ahead, while sidestepping the pretenders and those that will be left behind.

If you are an experienced investor, you may be formulating a plan of attack using the pain points we've identified in this chapter as a way of screening potential stock positions. There is no doubt the aging of the population gives rise to opportunities for healthcare companies, end-of-life-care companies, asset managers, and online investing platforms, as well as others. As you'll see, we'll be sharing techniques and procedures to help you identify the better positioned companies and how to determine which may be better for you—shares in a 9 percent dividend paying company or one whose shares are trading at a 30 percent discount to its price to earnings growth ratio?

Cocktail Investing Bottom Line

The economic climate has changed dramatically. The much-heralded savings and investing practices of past decades are no longer delivering the expected results. Frustration and even rage are evident across society as families look at the current state of their finances. The nation is facing a veritable crisis, as a significant portion of the population has not and is still not saving sufficiently or investing effectively, which will impact even those who have the good fortune to be otherwise well prepared. We present an accessible, alternative way to look at investing in a style that is enjoyable to read, exciting the mind as well as touching the heart.

At a time when people are living longer, many are increasingly concerned that they will not have enough money to last during their retirement years. According to data published by Fidelity Investments, the average 401(k) balance at the end of March 2014 stood at $88,600. This means that average investors will likely fall short in saving for their retirement unless they take a more active and informed role in saving and investing for their golden years.

- Whether you are raising children, saving for retirement, concerned over living a longer healthy life, or trying to make the most of your education let alone put food on the table and make ends meet, you need money.
- You can only work so many hours in a day and so many days in a week, and that means you need to make sure your money is working for you.
- Saving is a step in the right direction, but to grow your money over time in order to achieve your goals, you will need to invest to get the most from your money and get the life you want, be it debt free or enjoying the lifestyle you want in your golden years.
- Buy-and-sleep investing is over, and you need to be an active investor who is taking note of the ever-shifting series of landscapes.
- *Cocktail Investing* recognizes pain points as well as opportunities that arise from the intersection of several powerful forces—economics, demographics, psychographics, technology, policy, and others—that, when combined, give way to a powerful force that shifts the *what*, *where*, and *how* people and businesses are going about their daily activities. At the very core of these uber-catalysts, companies, be they business-to-business (B2B) or business-to-consumer (B2C), need to respond to the changing landscape and adapt their business models. That offers opportunity for investors like you.

Endnotes

1. 31 percent of Americans have no retirement savings at all.

2. http://www.prnewswire.com/news-releases/63-of-americans-cant-afford-500-car-repair-or-1000-emergency-room-visit-300200097.html.

3. Rebecca Smithers, "Cost of Raising a Child Rises to £218,000," *The Guardian* (January 26, 2012). Retrieved August 12, 2012. www.theguardian.com/money/2012/jan/26/cost-raising-child-rises-218000.

4. The Harris Poll, "Three-Quarters of Americans Worry About Having Enough Money to Retire" (July 10, 2014). http://www.prnewswire.com/news-releases/three-quarters-of-americans-worry-about-having-enough-money-to-retire-266550481.html.

Chapter 2

Getting Started

The secret of getting ahead is getting started.

— Mark Twain

Though no one can go back and make a brand new start, anyone can start from now and make a brand new ending.

— Carl Bard

Great love affairs start with Champagne and end with tisane.

— Honoré de Balzac

Hopefully, we have convinced you that you will be best served relying only on yourself for your retirement and that the investing wisdom of the 1980s and 1990s is no longer going to deliver the same types of results. Saving and investing for your future is a lot like ice skating for the first time—you can feel a bit unsure and wobbly at the start and it can take a bit more effort than expected, but once you get some momentum going, it can get a lot more comfortable and natural. So, where to start?

First Step: Saving

How's that for a topic heading to make you groan and skip ahead to the next section?

Saving: It is a dire imperative but calls to mind excruciating lectures by Mom and Dad accompanied by profuse finger-wagging and a desperate desire to stick one's tongue out—or maybe that's just us, but you have to admit spending can be fun. Out of respect for you, the reader, we'll make this as quick and painless as possible.

There are three types of savings, and everyone needs to have at least the first two of these three:

1. Emergency fund
2. Retirement savings
3. Special-purpose saving (buying a home, college for the kids, that dream vacation, man cave, or fantasy shoe closet, etc.)

Most financial advisors typically recommend stashing away at least three and preferably six months' worth of living expenses for your emergency fund. If your income tends to be more volatile, consider having closer to a year's worth. This isn't the "I-seriously-need-a-vacation-from-my-insane-boss emergency fund," but rather, savings intended to protect yourself in case of an unexpected loss of a job, a medical emergency, or an unanticipated home or auto expense.

According to a Bankrate.com study released in mid-2015, 29 percent of all Americans have no emergency savings, and of those who do, just 22 percent had "enough to pay for at least six months of expenses."[1] That's a big problem, because according to the National Endowment for Financial Education, about 60 percent of adults experience a financial emergency each year, 20 percent experience an unexpected transportation expense in a given year, 19 percent report having an unexpected home repair or maintenance issue, and 16 percent have unanticipated medical bills for an injury and illness. Medical debts account for about half of all the accounts in collection among U.S. adults.

Simple enough? You need emergency savings. Make it happen. Enough said.

As for retirement, the first question is, how much do I need to save per year? This is a question a lot of people ask themselves. Searching the phrase "How much do I need to save per year" in Google gives about

433 million results (we checked), so there are a lot of opinions out there. *MSN Money* has a great calculator to give you an idea of how much you need to save per month given your current income level, how much you already have saved, when you want to retire, and how long you expect to need your savings to last during retirement.

We recommend looking at a few of these various guides/calculators to get an idea of where you stand. The easiest way to put your savings plan into action is to actually have, somewhere, a separate bank account, for example, to sock away your current nest egg and to move funds every month. There is something rewarding about being able to see your retirement savings growing month after month. The best way to fund it is by having money automatically put into it every month, withdrawing from perhaps your day-to-day checking account. However you choose to do it, make it a consistent habit.

Sometimes, despite the most carefully crafted plans for the future, life can throw a curveball and you find yourself someplace you never expected to be, dealing with problems you never would have imagined. Bob, whom you met in Chapter 1, asked Lenore to meet with his daughter as she was dealing with a painful situation, one to which Lenore could unfortunately relate.

Sophia—Rebuilding a life and a plan for the future

Lenore met with Bob's daughter for dinner a few days after she had run into him, literally, at the UPS store. After commiserating about their failed marriages, Lenore tried to get a smile out of Sophia. "My marriage was also all about compromise. My ex got his way and I learned to live with it! After an argument with him, the only way I could keep my spirits up was to come up with a really great comeback. Unfortunately, one usually didn't dawn on me until a few days later!"

Sophia was in such a glum mood that the best she could do was a short laugh that was more of a hiccup. She mused, "Nothing has turned out the way I expected it to."

Lenore told her, "I know what you mean. Seems that they rarely ever do, but sometimes what I get ends up being better than my own plan. . . . Not what you want to hear now, though, is it? I hate it when people give you the, 'This will be such a growth opportunity' speech when all I really want to do is feel awful. Relationships seem to me to be a lot like algebra. I look at my X and wonder Y."

Understandably, Sophia groaned and rolled her eyes. Frankly we can't blame her.

Lenore laughed and told her, "Sorry, bad puns are a familial genetic defect. Now that you and your ex-husband have split, you can explore a life full of unexpected stories, some of which you hopefully won't be able to share," trying to coax a smile out of her. One of the great things about having something blow up so spectacularly is that you can cash in all that sadness for a ticket to do something you never thought you'd have the courage to do. If you were ever going to really shoot for something beyond your wildest dreams, why not go for it now?" she continued encouragingly, "Let's just make sure that before you go cavorting around the Tuscan hills writing the next great novel or becoming the next Picasso, your finances are in order."

After Lenore painted that picture, an awkward silence ensued while Sophia's eyes remained glued to the tabletop.

Lenore silently chewed her cheek, thinking of how to best navigate the minefield she'd apparently stepped onto. She asked, "Did your husband handle most of the finances for you two? It's pretty standard for one person in a marriage to handle it all."

Sophia let out a big breath, but continued to avoid eye contact while fidgeting with the wine list. Lenore stared awkwardly into her water glass, trying to think of some way to help Sophia feel less vulnerable. There is nothing like a painful divorce and the realization that you're not sure how the hell you're going to manage your life going forward to make a mess of one's sense of self-worth.

Being human is just not easy at times. There are days that we both wish we had our respective dogs' lives, being told daily how wonderful we are, plenty of head rubs and getting to feel exquisite joy from something as simple as the sound of a leash being picked up or the tail-tingling sight of a tennis ball.

Lenore stopped chewing on her cheek and asked, "Sophia, how about this? If you would like, you could come over to my office next week and we can go through your finances and figure out how to get everything in order so you know where you stand. I'm guessing that you are feeling totally overwhelmed and don't know where to start. My partner Chris and I can help. Let me know if you feel up to it. Most importantly, which bottle of wine shall we order? I think we need something special to toast the start of your next chapter in life. If you are up for it, it could become a real page-turner. . . . So what do you think of the salads here? I'm trying to get back into bikini shape, but so far the only member of my household with a personal trainer is the dog."

Sophia, one again, rolled her eyes. You are probably going to want to do the same occasionally during this book, as we just can't help ourselves sometimes.

Second Step: Investing

After some cajoling, we managed to get Sophia to join us for lunch to talk about how she could get back in charge of her finances.

We determined that Sophia had about five months' worth of emergency cash in a savings account, a reasonable-sized nest-egg for her retirement, and we came up with a plan for how much she needed to put away every month to augment her retirement savings. Next, we needed to help her decide how she wanted to manage her retirement savings.

We told her that there are a few things to think about when you decide how you want to invest. The first is how much time you can devote to your investments and the other is how comfortable you are with making decisions about what to invest in and when to buy and sell.

Sophia revealed that her ex-husband had handled most of their investments, so she didn't have a lot of experience, but was really not comfortable handing it all over to someone who she felt was just going to charge her a bunch of fees to do what she thought she could do herself, particularly since she wasn't sure she'd know how to even monitor what they would be doing for her. She'd heard horror stories about how so-called "advisors" had destroyed someone's life savings.

Investing Methods

We hear those stories, too, and believe investors are wise to be cautious. There are basically three options with differing levels of commitment:

1. Self-directed
2. Partially self-directed
3. Advisor-directed

If you choose to be *self-directed*, you are deciding to make all your investment decisions on your own. This is probably the right choice if you have less than $300,000 (that's Lenore's rule of thumb) and/or you feel comfortable choosing your own investments and are willing to devote the time necessary to monitor them. (We'll go over in later chapters just how to do this in a way that is as time-efficient as possible.)

You can also choose to be *partially self-directed,* which entails either using a broker who will give you advice and guidance on potential investments and your portfolio as a whole or using a service. There are a plethora of services and newsletters out there than can give you guidance on stocks, mutual funds, ETFs, bonds, and so on. These services run the gamut from giving you a complete portfolio, which you actively manage by responding to email alerts, to services that just suggest various stocks, bonds, or funds that an investor may want to consider for their portfolio without giving guidance on timing or how much of your portfolio ought to be invested in any particular security.

Finally, you can choose to work with an *investment advisor* who works either at a registered investment advisory firm (RIA) or at one of the bigger investment companies such as JP Morgan, Goldman Sachs, Merrill Lynch, and others. This also includes those who take advantage of the family office approach. A family office is a private company that manages the investments and trusts either for a single family, or in the case of a multifamily office, for more than one. These are typically used by relatively wealthy families and may include personal services such as managing household staff, legal services, day-to-day accounting and bill pay, philanthropic efforts, and so on.

When Sophia started to get that glazed look that often comes from such a riveting conversation, we told her to think of it this way. You know how the furniture you buy from Ikea comes in those little boxes that look so harmless up until you start trying to put it all together? Some people are really comfortable with a hex key and wooden dowels; they'll put together an entertainment center from Ikea without even looking at the instructions. Others prefer to follow the instructions step-by-step and may even look for tips and tricks on Google. Some prefer to just hire someone to put the whole thing together.

She told us that she thought she was more the instructions type, but was curious as to how the others work as well.

So we told her that before we even talk about opening up a brokerage account, she first needed find out if her employer offered a 401(k) plan, and if so, did the company do any sort of matching contributions? Money that goes into a 401(k) reduces taxable income, thus reducing the amount of your income that you lose to the government, and your 401(k) savings can grow without having to pay any taxes on investment gains or income until you start taking money out of it. This helps to grow your savings a lot faster. We'll show you how.

Since Sophia was self-employed, she wouldn't be able to take advantage of an employer 401(k) plan, but she was going to contribute to an IRA she planned to set up. When possible, maximize your allowable contribution to an IRA. Depending on your income and tax-filing status, you may be able to use some or all of your contribution as a tax deduction. Either way, the money within your IRA grows, like a 401(k), without having to pay any sort of taxes. Again, taxes are only paid on it when you take the money out.

Figure 2.1 shows the difference between growing your savings inside of a nontaxable IRA or 401(k) versus in a taxable account.

If we look at a three-year period, and for the sake of simplicity assume you get 8 percent returns every year, and that were the money to be in a taxable account, you would end up paying 15 percent in

Annual Return	8%		
Tax Rate	15%		
Non-Taxable		Taxable	
Initial		Initial	
Investment	$10,000	Investment	$10,000
		Pre taxes	$10,800
End of Year 1	$10,800	After Taxes	$10,680
		Pre taxes	$11,534
End of Year 2	$11,664	After Taxes	$11,406
		Pre taxes	$12,319
End of Year 3	$12,597	After Taxes	$12,182
Difference	$415		
	4%		

Figure 2.1 Investment growth in taxable versus pretax accounts

taxable gains. We will also assume that all the gains are long-term gains, which have a significantly lower tax rate than short-term gains, and again for simplicity, we'll assume that annual income in this example is below the threshold for "high-income" earners.

After three years, in this example, you would end up with an additional $415 or 4 percent more than you would in a taxable account. The difference is even greater if you are considered a "high-income" earner by the tax code. In that case, even if all of your gains are long-term, you would have to pay 23.8 percent, which would mean that over three years, you would lose 7 percent of your return (or $655) in taxes! Remember, too, that the extra 7 percent gets to grow inside your account, compounding the benefit! (See Figure 2.2.)

This led us to ask Sophia one of the most important questions. Just what kind of an investor are you? What kind of returns are you looking for, and what kind of risks are you comfortable taking?

These questions, or some form of them, are the most typical questions asked by investment professionals, and are probably the most widely misunderstood, both by those asking the questions and those on the receiving end!

Annual Return	8%		
Tax Rate	23.8%		
Non Taxable		Taxable	
Initial		Initial	
Investment	$10,000	Investment Pre taxes	$10,000 $10,800
End of Year 1	$10,800	After Taxes Pre taxes	$10,610 $11,458
End of Year 2	$11,664	After Taxes Pre taxes	$11,256 $12,157
End of Year 3	$12,597	After Taxes	$11,943
Difference	655		
	7%		

Figure 2.2 Investment growth in taxable versus pretax accounts at "high-income" tax rate

What these questions are meant to discern is what style of investing most suits you, based on your personality, your comfort with risk, and your individual financial needs and goals. Start first with your investing personality. One of the best ways to figure out just what type of investing will make you more comfortable is to think of it in terms of your personality.

Do you prefer to have a lot of more casual friendships, spending smaller amounts of time with a large number of people, or do you prefer to have a small set of very close friends with whom you have more intense relationships?

This is intended to identify just what type of portfolio you would be most comfortable implementing and monitoring. On the one hand, you could have 10 to 20 securities that you know really well and are committed to being with for a long time with the rest of your portfolio comprised of mutual funds or ETFs. If the price of one of your stocks were to decline significantly, you would be more likely to simply buy more of it rather than sell out quickly. On the other hand, you could have a lot more securities in your portfolio at any one time, most of which you tend to not stick with for more than a year. With those you would be more actively trading around movements in the stock, without having any particularly affinity for the company's long-term business potential, for example.

Understanding what style works best for you will help you narrow down where to look for help, be it a newsletter or trading-advice service or working with an advisor. It will also help you decide what type of brokerage account is best for you.

Another question that advisors often ask a potential client is about their risk tolerance. This is a really important point, but difficult for both parties to assess. What this comes down to is just how much money you can stand to lose in your portfolio before you start to lose sleep, or in the case of having an enviable ability to sleep regardless of life's woes, just how much you can lose before your long-term goals are threatened. When thinking about this, consider how volatile your income may be. If there is a reasonable chance you could lose your source of income for a sustained period of time, you need to have a less risky investment strategy than you would if your income was more stable and predictable.

Your timeline on your retirement savings is also a deciding factor here. The more time you have before you will start to tap into your savings, the more risk you are able to take. All of this, of course, is limited by just what makes you comfortable. That comfort is driven partly by having a portfolio that suits you and partly by understanding what your investment strategy is all about.

Regardless of whether you decide to go it alone, use some degree of outside advice, or turn your portfolio over to an investment advisor, you'll need to have a good idea of just what level of risk you are comfortable with and how to define just what levels and types of risk various securities have. We'll cover this in more detail in later chapters.

Now let's talk about a brokerage account, which is necessary if you want to buy stocks and exchange-traded, and highly useful if you only want mutual funds. The best place to start is with the online brokers such as Charles Schwab, Fidelity, TD Ameritrade, E*Trade, or Scottrade, among others. When looking at the various options, consider how often you plan to buy or sell securities and how much money in total you will have invested or in cash in your account, as that can affect the fees you pay. Some services, such as Schwab, charge no transaction fees or loads (fees charged by the mutual fund either upon purchase or sales of shares) to buy or sell some of the funds on their platform, which can help improve your returns.

If you decide to either go it alone or use some level of advice, you'll need to open up a brokerage account yourself. If you go with an investment advisor firm that manages your money for you, they will have a brokerage firm or firm(s) that they prefer to work with, so they would handle either opening up an account for you, transferring your funds into a brokerage that they work with, or simply adding themselves to an existing account if you are already using a brokerage with whom they work.

There are two different types of brokers: a traditional, full-service style and a discount style. Discount brokers are geared more toward the do-it-yourself investor. With this type, most of your trading is done online and you will not have a dedicated broker to execute trades for you. Some of these brokers do provide research information, but they generally do not offer any investment advice. Companies like E-Trade, TD Ameritrade, Charles Schwab, and Scottrade (we list these purely as an example and are not endorsing their services) all offer discount broker services and charge lower commissions on trades.

Another way you can get help outside of using a more traditional brokerage firm is by using investment advice services. These usually take the form of newsletters, weekly or daily publications, which are typically sent via email or published regularly for subscribers on a website. These services run the gamut from giving you complete portfolio with specific security buy-and-sell recommendations to services that give more general economic or market condition information or services that help assess your portfolio's strengths, weaknesses, and risks. You can use these services with a no-frills brokerage service or in addition to a full-service brokerage as an additional source of investment advice and guidance. These services can run the gamut from around $100/year to multiple thousands per year or more and are offered by well-known companies such as Morningstar, Forbes, TheStreet.com, by investment advisory firms such as Gluskin Sheff, and by independent groups such as Mauldin Economics. Full disclosure: As of the writing of this book, Chris and Lenore are co-portfolio managers for an advisory service at The Street.

Keep in mind that the investment advice industry, like every other aspect of life, has its share of good people and utter rats, so be careful when you are evaluating advice providers. Use your good sense and be cautious concerning those that offer "guaranteed returns" and/or returns that sound too good to be true. They probably are. Investing is tough; those who tell you they can get you massive returns easily because they know "secrets" are expecting you to ignore the realistic lessons of decades. We would advise you against believing there is one investing solution that takes care of all needs for all time.

History has shown there is no such silver bullet, and portfolio theory informs us that over time, not every investment in your portfolio will be generating positive returns. But that's the nature of investing. Still, the odds are better with a well-constructed stock portfolio than with the average venture capital portfolio. Generally speaking, a venture portfolio of 10 companies will make most of its returns from just one or two investments, while three to four generate solid returns and the rest tend to generate losses. When it comes to the investment newsletter and advice industry, look at the level of service offered and the track record rather than the folksy tone and one that spends more time promoting other things to you than helping you make sound investment decisions. Remember, too, that no matter how good the past performance might be, it's not an indicator of future performance.

In the Appendix, you will find a list of service providers to help get you familiar with this world. This list is only informational as we do not endorse any of the individuals or firms listed.

If you go with a traditional brokerage firm, you will have a personal stockbroker who will offer you investment ideas, research on industries, companies, and so on, will assess your portfolio, and will generate reports for you concerning your portfolio's performance. Ultimately, you will still be the decision maker concerning what to buy and sell for your portfolio, but your broker will advise you. In return for this extra level of service, you will be charged higher commissions and fees. Morgan Stanley, Merrill Lynch/Bank of America, Solomon Smith Barney, and Wells Fargo Securities all provide this type of service.

If you decide to go with a broker from one of these big brokerage firms, ask them directly about how they are compensated. Make sure you understand just what their firm rewards them for doing. Many companies unfortunately reward brokers for pushing specific securities or types of securities on their clients. Be aware of this practice and try to get as much information as possible about how your advisor may be personally motivated, either through a bonus system or through career progression. Also keep in mind that there is a historical trend for brokers within the larger companies to build up a good-sized client list, and then leave the firm and try to take clients with them. Their former employers obviously don't take kindly to this and try to prevent this from occurring, but it does happen, so be aware.

Your final choice is to use an investment advisor who will take responsibility for managing your entire portfolio. You can be as involved in the decision-making process as you like and as much as your advisor is willing to share. Some advisors like to have their clients be actively involved; others take a more proprietary approach and prefer to have little, if any, client involvement. The typical fee for investment advisor services is around 1 percent of the assets under management on an annual basis, with declining ratio as the size of the account increases. For example, an account with $1 million at 1 percent would be charged $2,500 every quarter, typically in advance of the quarter. Some advisors charge a slightly lower rate for that portion of the portfolio that is invested in fixed income. This type of compensation structure for investment advisors has an advantage over that for most brokers in that investment advisors make more money as they increase the size of their clients' portfolios, so interests are perfectly aligned. A broker may get additional compensation if he or she invests clients' funds in particular securities, which may or may not perform up to expectations.

If you do choose to go with either a broker or an advisor, here are some things they ought to be asking you about; if they don't, we suggest you look elsewhere:

- *Time horizon:* How long do you expect or need your money to be working toward your objectives? In other words, how long do you have until you start taking funds out?
- *Cash flow requirements:* What are your near-, medium-, and expected long-term income needs and sources?
- *Outside income:* Do you receive income from sources other than your portfolio? If so, how stable is that income, and how does it compare to your needs?

- *Outside assets:* Do you own other assets that should be considered when constructing your portfolio? For example, is the majority of your wealth tied up in an office building or in the stock of a privately owned company?
- *Taxes:* What is the tax basis for your various accounts? Do you have realized or unrealized gains or losses that we need to consider in the management of your portfolio?
- *Other restrictions or preferences:* Do you prefer to avoid investments in a particular geographic region or industry?

When you are looking for an advisor, keep in mind that this can be an awful lot like online dating where everyone puts their best foot forward, and all too often tries to be too many things to too many people. The best way to get good leads on advisors is often through friends and colleagues who have a similar financial situation as you do. Your accountants and legal advisors are also potential good referral sources.

Any broker or investment advisor should also provide the following:

- At a minimum, quarterly performance reports; some may provide monthly.
- A broker should also provide a report for every transaction performed for your account. An advisor who manages your money for you is unlikely to do this directly, but the brokerage service that holds your investments will do this for you so that you know what your advisor has done on your behalf.
- All of your accounts should be held at well-known, secure institutions specializing in asset custody. All of these accounts should be accessible to you at any time and you ought to be able to remove the broker's or investment advisor's access to your account at any point. For example, in Lenore's practice, the publicly traded investments for most all clients are held with Charles Schwab and a few at Fidelity. Clients are able to log on to Schwab's website or call Schwab at any time and get information concerning their account balances, securities held, transaction history, and so forth. Clients can also immediately remove her firm's access to their account any time they want. You should not trust any advisor who does not allow for this. Note that if you are investing in non–publicly traded investments such as hedge funds, they are held in a slightly different manner from securities such as shares of Apple.

In addition, investment advisors may provide the following types of services:

- Assist with retirement planning.
- Evaluate employer benefit options.
- Evaluate retirement offers or pension plan distribution options.
- Coordinate with your accountants to minimize your taxes and provide your accountants with year-end tax reports.
- Review your life insurance policies.

A final few words of caution about retirement planning and advisors: Commissions on life insurance policies can be quite surprisingly high, which can make it difficult for an advisor who is a licensed insurance agent to provide objective advice. We highly recommend that before agreeing to purchase a life insurance policy, you have the policy terms and financials reviewed by at least one additional advisor such as an accountant or an attorney and understand how the person selling you the policy will be compensated.

Never, *ever*, invest in something that you do not fully understand, and always make sure you understand exactly where your money is. Our rule of thumb is to never put money in something that cannot be explained with a crayon on a cocktail napkin. You should also be very clear where your money is at all times. The Bernie Madoffs of the world would not exist if their investors did not willingly accept returns out of a magical black box. Understand exactly how your money is being invested, know exactly where it is at all times, *and* always make sure that you can verify both of these through independent third parties. If not, you need to walk away.

You will find a list of suggested questions to go over with any potential broker or investment advisor in the Appendix of this book.

Cocktail Investing Bottom Line

You need to have at least two types of savings:

- Emergency fund (3–12 months' worth of living expenses, depending on the volatility of your income and job security)
- Retirement savings

An optional third type can be for special-purpose savings for things such as buying a home, college fund, vacation, and so on.

There are three methods of investing, listed in decreasing order of time commitment:

- Self-directed
- Partially self-directed
- Advisor-directed

Investing Guidelines

- You should always max out your pretax savings options (like an employer sponsored 401(k)), and when possible, place your savings into an IRA.
- You need to decide just how much money you can stand to lose in a given time frame to determine just what level of risk you are willing to take on.
- Consider what style of investing best suits you. Are you more comfortable holding specific securities for a long time, or are you more interested in taking advantage of potential shorter-term opportunities? Keep in mind that we do not recommend that anyone manage their savings by engaging in daily or even weekly to multi-week short-term trading strategies. Very few have ever been successful doing this, regardless of what late-night infomercials may imply.
- When assessing a potential advisor, understand how he or she is compensated, and make sure this does not lead to a conflict of interest between your advisor maximizing his or her annual income and doing what is best for your portfolio in the long-run.
- Never invest in something you cannot explain on a cocktail napkin with a crayon.
- Never invest your funds in something for which you do not fully understand the strategy and where you cannot readily verify your investment through an independent third party.

Endnote

1. Janna Herron, "Americans Still Lack Savings Despite Bigger Paychecks," www .bankrate.com (June 23, 2015).

Chapter 3

The Economy versus the Markets

Economics is half psychology and half Grade Three arithmetic, and the U.S. does not now have either half right.

— *Conrad Black*

There are a number of ways to pick your investments, from being a voracious reader of all things, to following the pundits of the day, to getting informal advice from your stylist/barber, to eavesdropping on line at Starbucks. One of the biggest mistakes is not having an investment process, and while that sounds rather daunting, once you see the world through the lenses that we'll share with you over the coming chapters, it will be like riding a bicycle or mixing your favorite cocktail; you will find yourself doing it naturally.

Before we continue, we have a question to ask you.

Have you ever tried to make a peanut butter and jelly sandwich by spreading the jelly on the peanut butter or vice versa?

If you've ever tried it, you know it doesn't work.

It's one of those rare occasions where doing it the wrong way is immediately obvious. We bet you've had some dangerously good cocktails and some that you couldn't bring yourself to sip more than once or twice. Odds are they were made with similar ingredients but there is art in that shaker.

We would argue the same holds true with picking investments and how they are combined; as the saying goes, if it were easy, everyone would be good at it.

Much like that peanut butter and jelly sandwich or a cocktail, you need to know where to start. Many individual investors start with the "hot stock" version of investing, which rarely ever works out when the assessment of that "hot stock" doesn't take into account the big picture. Over the course of our collective experience, and as President Bill Clinton once said, "It's the economy, stupid."

So just what is the economy?

Everyone talks about it, but what do they really mean?

According to Merriam-Webster, the economy is "the process or system by which goods and services are produced, sold, and bought in a country or region." So when we talk about the economy, we are talking about the system through which stuff gets made, bought, and sold. The growth of an economy is dependent on three things: (1) the quantity and quality of the labor pool; (2) the amount of available investment capital; and (3) the abundance and utilization of natural resources—talk about a mouthful! Simply put, that means, how many people can/will work. How much can they get done. How much money you've got to work with whatever kinds of resources are available, such as fertile land, oil, and minerals. How to best allocate and utilize those resources to create the stuff, pay people, invest in future production—that is the somewhat-art, somewhat-science of economics.

The ideas of economists and political philosophers, both when they are right and when they are wrong, are more powerful than is commonly understood. Indeed, the world is ruled by little else. Practical men, who believe themselves to be quite exempt from any intellectual influences, are usually slaves of some defunct economist. Madmen in authority, who hear voices in the air, are distilling their frenzy from some academic scribbler of a few years back.

John Maynard Keynes

Although economics often gets a bad rap in the media, particularly after the recent financial crisis, it impacts almost every aspect of our lives in that it provides the theories concerning what is economically beneficial to a society and just how those benefits are to be measured. In fact, outside of an all-out war, little else affects every single person in a society more than economics. Economic theory provides the *prevailing narrative* through which information is interpreted, what the information means, and if it is a good thing or a bad thing. Voting is for the most part all about economics. People vote for the candidates they think will enact policies that will make them better off, based on their assumptions of what makes an economy strong. The thing is, there isn't universal agreement on just what makes an economy robust, yet most candidates act like there is one school of thought that we all agree upon.

Before the age of the Kardashians, TMZ, and ever-so-realistic reality TV, economists were treated like today's rock stars, with John Maynard Keynes up in the Rolling Stones–type Hall of Fame category. Not yet convinced? How about this? War and economics have always been and will always be intimately linked. History teaches us that the more strained the economy, the greater the probability of conflict. Misguided economic thinking has often led to a devastated economy, which then leads to . . . . ? You get the picture now!

Remember in the last chapter we introduced you to Sophia, who was going through a divorce and had been introduced to us through her father, Bob, from Chapter 1. We next met her sister, Reilly.

Reilly learned the hard way just how important it is to identify the prevailing narrative, what school of thought drives it, and where it might have blind spots. Sophia asked us to meet with Reilly and her husband, Tyler, because they'd gone through a painful time with their investments, having lost over half their savings during the financial crisis as well as enduring an excruciating fall in the market value of their home. Those losses had put a lot of strain on their relationship, which, coupled with the loss of Reilly's mother and the strain between her and her father over his new romance with his neighbor, Madeleine, was making the entire family feel they were living in a Jerry Springer episode. We both can attest to having experienced similar moments with our own respective families—*ahhh*, the holidays!

When Reilly and her husband, Tyler, arrived, it was evident to us that Tyler had accompanied her under protest. As we talked with them, we learned that Tyler had been insistent on buying their home in 2006, even though Reilly was concerned that the home's price had increased over 40 percent over the prior five years. They'd put very little down, then after their home price rose another 20 percent, they took out a home equity line of credit to have cash to put into a real estate venture Tyler was confident would generate enormous returns. Unfortunately, the fund had eventually been shut down and they lost their entire investment.

Reilly opened with a question we've heard many times that dealt with why housing prices got hit so hard during the downturn, even though so many people in D.C. kept telling us things were getting better. Here are a few tidbits to show how those in government are just as fallible as everyone else. Their assessments and prognostications ought to be assessed just as thoroughly as those from any other source.

In 2003, Federal Reserve Chairman Alan Greenspan said of housing, "The notion of a bubble bursting and the whole price level coming down seems to me, as far as a nationwide phenomenon, really quite unlikely."

In 2005, Treasury Secretary John Snow said, "The idea that we're going to see a collapse in the housing market seems to me improbable."

In 2007, the new Fed Chairman Ben Bernanke said, "At this juncture, the impact on the broader economy and the financial markets of the problems in the subprime market seems likely to be contained."

It doesn't matter which side of the aisle they come from; bureaucrats are only human, and the economy is one very complex system. They were all relying on flawed economic ideology, but given their jobs, they had to rely on something to guide their actions. We don't want you, our readers, to suffer the same fate, so let's walk through just what we mean by economic ideology and what you need to know about the various schools of thought in order to successfully navigate your portfolio through all the misinformation and mistaken assumptions that pervade the headlines.

Economic Ideology

By economic ideology, we mean schools of economic thought such as Keynesianism, monetarism, socialism, and so on. All these schools are based on defined goals and a set of means to achieve those goals, but are limited by the constraints of reality, much the way an architect is limited by gravity; just as the Egyptians had to learn the rules of gravity often by trial and error, so does society have to learn economic reality through trial and error.

To understand how economic ideology affects investing, we have to first understand the goals of that ideology. For centuries, the goal of the prevalent forms of economic ideology was simply the personal goals and preferences of either the individual or group of individuals at the top of the power structure. Economics was all about what the person wearing the crown wanted.

Over time, this power structure has evolved, and the way people interact and view each other's innate rights has evolved.

This is the evolution from a kingdom-type structure, in which the purpose of society was to serve the whims of royalty, to socialism, which attempted to allocate resources so as to maximize the "good" for society as a whole, which of course was defined by those in charge. In order to achieve these goals, the expected and acceptable means have evolved from the use of force with the threat of injury or incarceration, to more subtle forms of coercion using societal pressures and the threat of ostracism. This is an evolution from the threat of a gun to the doctrine of political correctness.

Regardless of how angelic or demonic the goals and means may be, all economic ideology is faced with the simple constraints of human nature. A totalitarian regime, in which the minority dictates the use and allocation of resources, is constrained by the risk of a populace uprising. Whenever the ruling group goes too far, the subservient majority can use the sheer strength of their numbers to physically take over the mantel of power. Unfortunately, this process often results in a new group of despots taking over and the cycle continues. This threat of violent revolution has been the dominant constraint throughout most of history and becomes more likely the further day-to-day reality gets from societal expectations. We have seen such constraints take over in the recent Middle East uprisings.

As societies progress, the constraints evolve in something more subtle. These are based in the simple laws of human nature. For example, if income tax rates are increased from 30 percent to 90 percent, people will generate less income. No amount of political will can change this. It is a simple fact: Human nature innately evaluates effort expended to reward and if one can only keep 10 percent of one's efforts, a Netflix marathon becomes a lot more attractive.

In the United States in recent decades, the primary goals have been dominated by the identification of the best allocation of societal resources to maximize the "public good." From the 1990s, one of those goals has been increasing the level of home ownership.

We have been and are still living through the inevitable consequences of how those goals were implemented, which is all about economic ideology. We lived through a housing crisis, with home prices falling across the nation to a degree never before seen. In early 2012, a Wells Fargo report indicated that there were about 3.2 million homes vacant, about 85 percent higher than the normal levels, with another 1.6 million likely becoming vacant because of foreclosures.

Families were forced to go through a painful deleveraging process (paying off debts) after the low interest rate/free credit for everyone festival pushed household debt to income levels from their historic norms around 65 percent to a peak of almost 140 percent in 2007, per data from the Federal Reserve. That credit contraction slowed economic growth, so we saw household income levels falling while families struggled to pay down their debt.

The easy, but dangerous, way to assess the problems is to claim that those people, that political party, or that part of the government is dumb, evil, lazy, or whatever insult suits the situation.

The reality is that the economy is incredibly complex, in some ways more art than science. In science you seek to run experiments to determine the impact of something by holding all other variables constant. That is impossible when it comes to the economy. We will never know what would have happened without the TARP bailouts or without the Federal Reserve's quantitative easing programs; everyone has theories, including your authors here, but no one can positively know.

That being said, there really is no such thing as a free lunch, so when you see government efforts to push the market in a specific direction, know that there will be consequences, much the way there are consequences to diverting the path of a river. Our goal is to help you see ways to protect yourself from them and ideally to even profit from them. So let's walk through the different theories and where you can see their effects today.

Schools of Economic Thought

Earlier we told you that the growth of an economy is dependent primarily on three things: labor, capital, and resources. Since the dawn of mankind, there have been a lot of opinions about them, which can be organized into schools of economic thought. To understand what you read or hear about the economy, you need to understand these schools of economic thought. These theories impact the way we all think about the economy, especially those in the government, and maybe even more importantly, they affect the thinking of those who report to the rest of us what is going on and whether it is a good thing or a bad thing.

Most recently, the prevailing narrative has been that the Fed's quantitative easing (QE) programs would help get the economy back on its feet. We can never really know what would have happened without the program, whether economic growth would have been slower, faster, or the same because we'd have to be able to repeat that time in history, not have QE, while keeping everything else the same. The important thing was that the prevailing narrative believed QE was necessary, so the markets reacted as if it were true and beneficial to the economy as successive rounds were discussed and implemented.

Like religion, there are almost endless permutations of views on how an economy works or ought to work. Lucky for you we like to keep it simple and will just break them all down into seven major schools of thought:

1. Neoclassical economics
2. Fascism
3. Socialism
4. Keynesianism
5. Monetarism
6. Austrianism
7. Supply-side economics

There is no consensus about which is correct, and they overlap to varying degrees, but the one most widely followed by those who work in or closely with governments is Keynesianism. This makes intuitive sense, as Keynesianism ardently supports active government intervention in the economy, which validates what many politicians are already doing and are inclined to do, fair enough! Schools primarily teach neoclassical with a Keynesian slant, which is sometimes referred to as the neoclassical synthesis.

The following is a high-level overview of the different schools of thought. Keep in mind as you read these that since the study of economics is a "soft science," these theories don't have perfectly clear definitions with uniform consensus and tend to evolve over time. They are a bit like religion, where, for example, Lutheran, Episcopalian, Protestant, and Catholic all are variations of Christianity. Since we aren't talking about something objective like $E = MC^2$ or $2 + 2 = 4$, these definitions are of course subject to interpretation.

Neoclassical economics was developed in the eighteenth and nineteenth centuries and is a very broad term, lacking universal agreement on just what it encompasses. It includes the works of Adam Smith (author of *The Wealth of Nations*), David Ricardo, Thomas Robert Malthus, and John Stuart Mill. It holds that the value of a product depends on the costs involved in producing the product and, according to E. Roy Weintraub, rests on three assumptions:

1. People have rational preferences among outcomes that can be identified and associated with a value.
2. Individuals maximize utility and firms maximize profits.
3. People act independently on the basis of full and relevant information.

This approach focuses on the determination of prices, outputs, and distributions through supply and demand. This is where we get the concept of a supply curve and a demand curve, shown in Figure 3.1.

What the graph illustrates is that as the price of something goes up, those providing it will be willing to supply more of it. As the price of

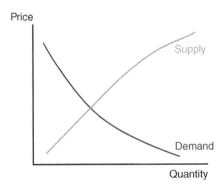

Figure 3.1 Supply and demand curves

something goes down, more people will buy it. The quantity suppliers are willing to supply at various prices can be charted as can the quantity that will be purchased at various prices. The point where they meet is the equilibrium price and output quantity.

You can think of this as similar to your basic physics class in which you were taught how things would work in a vacuum; if you dropped a feather and a bowling ball from the same height at the same time in a vacuum, they'd hit the ground at the same time. This provides the foundation for most of modern economic theory, but much like that bowling ball and feather, reality is a bit different from that perfect vacuum. Let's look at those three assumptions again:

- People have rational preferences among outcomes that can be identified and associated with a value. (*So it makes perfect sense that Gläce Luxury ice has been able to sell 50 cubes for $325. Enough said.*)
- Individuals maximize utility and firms maximize profits. (*Michael Jordan had a stint in the MLB and Time Warner merged with AOL, a profit destroyer of epic proportions.*)
- People act independently on the basis of full and relevant information. (*Housing was booming because, well, everyone was buying a house and of course they will continue to do so in the future. Full and relevant information? If the markets had full information, we wouldn't have insider trading laws.*)

In contrast to the focus on the individual in neoclassical economics, *fascism*, which originated in Italy after World War I, places the "State" above all else; thus, governments are free to do whatever they deem necessary. There are no limits. It typically involves a mixed economy, with government interference deemed necessary to ensure national self-sufficiency and independence. In this ideology, an individual is primarily viewed simply as a tool to further the "best interests" of the State.

The original symbol of this ideology is a bundle of sticks tied together, which in Italian is called a *fascio* (plural is *fasci*), sometimes including an axe with its blade emerging. The symbolism here is that one rod alone may be broken easily, but together they are much stronger—in other words, "strength through unity." You can see this symbol of a tied bundle of sticks at the Lincoln Memorial, symbolizing the president that kept the union together.

The most extreme example of fascism is Nazi Germany. The core of fascism is so simple, and can be so deceptively seductive, that it is usually found weaving its way through other schools of thought, particularly in challenging times. At the end of World War II, the ultimate consequence of this model was made heartbreakingly clear, but remnants of it can still be seen today as political leaders proudly claim they will "do whatever it takes," to which we like to sarcastically add, "and be damned the consequences as I'll most likely be out of office when they arrive!" Try throwing that one out at your next dinner party after everyone has had a drink or two.

Socialism essentially believes that the free markets are inherently unfair and prone to disaster. Implicit in these assumptions is the belief that a select group of people in government can and should decide what is more "fair" than would exist without intervention and that manipulation to bring about a more "fair" state is a moral imperative. This also assumes that more "fair" is an objective truth, rather than a subjective opinion developed by those in power. This paradigm requires that masterminds control the money supply, interest rates, production, employment—basically, most aspects of the economy. Implicit in this is the belief that these masterminds are capable of running thing better than would otherwise be the case, and that such omniscient and benevolent masterminds will be in continual supply. Basically, this theory believes that society is best served when government takes things away from some individuals and gives them to others in order to rectify the innate unfairness of life.

In today's world, the *Declaration of Principles* of the Party of European Socialists gives a good idea of how this ideology is currently implemented:

- The welfare state and state-provided universal access to education and healthcare are society's greatest achievements.
- A strong and just society must ensure that the wealth generated by all is shared fairly, as determined by the state.
- Collective responsibility makes society stronger when people work together, and all people are enabled to live a dignified life, free of poverty and protected from social risks in life.

Anytime you hear discussions around "fair share," you are hearing the influence of socialism.

Keynesianism is named after the British economist John Maynard Keynes (June 5, 1883–April 21, 1946), who was an advisor to Franklin Roosevelt. His economic theories were developed primarily in the 1930s, during the Great Depression. Keynesianism overturned the older ideas of neoclassical economics that were widely adopted by leading Western economies after World War II. Keynes was even included in *Time* magazine's list of the *100 most influential people of the twentieth century*. His theories propose that governments are obligated to use monetary policy (meaning money supply) and fiscal policy (meaning government spending) to alter the economy from how it would otherwise behave. He strongly supported government deficit spending as a way to solve unemployment (remember his theories were developed during horrific levels of unemployment in the Great Depression) and provided the theoretical basis under which sovereign debt has grown to its current levels across most of the world. Keynes versus Bono—now that would be an interesting battle of global influence!

We like to sum up the Keynesian viewpoint this way: "Free markets are volatile and don't produce the greatest 'general good' possible. Governments are obligated to and are able to successfully manipulate economic factors to provide a less volatile economy and make everyone better off than they would have been without the intervention." There is an underlying assumption here that an objective state of highest "general good" exists as a singular truth and that individuals in government are able to consistently identify that state and alter conditions to move toward this truth. Keynesianism is a somewhat lighter version of socialism in that it focuses more on altering economic factors where socialism looks at both economic and social issues. While Keynesianism often gets the lion's share of the blame for the recent global financial meltdown, governments worldwide have relied heavily on it to justify their responses that crisis. When you hear anyone talk about how government must do what it can to help the economy through stimulus, think Keynes.

Monetarism is sometimes also referred to as the Chicago School (of economic thought). Monetarism is most widely associated with Milton Freidman and supports primarily a free market economy with little government intervention save for, as the name would imply, monetary policy (money supply). The concern of the monetarists is that as productivity increases, without an increase in the money supply prices will fall. Think of a simple economy that produces 10 items this year and has $100 as the total money supply. Over the year, those 10 items are produced and exchanged, but the supply of money remains $100. Next year, due to productivity gains (in general people are able to produce more as they get better at what they do—better known as moving down the learning curve), 12 items are produced in this society. The price of all 12 items still can only add up to $100. Thus, a fall in some if not all prices must occur. This theory assumes that chronically falling prices is a bad thing, as it will deter buying, with the buyer asking the question, "Why buy today when the price will be lower tomorrow?" If all buyers were to behave in this way, the economy would come to a standstill.

The goal of a monetarist is to keep the money supply growing at roughly the same pace or slightly faster than the economy so that in general prices remain relatively stable or increase just a little bit year after year. Think monetarist when you hear talk of a "target inflation rate." This assumes that if you think the price of something will increase in the future, you are more likely to buy it today and that, for the economy, buying today is better than buying tomorrow.

Implicit in this theory is the assumption that individuals in government are able to predict with reasonable accuracy the growth in productivity over time and can also accurately expand the money supply to match increases in productivity. It also assumes that individuals in this position of considerable power will be able to resist pressures to waver from this goal. Recall the recent massive expansion in the money supply in response to the financial meltdown of 2008.

An interesting challenge for the monetarists is *malinvestment,* which refers to poorly allocated business investments due to either artificially low cost of credit or an unsustainable increase in money supply. Classic examples include the dot-com bubble and the U.S. housing bubble. The additions to the money supply are not evenly injected into the economy. Think of the economy as a big bowl of whip cream. The additions to the money supply are like dollops of cream tossed into the bowl. Those dollops don't immediately spread out evenly, but instead form little "cones of malinvestment," meaning money flows unevenly into very specific areas at first. Only over time do the dollops melt down, and eventually, the level of the entire bowl rises.

Austrian economics, or *Austrianism*, gets its name from its founders and early supporters, who were citizens of the old Austrian Habsburg Empire. Best-known Austrians are the 1974 Nobel Laureate Friedrich Hayek and his mentor, Ludwig von Mises. In economics, the Austrian paradigm is the philosophical descendant of Adam Smith and the other so-called classical liberals, today referred to as libertarians. In politics, the Austrian School is often considered the descendant of Patrick Henry, James Madison, Thomas Jefferson, and the other American founders. The Austrian school has received greater attention in recent years, as many proponents of this school predicted the financial crisis years in advance. Contrast this to an interview with Ben Bernanke (a monetarist with, we believe, Keynesian leanings) in July 2005, in which he stated that the global economic fundamentals were extremely strong and expected continued strong growth. Arthur Laffer (a supply-sider) in a 2007 video claimed the U.S. economy had never been in better shape.

Austrians view the economy as a living ecosystem rather than a machine. They believe the mastermind concept implicit in every other doctrine is deeply flawed and contend that it is not possible for political leaders to know what is best for each individual and that any manipulations in an attempt to produce a "greater good" will only cause harm. Thoreau summed up the Austrian perspective when he said, "If I knew for a certainty that a man was coming to my house with the conscious design of doing me good, I should run for my life."

The emphasis of this school is on individual rights, with government's only legitimate function being their protection thereof. It differs from many other schools in that while fascism, socialism, and the like paint a utopian end-state that can be achieved if the group in power is just given the ability to do what needs to be done, the Austrian school holds that no such utopian end-state exists and that the best society can achieve is to basically let each individual live as he or she chooses and that the natural level of "unfairness" that exists cannot be improved by government intervention.

Supply-side economics developed during the 1970s during a period of stagflation (a period of inflation and stagnant economic growth) and as a response to the perceived failure of Keynesian economic policy. It is a mixture of Austrian and neoclassical economics and proposes that production or supply is the key to economic prosperity and that consumption or demand is only secondary. This idea is summarized by

Say's law of economics, which states: "A product is no sooner created, than it, from that instant, affords a market for other products to the full extent of its own value." The theory focuses on low taxes and less regulation in order to stimulate the supply side of the economy. It also strongly supports the theories of Arthur Laffer, who is given credit for the Laffer curve, which states that tax rates and tax revenues are separate and that increasing tax rates above a certain level leads to decreasing tax receipts. This theory was supported by the drop in capital gains tax rates from the late 1970s and into the 1980s, during which time each drop was met by an increase in tax receipts. This theory gained notoriety under President Ronald Reagan, who lowered income tax rates with the theory that a drop in tax rates would result in increased economic growth, which would then lead to increased tax receipts.

Comparing Economic Theories

We like to compare the Austrian perspective to the other schools of thought, with the exception of neoclassical and supply-side, using an ecosystem analogy. Austrians look at a forest and say it is complicated, messy, unpredictable, and doesn't consciously follow any concept of fairness. That being said, any manipulations will only do harm. The forest system is too complicated for any human intervention to be able to consistently improve what exists naturally without eventually causing great harm, often through unintended consequences. Fascists, socialists, Keynesians, and monetarists look at the forest and say, "I can do better." They just differ on what needs to be improved and what tools they are willing to use.

A primary difference between Austrian and neoclassical concerns the relationship between cost and price. Recall that neoclassical economics holds that the price of a good is based on the costs incurred to produce it. An Austrian would say that's all well and good when deciding whether or not it is worth your while to produce something, but once the good is produced, costs have no relevance and the only thing that determines price is what someone is willing to pay for it. Imagine you build a house with the intent of selling it once it's built. The neoclassical economist would say that your price will be based on your costs plus some target profit. The Austrian says once it is built, you'll end up selling it for the best price you can get, regardless of cost. That price may be above your costs, generating a profit that exceeds your expectations, or below your costs, generating an unanticipated loss. Thus, cost and price are in the end, independent.

While Austrian economist and supply-side economists often end up in the same place, Austrians criticize the supply-siders for not being more critical of government spending. The two schools are quite similar, however, with slight differences in the areas they emphasize.

The way an Austrian economist thinks can be best summarized using a quote from author P.J. O'Rourke: "Giving money and power to government is like giving whiskey and car keys to teenage boys."

Supply-side focuses on the—big surprise here—supply/production side of the economy, while Keynesian focus on the demand side in terms of fiscal policy to generate higher employment rates, thus more consumption/demand.

Whenever you hear economic information presented in a newspaper, on television, or in a magazine, keep in mind that how the information is being presented and the assessment of the policies around it will be affected by the biases of the person presenting the information coupled with the prevailing narrative (what the majority believe to be the truth of the day) and just how much the individual wants to agree with or disagree with that narrative. These narratives aren't necessarily true, so investors need to keep a focus on the fundamentals of an economy or a stock, but understand that even a completely incorrect prevailing narrative can dominate the fundamentals for some period of time.

> We often find that when we get to this point, we are often asked how it is that even when the economy hasn't been all that strong, the stock market can go on a serious tear. How can that be?

The Economy versus the Market

The market is like the weather while the economy is like the climate. We can enjoy an unseasonably warm day in the middle of winter or shiver through an exceptionally cold day in the middle of summer, but that doesn't change the season or latitude. The prevailing narrative in the markets may push investments into an area beyond that which the fundamentals will support, sending returns higher and higher as everyone jumps for their seat on the rocket, igniting ambitions in much the same way as the gold rush of the 1840s and 1850s. Unfortunately for those who hop off too late, eventually reality, the inescapable gravity of economic fundamentals, exerts its pull and the prevailing narrative suddenly switches with the new version exclaiming how all along we knew the prior one was only for fools! The bubble bursts, followed by much handwringing, finger pointing, and adamant pledging, "This must be addressed!" by politicians ensues. That is, until the next Dutch Tulip Tornado (1637), South Sea Shindig (1720), Mississippi Mania (1720), Roaring 1920s, Computer/Tech Craze (1980s), Dot-com Dementia (1990s), and Real Estate Rage (2000s) ignites, and off we go again. Prudent investing requires separating the weather from the climate, taking advantage of unseasonable trends, while always being wary of the inescapable gravity of economic reality.

What Does It All Mean?

As advisors and investors, we attempt to maintain awareness of the implications of all these varying schools of thought, of the malinvestments that can often occur as governments attempt to improve upon what would otherwise occur, and take advantage of those opportunities as they arise while avoiding the hubris of overconfidence. For the active investor, a portfolio ought to be designed to take advantage of trends you see coming while maintaining a level of protection just in case you are wrong or if something unexpected occurs. We live in dynamic times, where seemingly impossible events, Nassim Taleb's *black swans,* occur more often than expected. Ask your advisor about their views on the different economic theories. This will give you valuable insight into how they develop their investment strategies. Be wary of any advisor who *knows* with certainty what is coming next. Investing is all about probabilities, not guarantees or absolutes.

The world is a complicated place, and we humans have so very much to learn. All these schools of thought were developed through the work of exceptionally intelligent individuals who were usually well-intentioned, but like the rest of us fallible humans who couldn't possibly be expected to get it all right. Personally, we like to tread slowly and cautiously, with awareness of all that we do not yet know, but still are required to make decisions in the face of such uncertainty.

Helping us make those decisions is data, the focus of our next chapter, in which we look to find either confirming data, which increases the probability of our hypothesis, or contradicting data, that reduces the probability that we are on the right path.

Cocktail Investing Bottom Line

- Economic growth is driven by three factors: labor, capital, and resources.
- Economic theory provides the prevailing narrative through which information is interpreted, what the information means, and if it is viewed as a good thing or a bad thing.
- Be aware of the prevailing narrative, how different parties (governments, companies, and so on) will speak to you in a particular economic theory voice, and how it differs from the actual data.
- Economics and investing is about probabilities, not absolutes, so it is important to look for data that confirms (or refutes) your hypothesis to increase the chances that you are on the right (or wrong) track.
- We would also recommend searching for data that may contradict your hypothesis to identify any potential flaws. In our experience, this helps us think through the hypothesis from several angles. If the confirming data outweighs the contradictory data, you are more likely to be on your way to a well-thought-out and solid hypothesis.

Chapter 4

Read the Economy
Like a Pro

The future ain't what it used to be.

– Yogi Berra

An economist is a man who states the obvious in terms of the incomprehensible.
– Alfred A. Knopf

We've already talked about how successful investing requires a bigger view than just the latest "hot stock" tip and gave you the background to understand the biases and assumptions hidden in the way information concerning the economy is presented. Like so many, Reilly and Tyler's savings were seriously damaged because they reasonably believed that the so-called experts they saw on TV or whose articles they read were reliable. Having been so devastated they are understandably unsure of where to turn for information, making decision-making painful and putting additional strain in their marriage.

In this chapter we are going to show you how to understand the current state of the economy and, even more importantly, how to look forward using Chris's two favorite words: vector and velocity. You will come to see that understanding these two things is critical for successful investing and that you cannot simply go with "information" from the headlines.

Before we go further, though, we need to make one thing clear. Remember to always keep in mind that for at least the near to medium term, it really doesn't matter what we think or what you think about the way the world works. The only thing that matters is what the market thinks about the way the world works—up until the point when the market discovers it's wrong. Think of it as akin to the celebrity phenomenon; at some point, someone becomes famous just for being famous, until one day you realize, often with relief, they haven't graced the headlines in ages. You mean you're not wondering what's up with Paris Hilton anymore?

Here, we will teach you to see what is truly going on so that you will understand the difference between the prevailing narrative and reality, and more importantly be prepared to deal with both. It is important to have an independent viewpoint grounded in the fundamentals, otherwise, you will be constantly whipsawed back and forth as the prevailing narrative bends and shifts, much like Hollywood's favorite romantic leads, but you can never ignore the prevailing narrative or, even more dangerous, stick to your own viewpoint for too long, which turns out in the end, to be wrong. Like most things in life, this is a balancing act.

Are we interested in the data? Hell, yes, in all its various forms and sources!

We bet that you too will soon be hooked, because it's the data that tell us how the economy is really performing now and where it is headed in the future.

Do we rely on the pundits and tweets, which simply regurgitate headlines that lack substance and context? Hell, no!

We're far less interested in all of the loud but disparate voices that lace their comments with political undertones and flawed economic ideology while trying to grab headlines and your attention. Chris does, however, enjoy how riled up Lenore can get when she listens to one of them spouting drivel while he looks for the fatal flaw in their "logic." That being said, those tweeting pundits do provide you with easily accessible versions of the various prevailing narratives, of which you must always be aware. And every so often they do pass or tweet along a good nugget of data that we find useful.

Don't Trust the "Experts"

Man will occasionally stumble over the truth, but most of the time he will pick himself up and continue on.

— *Winston Churchill*

Time and time again, we are amazed at how the "smart money" and those supposedly "in the know" continue to misread the economy. We're not talking about the president, who is most likely just as out of touch with what is going on in the real-world as was his predecessor and most every other president, nor are we pointing the finger at Congress, although sometimes we feel like blowing raspberries their way. Let's face it—with the now non-stop campaign cycle, most of them have little time to sweat the details of the economy, let alone the needs of their constituents.

We are talking about the group most able to move markets today with the tiniest shift in word choice, the Federal Reserve, which is composed of a group of very bright minds focused on monetary policy and the economy. If you haven't heard of or if you are unfamiliar with the Fed, we'll give you the scoop in the next chapter.

But for now, looking at the Fed's track record on forecasting changes in the economy or predicting an impending crises, saying the Fed is out of touch is like asserting that reality TV isn't all that realistic—you think?! Chris has often wondered how it is a "reality" show needs to have scripts. For example, you may have heard how the Fed looks at inflation. It excludes food and energy, which makes sense because really, how many Americans are affected by the price of food or energy? Seriously? Perhaps one of the benefits of being inside the Fed is you don't have to buy your own food or gas, or perhaps they are simply paid so much more than the average person. To be fair, those two are excluded because commodity prices, things like oil and corn, can be very volatile in the short-term, thus their inclusion could give misleading cues, but to utterly ignore two large expenditure areas for the average person, while making sense in theory, simply doesn't accurately reflect the realities of daily life. As for accurately predicting the future direction of the economy, the Fed hasn't correctly predicted on recession since it was created in 1913.

According to the textbooks that Chris uses in his graduate Financial Institutions and undergraduate Capital Markets & Financial Institutions classes, the Federal Reserve's role is to promote full employment, economic growth, price stability, and a sustainable pattern of international trade. Those are some pretty big plates to spin all at once, and as you might imagine, there are several trade-offs. A Keynesian would say that the Federal Reserve has to balance its monetary policy efforts, which historically have led to economic growth and higher employment, against overheating the economy and driving prices and wages higher—in other words ... inflation.

Lenore would argue that the policies of the Fed, driven in no small part by the pressures it faces from Congress and presidents, have led to considerable inflation, and it is difficult to estimate just what the growth of the U.S. economy could have been otherwise. In fact, using the government's published Consumer Price Index (CPI) data as a measure of inflation, in 2014 it took $23.80 to buy what $1 would have bought in 1914. That's an inflation rate of 2,280.3 percent over a 90-year period, and that's called price stability? Perhaps the Fed needs a new definition of the term.

Since the prevailing narrative in the United States is mostly Keynesian, depending on how weak or robust the economy is, the Fed is expected to be able to successfully adjust interest rates and/or the money supply to keep things running smoothly. It follows, then, that assessing the economy accurately would be crucial to getting monetary policy right. How could they know what to do if they don't know what's causing today's problems or what problems are next?

Yet, for all the data available at its fingertips, it seems the Fed has perpetually been too optimistic regarding the economy, which isn't surprising given the political pressures it faces. In the last chapter, we gave you examples of Fed Chairmen Greenspan and Bernanke being dead wrong, as was former Treasury Secretary John Snow. They aren't unique, and those situations aren't unique. Always be skeptical of what the bureaucrats, pundits, and analysts say is going to happen, as they are often influenced by agendas that supersede the desire for accuracy.

Vector and Velocity

To get a firm grasp on any economy or sector within the economy, you need to know the vector and the velocity. Any pilot will tell you the vector is the direction in which we are heading and velocity is how fast we're moving. When it comes to the economy, by combining both vector and the *rate of change* in velocity, you will see that there are actually four primary stages of the business cycle that you need to be aware of:

- *Early* (Vector sharply up with an accelerating velocity)
  Activity rebounds with a typically sharp recovery from the last recession. Industrial production (IP) and income start to grow at an accelerating pace. Sales improve, while business inventories are low and profits improve rapidly. Monetary policy tends to remain stimulative, with credit conditions/lending expanding.
- *Mid* (More moderately upward vector with a slowing velocity)
  This is typically the longest phase of the business cycle with a positive, but more moderate rate of growth. Sales and inventory growth reach equilibrium with healthy profits. Monetary policy is shifting from accommodative to more neutral while credit growth remains strong.
- *Late* (Only slightly upward vector with velocity eventually stalling)
  This is often referred to as the *overheated* economy, where inflationary pressures emerge while growth starts to slow with credit now tightening (lending rates slowing). Corporate profits weaken as sales growth slows while inventory levels unexpectedly increase. Capacity utilization starts to decline as economic growth slows. Monetary policy becomes contractionary.
- *Recession* (Downward vector initially at high velocity)
  GDP growth has been negative for two quarters, at least with economic activity declining. Sales levels are low while inventory levels fall. Capacity utilization levels fall significantly; factories may even be shut down. Credit becomes difficult to obtain, which induces the government to now have more expansionary monetary policy.

The economy is in many ways just like any other living ecosystem. Think of it like a forest. The business cycle is the economic equivalent of the seasons, perfectly normal, with each season having its purpose, its pleasures, and its pains. Whereas seasons in nature tend to last for months, economic seasons last much longer.

Table 4.1, using data from the National Bureau of Economic Research (NBER), shows the length of these cycles. Think of the peak as the height of spring, when everything is blooming like mad. The trough is the darkest winter night, when barely a creature moves and all seems frozen over.

That's a lot of numbers to look at, so let's walk through it. Notice first that the contraction, when summer fades to fall, then into the darkest winter night, has always been shorter than the expansion period from winter to the height of spring; overall there are more swimsuit days than mitten days. Even more fascinating is how these have changed over time.

The breakout at the bottom of the chart separates business cycles into those that occurred under different types of economic policy. Pre–World War I, the government had little influence on the economy, thus the business cycle was primarily driven by the private-sector, which led to more frequent booms and busts that were simply allowed to run their course; some were small and some were large (mild winters and dear-God-please-stop-snowing ones). After World War I, the government became more involved in running the economy, with government spending and taxation as a percent of GDP rising from less than 5 percent to 43.6 percent by the mid-1940s. The Great Depression in the 1930s greatly impacted our understanding of the economy and how government actions affect it. Post–World War II policy, from 1945 to the present, has been focused on stabilizing output and employment, appearing to have counteracted some shocks and either prevented or reduced the pains from recessions. Table 4.2, using NBER data again, shows the degree of contraction from peaks going back to 1890.

From 1854 to 1919, contractions in the economy lasted on average 21.6 months while expansions lasted 26.6 months, an average difference of only 5 months, or contractions lasted 80 percent as long as expansion with the entire cycle just under 49 months long. From 1919 to 1945 contractions took about half the time of an expansion, with the entire cycle lasting on average 5 months longer. *From 1945 to 2009, contractions*

Table 4.1   Length of Economic Cycles 1902–2009 from the U.S. National
Bureau of Economic Analysis

Peak Month	Trough Month	Duration, Peak to Trough	Duration, Trough to Peak	Duration, Peak to Peak	Duration, Trough to Trough
September 1902	August 1904	23	21	39	44
May 1907	June 1908	13	33	56	46
January 1910	January 1912	24	19	32	43
January 1913	December 1914	23	12	36	35
August 1918	March 1919	7	44	67	51
January 1920	July 1921	18	10	17	28
May 1923	July 1924	14	22	40	36
October 1926	November 1927	13	27	41	40
August 1929	March 1933	43	21	34	64
May 1937	June 1938	13	50	93	63
February 1945	October 1945	8	80	93	88
November 1948	October 1949	11	37	45	48
July 1953	May 1954	10	45	56	55
August 1957	April 1958	8	39	49	47
April 1960	February 1961	10	24	32	34
December 1969	November 1970	11	106	116	117
November 1973	March 1975	16	36	47	52
January 1980	July 1980	6	58	74	64
July 1981	November 1982	16	12	18	28
July 1990	March 1991	8	92	108	100
March 2001	November 2001	8	120	128	128
December 2007	June 2009	18	73	81	91
1854–2009 (33 cycles)		17.5	38.7	56.4	56.2
1854–1919 (16 cycles)		21.6	26.6	48.9	48.2
1919–1945 (6 cycles)		18.2	35.0	53.0	53.2
1945–2009 (11 cycles)		11.1	58.4	68.5	69.5

SOURCE: National Bureau of Economic Research

lasted less than one-fifth the time of an expansion, with the entire cycle lasting 20 months longer than from 1854 to 1919! Swimsuit time has lengthened while mitten usage has declined. Keep this in mind whenever you hear people talk about business cycle norms; those norms have changed and will likely continue to do so as the Federal Reserve, and central banks in

Table 4.2 Degree of Economic Contraction
from Economic Peak from the United States
National Bureau of Economic Analysis

Year of NBER Peak	% Decline in Industrial Production
1890	−5.3
1893	−17.3
1895	−10.8
1899	−10.0
1902	−9.5
1907	−20.1
1910	−9.1
1913	−12.1
1918	−6.2
1920	−32.5
1923	−18.0
1926	−6.0
1929	−53.6
1937	−32.5
1945	−35.5
1948	−10.1
1953	−9.5
1957	−13.6
1960	−8.6
1969	−7.0
1973	−13.1
1980	−6.6
1981	−9.4
1990	−4.1
2001	−6.2

SOURCE: National Bureau of Economic Research

general, have greatly expanded their influence over economies and stock markets.

Now you have an understanding of the phases of the business cycle and have an idea of how long they last. Just as different types of plants and animals thrive during each season, each phase in the business cycle gives rise to different investment opportunities. If you were to follow this pattern exclusively as an investment strategy, you would be a *cyclical investor*. Figure 4.1 shows which sectors tend to do best during each phase of the business cycle. Keep in mind that like all things in life, *tend to* does

Sector	Early	Mid	Late	Recession
Financials	1	0	0	−1
Consumer Discretionary	2	0	−2	0
Technology	1	1	−2	−2
Industrials	2	1	0	−2
Materials	0	−2	2	−1
Consumer Staples	−1	0	1	2
Healthcare	−1	0	2	2
Energy	−2	0	2	0
Telecom	−2	0	0	2
Utilities	−2	−1	1	2

Figure 4.1 Typical sector performance per business cycle phase

not mean *always*. A sector can underperform or outperform relative to typical cycle trends thanks to any number of unique situations.

Figure 4.1 shows the relative performance of each major sector during different phases of the business cycle. A positive 2 means that sector usually produces positive returns during that specific phase of the business cycle, whereas a negative 2 means typically experiences losses. A positive 1 or negative 1 means often, but not always, a positive or negative return. A 0 means there is no consistent historical pattern. Keep in mind, though, that these are probabilities and not guarantees. A sector showing a positive 2 above could very well generate negative returns during that cycle in the future as returns are more complex than just about economic cycles.

Over time you could generate favorable investment returns with that strategy alone, but if it were your only strategy, you would have missed opportunities with a number of disruptive companies like Apple, Google, Qualcomm, Facebook, and hundreds of others. We'll talk more about how to spot those types of opportunities in Chapter 6.

Breaking It Down

There are three major participants in an economy: businesses, households, and government (see Figure 4.2). To understand the vector and velocity of an economy, you need to understand what is happening with each of these participants.

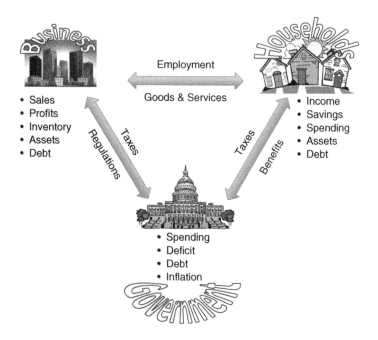

Figure 4.2   Major participants in an economy

Households

Households refers to all of us and the people we live with. Individuals in a household work, generating income that can then either be saved or spent. They may own assets such as homes and cars and may have taken on debt such as mortgages, auto loans, student loans, and/or credit card debt. These households pay the government through taxes and/or receive benefits from the government such as unemployment benefits and Social Security, or some form of welfare such as food stamps. To understand what is happening in the economy, it is necessary to understand the vector and velocity of these various aspects.

When we look at households, the two most important metrics reflect what portion of society is working and how much they are making (wages) and how those two have changed over time. To understand that, we need to look at not only what percent of the population has a job, but also the directional trends in job creation and how confident people are that they can find a job, which is reflected in the voluntary quit rate. We also want to know how much people are working and what kind of jobs they are performing—lower wage jobs, part-time or full-time jobs and so on. We refer to this as the "quality of job creation"—the more full-time jobs the higher the quality, and vice versa. We also want to know if wages are growing, stagnating or falling. If we see an increase in new job openings and increasing rates of employment, it would be reasonable to expect that income levels would next start to rise as businesses are forced to compete for employees.

The metrics in Table 4.3 will give you a very good understanding of the overall financial health of households. This is a rather complete list,

Table 4.3   Suggested Metrics for Financial Health of Households Application Example

Area	Indicator
Income	*Percent of population employed
Income	*Unemployment rate
Income	*Initial claims for unemployment insurance
Income	JOLTS Report
Income	Disposable income (percent change)
Income	*Median household income
Income	Hours worked
Savings	*Household savings rate
Spending	Retail sales ex-auto
Spending	*Consumer spending
Spending	Average daily spending by income
Assets	*Home ownership rates
Assets	*Case-Shiller home price indices
Assets	Housing starts
Assets	Single family housing starts
Assets	*New home sales
Assets	*Existing home sales
Assets	Average age of vehicles on the road
Assets	Auto sales
Assets/Income	*Percentage of homes purchased by first-time home buyers
Debt/Income	*Household debt-to-income levels
Debt	Mortgage rates
Debt/Income	*Mortgage delinquency rates
Debt/Income	*Auto loan delinquency rates
Debt/Income	*Credit card delinquency rates
Debt	Student loan levels
Debt/Income	*Student loan delinquency rates

so if you'd like a more cursory view, just look at the ones that are starred. More detailed explanations of these metrics and links to data sources can be found at the website for this book, CocktailInvesting.com. Most of these metrics are updated on a monthly basis and should be regularly monitored. We like to think that stringing several data points for each metric creates a trend that paints the picture of what is happening.

Households can either spend or save the income they've earned. The financial health of households can be assessed by looking at how their income is changing, to what degree they spend, save, and borrow, and changes in their assets such as cars and homes.

In the prior chapter we discussed how Reilly and Tyler were frustrated that they had bought their home near the peak of the market. One indicator that could have told them things were off in the housing market and the growth in home prices was not on a sustainable trend would have been the data shown in Figure 4.3 from the St. Louis Federal Reserve's program called "FRED." The affordability of a home, for the vast majority of families, is based on their household income.

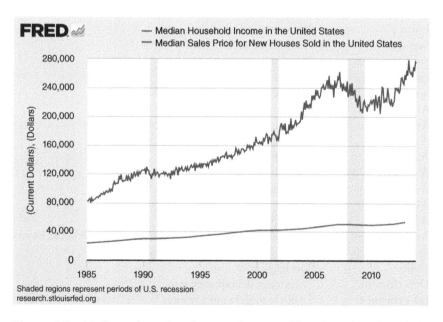

Figure 4.3 Median sales price for new houses sold and median household income in the United States from the Federal Reserve
SOURCE: St. Louis Federal Reserve

See how home prices have risen much more rapidly than incomes? Clearly, that isn't a trend that can continue indefinitely. At some point, people just give up trying to buy a home, as the prices are just impossible, given their income levels. As they give up, we would see this reflected in data for existing home sales as well as new home sales. The tough part is that there is no way to predict exactly when that moment will come. All you can say is that as home prices continue to rise faster than incomes, it becomes more and more likely that prices are going to fall.

Home prices fell substantially during and after the financial crisis, but then once again started to rise at an even more accelerated rate that grossly outpaced income levels. In fact, according to a report by RealtyTrac, in 2013 and 2014 home price appreciation nationwide outpaced wage growth by a 13:1 ratio, with median weekly wages rising 1.3 percent versus median home price increase of 17.31 percent. This trend of home prices rising faster than income levels continued in 2015. Once again, we see something that is simply not a sustainable trend.

Understanding the vector and velocity of delinquent mortgages can also tell you a lot about the housing market and the overall health of the consumer. If delinquency rates are falling and you see that income levels are improving while household debt-to-income levels are also improving, then you could likely expect to see an improvement in the housing market as well as overall consumer spending. You'd want to confirm that the consumer is looking to be in better financial shape by examining unemployment levels, and if there are increasing voluntary quits, you know that confidence in the job market is improving.

Real-Life Example of Putting It All Together for Households. Many investors, Chris included, thought the housing rebound would continue in 2015. In his mind, it was simple supply and demand— the supply of homes shrank and, given the level of demand, prices got ahead of themselves. Heading into 2015, data from the National Association of Home Builders showed that the available inventory of single-family homes for sale had reached multiyear lows (see month's supply for December 2013, circled, in Figure 4.4). Looking at the data, Chris thought that homebuilders—both publicly traded like D.R. Horton (DHI), Toll Brothers (TOL), and others as well as private ones—would see the market for what it was and build more affordable housing.

New and Existing Home Sales, U.S.

	NEW HOMES				EXISTING HOMES									
	SOLD	SOLD	FOR SALE	MONTHS' SUPPLY	SALES				INVENTORY			MONTHS' SUPPLY		
					TOTAL	TOTAL	SINGLE-FAMILY	CONDO-MINIUMS	TOTAL	SINGLE-FAMILY	CONDO-MINIUMS	TOTAL	SINGLE-FAMILY	CONDO-MINIUMS
	(1)	(2)	(3)	(4)	(5)	(6)	(7)	(8)	(9)	(10)	(11)	(12)	(13)	(14)
2010	321	321	189	7.0	4,183	4,182	3,708	474	3,020	2,590	429	9.4	9.0	11.9
2011	306	305	150	5.3	4,278	4,263	3,786	477	2,320	2,030	291	8.3	8.1	9.7
2012	368	369	148	4.5	4,657	4,656	4,128	528	1,830	1,610	224	5.9	5.8	6.3
2013	430	429	186	5.1	5,074	5,087	4,484	603	1,860	1,640	222	4.9	4.9	4.7
2014	440	439	212	5.1	4,920	4,935	4,344	591	1,860	1,640	216	5.2	5.2	5.1
2014 – Sep	459	37	209	5.5	5,100	436	4,500	600	2,280	2,020	257	5.4	5.4	5.1
Oct	472	38	208	5.3	5,160	443	4,540	620	2,240	1,980	261	5.2	5.2	5.1
Nov	449	31	210	5.6	4,950	351	4,350	600	2,080	1,850	227	5.0	5.1	4.5
Dec	495	35	212	5.1	5,070	413	4,500	570	1,860	1,640	216	4.4	(4.4)	4.5
2015 – Jan	521	39	208	4.8	4,820	281	4,280	540	1,860	1,670	194	4.6	4.7	4.3
Feb	545	45	204	4.5	4,890	295	4,350	540	1,900	1,660	238	4.7	4.6	5.3
Mar	485	46	205	5.1	5,210	405	4,600	610	2,010	1,750	263	4.6	4.6	5.2
Apr	508	48	207	4.9	5,090	449	4,480	610	2,220	1,960	257	5.2	5.3	5.1
May	513	47	210	4.9	5,320	495	4,710	610	2,280	2,030	254	5.1	5.2	5.0
Jun	469	44	217	5.6	5,480	572	4,830	650	2,250	2,000	247	4.9	5.0	4.6
Jul	503	43	217	5.2	5,580	551	4,950	630	2,260	1,990	269	4.9	4.8	5.1
Aug	529	43	216	4.9	5,300	504	4,680	620	2,270	2,010	255	5.1	5.2	4.9
Sep	468	36	225	5.8	5,550	471	4,930	620	2,210	1,960	248	4.8	4.8	4.8

For greater detail and analysis of these and other data, go to HousingEconomics.com

(1), (2), (3) & (5)–(11) Data are in thousands of units.
(4) & (12)–(14) Number of months.
(3) & (4) Monthly data are seasonally adjusted.
(1), (5), (7), (8) Monthly data are seasonally adjusted annual rates.
(2), (6) & (9)–(14) Monthly data are not seasonally adjusted.
(1) & (5) Annual data are an average of monthly data, seasonally adjusted.
(2) & (6)–(8) Annual data are the sum of monthly data, not seasonally adjusted.
(3), (4), & (9)–(11) Annual data are December data, not seasonally adjusted.
(12)–(14) Annual data are an average of the monthly data, not seasonally adjusted.
(NA) = Not available.

Figure 4.4 New and existing home sales 2009–2015

SOURCES: (1), (2), (3), and (4) from the U.S. Bureau of the Census; (5) through (14) from the National Association of Realtors. Prepared by the Economics Department of NAHB. Available at www.HousingEconomics.com.

Keep in mind the severe winter weather in early 2015 exacerbated the housing pain and conventional wisdom led many to think pent-up demand had been created—historically that's how it had typically worked.

Yet by late 2015, as Figure 4.5 shows, home ownership rates were back down to where they were 20 years prior.

So let's look at the condition of potential homebuyers. By the end of the post–financial crisis Great Recession, the unemployment rate had risen to just over 10 percent. By the latter part of 2015, it had fallen back down to 5 percent (see Figure 4.6), which sounds like a good thing for the housing sector, yet we still weren't seeing the expected boom.

The problem with just looking at the unemployment rate is it only reflects those who are actively looking for a job but can't find one. It doesn't take into account those who have simply given up or "fallen out of the labor force," to use Labor Department terms, nor does it take into account the income level of the previously unemployed person's new job relative to their prior job. For example, someone who loses a $200,000-a-year job who a year later can only find a job that pays $25,000 a year, while technically no longer unemployed, is in a

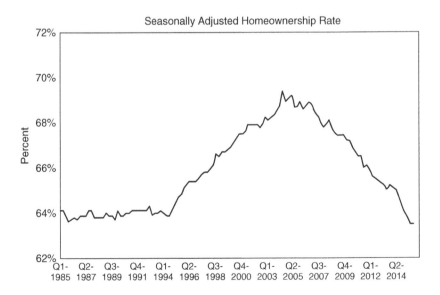

Figure 4.5 Quarterly homeownership rates for the United States 1995–2015 from the U.S. Census Bureau

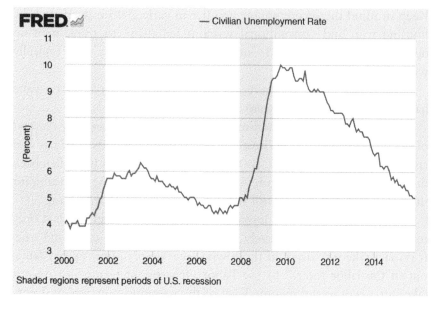

Figure 4.6 Unemployment rate
SOURCE: U.S. Federal Reserve

very different financial position than before losing his or her job. This is why earlier we mentioned that the most important metrics when thinking about households are the percentage employed and how much are they earning.

The chart in Figure 4.7 shows that the percent of the population employed rose from 1975 to 1999, but fell dramatically through 2012, only rising slightly by late 2015. The percent of the population employed toward the end of 2015 was back where it was during the early 1980s, and well below the peak at the end of the last millennium. With a lower percentage of the population working, the potential for the economy would necessarily be lower than it was in 1999. That's fairly intuitive. If there are 10 people in a boat, when 8 are rowing the boat can move a lot faster than when 6 are rowing.

There are a number of other employment indicators with one of the better-known ones coming from payroll processing firm ADP. One of our favorite "alternative" measures of job creation and employment is Gallup's Employment to Population Index, which is similar to the one above, but sidesteps all the math games of how many people are in the

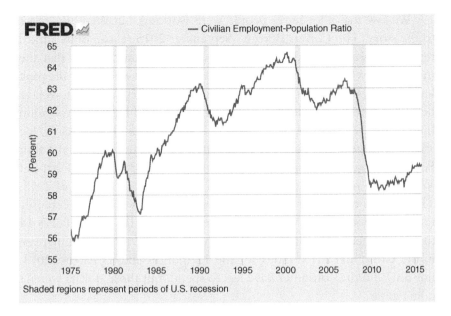

Figure 4.7 Employment-to-population ratio
SOURCE: U.S. Federal Reserve

labor pool and how many are not employed to focus on the number of people with jobs versus the entire U.S. population. We also watch payroll-to-population data published by the Bureau of Labor Statistics each month like hawks and we also keep close watch on other job creation data buried in monthly reports from Markit Economics and the Institute for Supply Management.

As you can see, in 2015 the financial state of the consumer and the availability of mortgages had changed, which is why it is so important to look at more than just a few pieces of data. Even if Joe and Jane Consumer wanted to buy a home, they couldn't afford to, couldn't get a loan, remained too shell-shocked from the previously unprecedented fall in home prices across the country to muster the courage, or knew they were facing (or soon to face) other financial hurdles.

We also saw a change in the usual makeup of those buying homes, with those buying a home for the first time much lower than we'd seen in the past. According to the National Association of Realtors, toward the end of 2015, the first-time buyer had fallen to the lowest level in nearly three decades at just 32 percent of all purchases.[1]

We saw that a lot fewer people were working, but there was more to the story. The Census Bureau's September 2015 release of its annual report on "Income and Poverty in the United States" stated that the median household income in 2014 was $53,657, still well below the peak level 15 years prior in 1999 at $56,895. Cardhub reported that average household credit card debt in the United States had hit a post-recession high of roughly $7,500 per household at the end of 2014.[2] Clearly, Joe and Jane Consumer were having a tough time. The Bureau of Labor Statistics showed median weekly earnings in second quarter of 2014 at $780, down roughly 1 percent from $786 in the third quarter of 2013. The drop in weekly earnings was bad enough on its own, and certainly took some wind out of "all the jobs created" during the first half of 2014 that was touted on Capital Hill, but compared to the 1.7 percent increase in the Consumer Price Index for the 12 months ending August 2014, not only did the consumer have less to spend, but those dollars weren't going as far.

There was also a problem with underemployment. A survey by Accenture released in May 2014 of 1,000 workers who graduated from college in 2013 reported that 46 percent claimed they were in a job that didn't require their degree, a 5 percent increase from the prior year's survey. The Federal Reserve reported in early 2014 that 44 percent of working recent grads were deemed underemployed in 2012. Those who think their job is well below their skill set may not feel confident in their earning abilities, which could make them less likely to take on the risk of buying a home.

Figure 4.8 from the Bureau of Labor Statistics shows how changes in productivity levels rose more than is typical during 2009, but then continued to oscillate below pre-crisis normal levels. The productivity of labor is, to a large degree, a function of capital investment by companies, which again is rather intuitive. With the latest and greatest tools, employees can normally accomplish a lot more than with tools from 10 or 20 years ago.

Productivity isn't exactly stellar looking in that chart. In fact, double-checking with the Commerce Department, we found that by the end of 2014, the average age of fixed assets, such as plants and factories, is about 22 years old, the oldest average going back to 1956! Of course, productivity would be challenging. Think about how much you can accomplish with your smartphone versus a rotary phone!

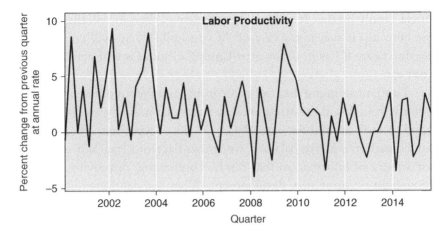

Figure 4.8 Labor productivity from the United States Bureau of Labor Statistics
SOURCE: Bureau of Labor Statistics

Putting all these charts together, we can deduce that there is room for improved labor productivity given that it has not been growing all that strongly. But, the contribution of labor into overall economic growth is limited until a higher percentage of the population is working, as those currently with jobs are working at nearly the same level of hours as before the crisis, when the economy was strong. Overall, a lower percentage of the population was working than before, income levels are below historical levels, and an awful lot of workers felt they were underemployed.

That's a very different picture than the one painted by the headlines claiming enormous strides in the employment situation. Sherlock Holmes was able to solve the mystery because he took in so many more data points, picking up on details that Inspector Lestrade never saw. Throughout this book we will not only be showing you what details you ought to look at, but also teach you to have a Holmes-like process.

As the data we just walked through became available, Chris's view on the housing sector softened, which goes to illustrate several points we want to highlight to you. First, the economy is a dynamic and living thing—parts of it can grow or expand while other aspects can shrink or come under pressure. Second, look for a relationship between different parts of the economy. In this case, there was a direct example largely because, for the most part, consumers are the ones who buy single-family homes. If consumers are hurting, then so will the demand for housing. It was not a case of "if you build it, he will come," and we don't care if Kevin Costner or James Earl Jones is whispering this in your ear.

Third, meaningful data can come from a number of different sources, not just from data that correspond to a particular industry, and it is always good to look around for extra data to verify a hypothesis. As we mentioned earlier, we love data and we always have our eyes and ears open for a piece of information that can be confirming, disproving, or shed some light on some new development. When we get these nuggets, we ask ourselves the following:

- What does it mean? (One of Chris's favorite questions.)
- How does this fit with the other data that we are seeing or have collected?
- Does this tell me anything new or different, or does it simply reinforce what we already know?
- Who does this affect? A demographic cohort, certain industries, both, or more?
- How well known or widely distributed is this piece of information?

Finally, when you think about the household part of the economy, keep in mind the context for where families spend money. You have probably heard that the U.S. economy is driven primarily by personal consumption, which accounts for around 70 percent of gross domestic product. Well, if that's the case, just what are households spending it all on? You'll see from Figure 4.9 that the largest portion of household spending goes to shelter at 20.2 percent, which helps make it clear why the boom and subsequent bust in home prices during the Great Recession was so painful. Conversely, apparel and services account for all of 3.8 percent of average expenditures, so a doubling of cotton prices isn't likely to have a big impact on the economy.

As the John Maynard Keynes saying goes, "When the facts change, I change my mind. What do you do, sir?"

Remember, we told you to focus on vector and velocity. This shows the importance of adding in one more concept when looking at individual metrics or parts of the economy—magnitude. Cotton prices could be moving in all kinds of wild directions, which will have a significant impact on companies in the apparel industry, but given the magnitude

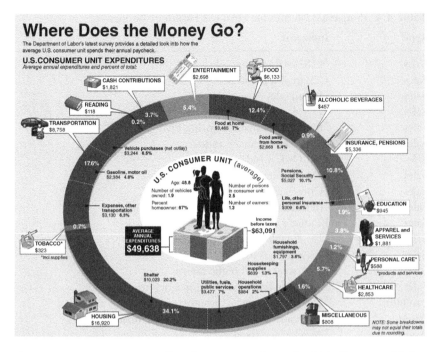

Figure 4.9   Consumer spending by category from the U.S. Bureau of Labor Statistics and the U.S. Department of Labor

of the apparel industry on the average family, cotton prices alone aren't going to significantly impact the average family's spending habits. So now let's take a look at the part of the economy that provides all those goods and services we buy.

Business

The second of the three participants in an economy, businesses, generate sales to earn profits, which they then reinvest into the business, use to pay down loans, or pay out to the owners or shareholders as a return on their investment. They have inventory, such as food and drinks at a restaurant. They have money invested in assets, such as kitchen appliances, tables, chairs, and linens for that restaurant. They may also have debt from borrowing to finance the purchase of perhaps a new refrigerator or to improve or even expand the dining room for that restaurant. Businesses employ people, who in turn pay businesses for products and services.

Table 4.4   Suggested Metrics for Financial Health of Businesses

Type	Indicator
Sales	*U.S. total business sales
Sales	U.S. total retail sales
Sales	*Retail sales ex-auto
Sales	*U.S. e-commerce sales
Sales	*Markit U.S. manufacturing PMI
Sales	ISM Manufacturing Index
Sales	ISM Orders Index
Sales	ISM Manufacturing Price Index
Sales	*Core capital goods orders
Sales	*Industrial production—Manufacturing
Sales	Producer Price Index
Sales	U.S. durable goods new orders
Sales	U.S. retail gas prices
Sales	AAR weekly rail traffic report
Sales	American Truck Association truck tonnage index
Inventory	*U.S. Total business inventories/Sales ratio
Assets	*U.S. capacity utilization—Manufacturing
Assets	*Average age fixed assets
Debt	U.S. debt outstanding nonfinancial sector—Business corporate

Businesses pay taxes to the government and are controlled to varying degrees through laws and regulations. We'll talk more about the relationship between businesses and the government later when we discuss government as the third participant in an economy.

As we did with households, the metrics in Table 4.4 will give you a good understanding of the overall condition for businesses. This is again a rather complete list; so if you'd like a quick cursory view, just look at the ones that are starred. More detailed explanations of the metrics and links to their sources can be found at the website for this book, CocktailInvesting.com. Most of these metrics are updated on a monthly basis, a few are weekly, and should be regularly monitored.

Application Example. Earlier in this chapter, we talked about the business cycle and the four states of the cycle: Early, mid, late, and recession. The metrics in Table 4.4 can help you identify just where we are in the business cycle.

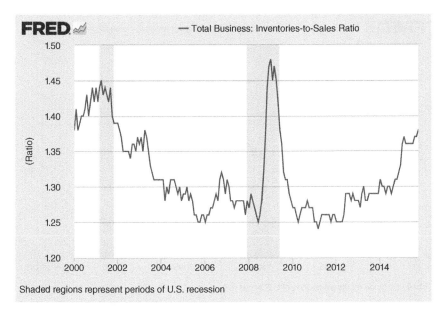

Figure 4.10   Business inventory-to-sales ratio, 2000–Q3 2015
SOURCE: U.S. Federal Reserve

Figure 4.10 shows the inventory-to-sales ratio from January 1, 2000, to September 2015. The trough of the first cycle below was November 2001. Notice how from 2001 to 2006 inventories relative to sales declined as the next cycle kicked off. Then in 2006 and 2007 inventories jumped up, which is typical for late stage, then as the recession hit, sales plummeted, so this ratio would naturally jump up significantly as businesses can't sell during a recession what they already have in inventory. During the recession businesses let their inventories fall much lower than during a strong economy, so when sales pick up, this ratio can improve rapidly.

Taking an even further step backward, Figure 4.11 shows an even more interesting trend in inventories that spans across multiple business cycles, with recessionary periods shaded gray.

You'll notice that businesses have been able to reduce their inventories on a fairly consistent basis over the past few decades. That's good news for the business owners, as inventory that just sits on the shelf is a poor use of a company's money. In a perfect world,

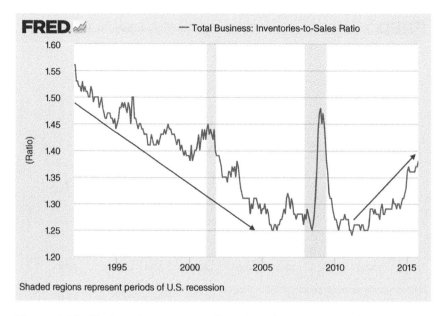

Figure 4.11 Business inventory-to-sales ratio and recessions, 1992–Q3 2015
SOURCE: U.S. Federal Reserve

inventory comes in one door and immediately goes out the other to the customer. Figure 4.11 also gives a great appreciation for the magnitude of the shock caused by the Great Recession. Since then, the trend of ever-falling inventories appears to have been reduced somewhat, with inventory levels rising since 2011.

We also mentioned how capacity utilization levels change throughout the business cycle. Figure 4.12 shows capacity utilization levels from 1990 through September 2015, again with recessions shaded in gray.

Notice how going into a recession, capacity utilization rates fall dramatically and fast. When people stop buying, factories slow down, lay off workers, and sometimes even have to shut down. As the recession ends and the recovery begins, the snows thaw, green shoots appear, and those factories get humming again.

Real-Life Example of Putting It All Together for Businesses. Part of the process of analyzing these data points is to not overextend a trend. Parts of the economy often do not move in tandem; for example, a few pages back, we mentioned the weaker than expected tone of the

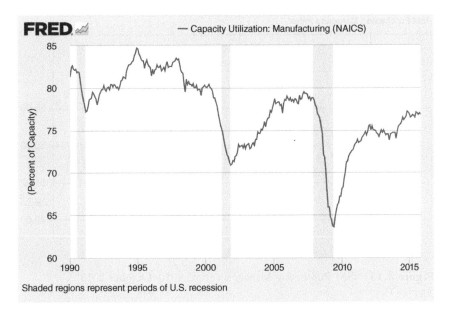

Figure 4.12 Manufacturing capacity utilization, 1990–Q3 2015
SOURCE: U.S. Federal Reserve

U.S. housing market reflected in the pressure being felt by the consumer. If that was all you knew, you might think that 2014 was not a good year for the U.S. economy. Although household income restrained overall growth, there were other factors that were spurring the economy along, including strength in auto and truck sales as well as aerospace demand and, generally speaking, overall manufacturing activity was improving.

The Institute of Supply Management (ISM) publishes the Purchasing Managers Index (PMI) on a monthly basis (Figure 4.13), which is widely considered a good indicator of the economic health of the manufacturing sector and is based on five major indicators: new orders, inventory levels, production, supplier deliveries, and employment conditions. A PMI reading of 50 or more represents expansion, under 50 signals a contraction, while an even reading of 50 means no change. We watch this metric out of both Markit and ISM every month.

Remember we mentioned vector and velocity. From 2011 to mid-2013, the ISM PMI was overall falling. During most of 2014, it looked to be improving significantly, but then once again starting falling dramatically at the end of 2014 and throughout 2015. If we look at the

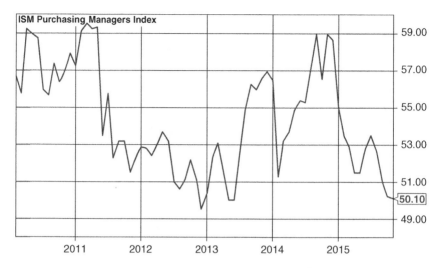

Figure 4.13   ISM Purchasing Managers Index, 2010–October 2015
SOURCE: YCharts

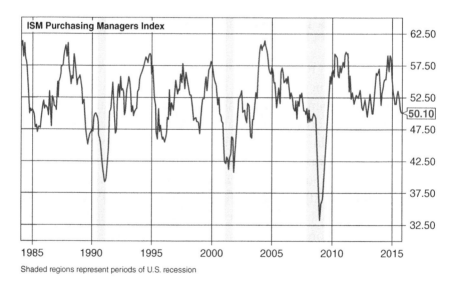

Shaded regions represent periods of U.S. recession

Figure 4.14   ISM Purchasing Managers Index, 1984–October 2015
SOURCE: YCharts

PMI on a longer time frame to get more historical context, we can see that in fact, by the latter part of 2014, it was in the region where it normally peaks out, so for those who were paying attention, the slide throughout 2015 would not have been a surprise. Figure 4.14 also gives you a better appreciation for the magnitude of the contraction from the Great Recession (note recessions are shaded gray).

So manufacturing was looking better, but just how impactful that is for the economy is another question. Remember to always keep things in context, so we need to look at just how impactful a strong manufacturing sector is on the rest of the economy. The Bureau of Economic Analysis provides quarterly and annual data on GDP by industry. Table 4.5 shows a summary of that data.

Here we can see that manufacturing had declined as a percentage of GDP from 16.1 percent in 1997 to 12.1 percent in 2013 and 2014, so while a positive PMI is a good sign for the economy, it doesn't necessarily speak for the entire economy.

Table 4.5 GDP by Industry as a Percent of Total Contribution, 1997–2014, from the U.S. Bureau of Economic Analysis

Industry Title	1997	2000	2010	2013	2014
Gross domestic product	100.0	100.0	100.0	100.0	100.0
Private industries	86.7	87.1	85.7	86.8	86.9
Agriculture, forestry, fishing, and hunting	1.3	1.0	1.1	1.4	1.2
Mining	1.1	1.1	2.2	2.6	2.6
Utilities	2.0	1.8	1.8	1.6	1.6
Construction	4.0	4.5	3.6	3.7	3.8
Manufacturing	16.1	15.1	12.2	12.1	12.1
Wholesale trade	6.2	6.1	5.8	6.0	6.0
Retail trade	6.8	6.8	5.8	5.8	5.8
Transportation and warehousing	3.0	3.0	2.8	2.9	2.9
Information	4.6	4.6	4.9	4.6	4.8
Finance, insurance, real estate, rental, and leasing	18.9	19.4	19.7	20.2	20.0
Professional and business services	9.8	10.8	11.6	11.8	11.9
Educational services, healthcare, and social assistance	6.8	6.6	8.3	8.2	8.2
Arts, entertainment, recreation, accommodation, and food services	3.5	3.8	3.6	3.7	3.8
Government	13.3	12.9	14.3	13.2	13.1
Federal	4.5	4.1	4.7	4.2	4.1
State and local	8.8	8.8	9.6	9.0	9.0

SOURCE: Bureau of Economic Analysis

We next look for corroborating data on the health of the manu-facturing sector. When a company manufactures something—a part, component, subassembly, or even a finished product—it not only has to get the building blocks to create its product, but the product must be transported to the customers, be they other manufacturers, distribu-tion centers, or retailers. That means paying attention to transportation activity data that are widely available to you and me.

Two such pieces of information that we like to track are weekly rail car loadings and truck tonnage. The American Association of Railroads[3] not only does a great job of publishing the weekly and year-to-date load-ings data, but it also offers several views on the data including intermodal loadings and a deeper dive on 10 carload commodity groupings. It's data like these that offer near real-time insight.

According to the American Association of Railroads, in the second quarter of 2014 U.S. intermodal volume was strong and through the week ending July 12, those car loadings were up 6 percent on a year-to-date basis.[4] For those who are unfamiliar with the term, intermodal freight transport involves the transportation of freight in an inter-modal container or vehicle, using multiple modes of transportation (rail, ship, and truck), without any handling of the freight itself when changing modes. We think it is a great measure of economic activity.

Intermodal was not alone, as U.S. freight carload traffic also rose 4.8 percent for the week ending July 12, 2014.[5] That was well above the year-to-date average of 3.4 percent as of July 12.[6] Comparing year-to-date figures at various points during the year lets us know if the traffic and subsequently the economy were picking up speed or not. In this case, it was—the 2014 year-to-date 3.5 percent increase in freight carload traffic for the first 28 weeks of 2014 compared to 2.2 percent for the first 24 weeks of the year.[7] Some simple math tells us, the economy had indeed picked by mid-July.

The second metric we mentioned was truck tonnage. According to the American Trucking Association, trucks hauled nearly 70 percent of all the freight tonnage (over 9.2 billions tons) moved in the United States.[8] That makes trucking activity a key barometer of the U.S. econ-omy. Each month the American Trucking Association publishes its truck tonnage index and just like the weekly rail traffic report, it's one we watch for each month.

Around the same time rail data was improving, the data also pointed to a pronounced pickup in the economy. The May 2014 tonnage index reading was up 3.3 percent year-over-year. Even though the June 2014 truck tonnage reading declined 0.8 percent month-over-month, the year-over-year comparison still showed an impressive 2.3 percent improvement. Through the first half of the year, compared to the same period in 2013, the truck tonnage index was up 2.8 percent.[9]

Put the truck tonnage and intermodal commentary together and you can imagine that it would have been a good time for companies such as J.B. Hunt Transport Services (JBHT), which gets more than half of its revenue from intermodal shipments; booming rail traffic means more truckloads to and from the railyard. In 2013 and 2014, it would be difficult to have a discussion of rail traffic without mentioning the proposed Keystone pipeline and all the political strife surrounding it, which brings us to our third and final participant in the economy, the government.

Watching both of these metrics—truck tonnage and weekly rail traffic—in 2015, however, painted a much different picture. For the first 10 months of 2015, total rail traffic volume in the United States was 23.5 million carloads and intermodal units, down 1.4 percent from the same point in the prior year.[10] The truck tonnage index hit a reading of 135.1 for September 2015,[11] well off the peak of 135.8 reached in January 2015. Putting these two indicators together tells us the economy cooled dramatically in 2015 compared to 2014, and we see that in both Figures 4.13 and 4.14. As we said before, the economy is a living, breathing dynamic beast, and as investors we need to be aware of its ever-changing vector and velocity.

Government

Earlier in this chapter, we discussed how the business cycle has changed significantly over the past 150-plus years. Between 1900 and 2013, federal government receipts (meaning money collected from taxes) increased from just 3 percent of GDP to over 17 percent for 2014 (estimated). Federal government spending grew from less than 3 percent to nearly a quarter of the economy by 2009, down to just over one fifth by 2014. If we add in spending by state governments, by 2014, it is estimated that total government spending accounted for around

35 percent of GDP—that's more than one-third! In addition, the Federal Reserve didn't even exist in 1900. Now the Fed is all but able to dictate interest rates, a key factor of any economy. Now that government spending accounts for over one-third of the economy, and given that the Federal Reserve is able to have an enormous impact on prevailing interest rates as well as dictating many aspects of bank lending, it is a participant worth our attention. In the next chapter, we'll go into more detail on how government policy affects the investing climate, so for now we'll just focus on what metrics to watch.

Governments collect taxes from businesses and households. That reduces the money those two participants (the private sector) can spend, save, and invest. Government then gives a portion of the taxes it has collected to other households through various benefits such as Social Security, unemployment benefits, food stamps, and so on, or it can use the money to provide subsidies and/or loans to businesses. One of the arguments for government support of the unemployed during tough economic times is that those subsidies can help bolster consumer spending. Government impacts the behavior of both businesses and households through taxes, regulations, and laws. The metrics for government, as shown in Table 4.6, are quite a bit slower to change than for households and businesses, so these are things that you need to be aware of and think through, but not on a monthly basis like many of the other metrics—quarterly to annually for most data points is sufficient.

Application Example: Housing Industry. One way that the U.S. government supports the housing industry is by making a portion of mortgage payments tax deductible. This effectively reduces the cost of a mortgage. For example, you are assessing whether to rent a house for $1,000 a month or buy a home and have a $1,000 monthly mortgage payment. For simplicity's sake, we'll ignore the impact of a down payment. The mortgage deduction makes owning less expensive, given that a portion of that $1,000 can be used to reduce how much money you pay in taxes. On the other hand, you may have to pay property taxes when you own, which raises the cost of owning, but you get the idea. Changes in the deductibility of interest payments on mortgages change the effective cost of owning a home, and thus will impact the desirability of owning versus renting.

Table 4.6 Suggested Metrics for Government

Type	Indicator
Spending	U.S. federal spending as % of GDP
Deficit	U.S. federal deficit as % of GDP
Debt	U.S. public debt as % of GDP
Debt	U.S. public debt per capita
Debt	Fiscal year-end interest expense
Debt	10-year Treasury rate
Inflation	Excess reserves of depository institutions
Inflation	Federal Reserve total assets
Inflation	U.S. monetary base
Inflation	Velocity of M2 money stock
Taxes	Changes in individual income tax rates
Taxes	Changes in taxes on consumer goods
Taxes	Changes allowable deductions such as the mortgage deduction
Taxes	Changes in business rates taxes and deductions

Remember in Chapter 3 how frustrated Reilly and Tyler were to see the market value of their home plummet after having purchased it in 2005? How could they have known just how much home prices were going to fall? They knew that they were not exactly buying at the bottom of the market, but everyone they spoke to told them not to worry, that perhaps their home value could drop a bit in the years to come, but not enough to worry about. Ten years later and according to Zillow, the estimated sale price for their home is still less than what they paid for it.

Looking at the data, Reilly and Tyler weren't alone! So very many people were caught up in the home-buying frenzy and we bet that for many, they were simply at a time in their lives when they wanted to settle down in a home for a while, so they went ahead with buying a home, even though they intuited that it wasn't the best time. Looking at the historical trends in home prices before the financial crisis, there never had been a significant and long-lasting downturn in home prices on a national level.

Housing prices in a heated market can go up for a while simply because everyone believes they will continue to rise, but generally there is some fire behind that smoke, something that kicked off the entire process. This was the case with the runup in home prices. In Figure 4.5

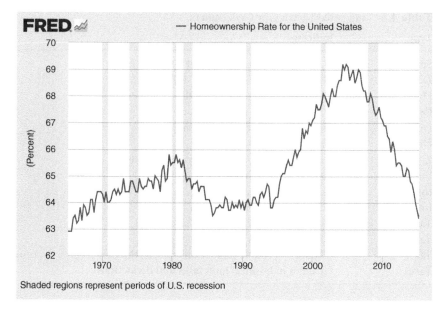

Figure 4.15   Home ownership rates, 1980–October 2015
SOURCE: U.S. Federal Reserve

we showed how home ownership rates had changed over time. In Figure 4.15, let's look at that data again, but from an even longer-term perspective.

Here we can see that home ownership rates rose dramatically from the latter half of the 1990s to peak in 2004 and have been falling continually since then. Why? Is this good or bad?

Before we answer that, let's remember that in the mid-1990s, home-ownership was a major push by both the Democrats and the Republicans over the ensuing decade that led to low to no down payments and pushed for lenders to give mortgage loans to first-time buyers with shaky financing and incomes. Hindsight being 20/20, it's clear the erosion of lending standards pushed prices up by increasing demand, and later led to waves of defaults by people who, for a variety of reasons, never should have bought a home in the first place.

Our interpretation of the data indicates that the peak of home ownership is not something to which we ought to aspire. Not every household should own the place in which they reside, as the costs and risks can easily outweigh the potential benefits. Homeowners can't easily move if they need to change jobs, something we saw coming out of the Great Recession, and we've seen the impact of this in the way the labor market post–financial crisis has been the most inflexible in history with respect to geography. People are unable to rapidly react to changing conditions in the economy that affect their household finances, not to mention the hassle of home ownership and all the costs that are unimaginable beforehand.

Why did home ownership rates increase so much before the financial crisis, to levels that were clearly unsustainable and caused so much pain for so many? Was it just those evil, greedy bankers that somehow tricked people into buying homes? Well, that's partially true. There are some rats in those banks, but that is only part of the story, and a misleading take on all that happened.

You can also thank the federal government. Traditionally, non-FHA mortgages required a minimum of 20 percent down, but in 1994 the Department of Housing and Urban Development (HUD) ordered Fannie Mae and Freddie Mac to supplement and eventually to far surpass the FHA's efforts by directing 30 percent of their mortgages to low-income borrowers, when previously the number had been much lower.[12] This became pretty tough to do, so to meet that goal, Fannie Mae introduced 3 percent down mortgages in 1997.[13]

In 2000, HUD increased the low-income target to be 50 percent of all loans. Now think about that: What bank in their right mind would want to make 50 percent of their loans for the year to low-income families with exceptionally low money down? That means 50 percent of your loans are in the riskiest category! To accomplish this, Fannie launched a 10-year, $2 trillion "American Dream Commitment" program to increase home ownership rates among those who previously had been unable to own homes. So when the government gets itself all focused on getting people who previously couldn't afford a home into one, is it really all that shocking that home prices rose like crazy?

In 2002, Freddie joined the party with the "Catch the Dream" program to accomplish essentially the same thing. Then in 2005, HUD increased the target for low-income loans again to 52 percent! Now here's a bit of irony. The government wanted more people to own homes, so it makes it easier and easier to get a loan. Now we've got more people out in the market to buy homes. Son-of-a-gun, prices go up. Well now, isn't that exciting! Buying a home looks like a really great investment because the prices are just going through the roof! But wait—rising home prices are great for only half the equation. They are great for the owner who looks to sell, but not much fun for the person trying to buy. So in their attempt to increase home ownership by making it easier to buy a home, the government made homes even less affordable.

Oh, but that's OK, as Fannie and Freddie are there to save the day and get you into that home that you really cannot afford with little to no money down and a variable rate mortgage that isn't a ticking time bomb at all! All these subsidies increased the supply of mortgages to low-income aspiring homeowners, but what was the source of the money to fund these loans? Welcome to the mortgage-backed securities (MBS), those weapons of mass destruction. Banks would pool together mortgages that could then be sold as an MBS, and with HUD's desire to get Fannie and Freddie to increase homeownership in the subprime areas, these two agencies were more than happy to back the MBS, which, because they are government-sponsored entities, turned subprime loans with very little money down into AAA-rated bonds!

Serious fairy dust, isn't it?

Now the banks were running around gobbling these things up like there's no tomorrow. Why, you ask? Well, according to the Basel Accords, banks could seriously lower their reserve requirements by holding these GSE (government-sponsored entity) AAA-rated bonds, which improved their profit margins. A bank's reserve requirement is a central bank regulation employed by most of the world's central banks, including the U.S. Treasury, that sets the minimum fraction of customer deposits and notes that each commercial bank must hold as reserves, rather than lend out. Anything that lowers reserve requirements lets a bank lend out more, thus, all things being equal, improving their profit margins.

So What Does All This Mean? *Subsidies distort markets in that they artificially increase demand.*

This artificial boost in demand raises prices and pushes the market to allocate more resources (workers, money, equipment, land, etc.) into the subsidized industry than it otherwise would have. When the subsidy ends, as they usually do, the extra resources that were allocated thanks to the subsidized demand have to go elsewhere, but the shift can take considerable time and be very painful.

In the recent housing crisis, the subsidies added a lot of workers to the payrolls of construction firms and mortgage companies and induced investments, such as in extra home-building, that would have otherwise gone elsewhere. When it all came crashing down, those workers had to find jobs in other industries, and the skills they'd developed in construction or mortgage generation became much less valuable, and a lot of the money invested in construction projects was permanently lost.

Regulations alter incentives.

Regulations are typically implemented to keep people safer than is believed they would be without the regulations. This theoretical protection can range from hazardous products to the impacts of foreign competition or financial irresponsibility. Without regulations, companies will behave according to their individual views on the opportunities and risks in the marketplace. Their views and corresponding actions may be contrary to what a regulator or regulation deems appropriate. However, the unfettered behavior in the free markets, which some may argue is more risky, tends to create a diversified set of positions, which helps prevent industrywide failure. All participants don't put all their eggs in the same basket, as companies tend to follow different tactics to gain a competitive edge. Regulations are intended to force companies to all behave in a similar manner with respect to the regulated area, so now everyone has their eggs in the same basket. Thus, the industry as a whole may be more vulnerable to systemic changes that are not anticipated by the regulation.

We'll talk more about how governments and regulations can impact the economy and your investments in the next chapter.

Application Example: Corporate Funding. Government also impacts the way businesses fund themselves and provide investment returns to shareholders. To grow, a business can either borrow money or take equity investors. The U.S. tax code affects the cost of debt funding relative to equity funding because, much like with a mortgage, interest payments on money a business borrows are tax deductible, whereas payments to equity investors to compensate them for the money they have invested are not. This can make debt funding relatively less expensive for the business than equity funding. In addition, the government taxes interest payments (for a loan) to lenders differently than dividends paid to equity investors. Investors must seek out the best returns available for any given level of risk. Thus, taxation that lowers net returns impacts where investors are willing to put their savings and what kind of returns they will demand for their investments. In Chapter 9, we will show you how the different tax treatment for interest payments versus dividends paid to shareholders has affected corporation behavior, particularly in recent years with interest rates at historical lows.

Application Example: Government Debt. You have also probably heard about the large and ever-growing federal debt. As of the end of 2014, the federal public debt was over 100 percent of GDP and it remained that way exiting 2015—just check one of our favorite sites on the Internet, USDebtClock.org. As you look at government debt, keep in mind that the largest holders of government debt throughout most of the world are banks. This is particularly true throughout much of Europe. One of the main holders of sovereign debt is the banking sector. Now here's the thing: As we mentioned in the earlier example and as you'll learn further in the next chapter, banks are highly regulated. When you give them money through deposits like a checking account, they turn around and either give that money to someone else in the form of a loan or invest in other assets like Treasury bonds. They get extra special bonus points, detailed in the next chapter in the section on fractional reserve banking, for holding sovereign debt, similar to the way, as we discussed in the earlier example, they received extra bonus points for holding mortgages guaranteed by Fannie Mae or Freddie Mac. So they can either lend to someone buying a home, starting or growing a business, or to the government. Keep that in mind when you look at the growth of sovereign debt and bank regulations; in a way they are competing against you for loans from banks.

Getting back to vector, velocity, and magnitude, when you look at changes in government spending, deficit, debt, taxes, and their impact on various sectors of the economy on down to companies, it boils down to looking at the direction of the change, the degree of change, and just how impactful it will be. An increase in cigarette taxes, while painful for the smoker, would not impact the overall economy. Removal of the home mortgage deduction would have a significant impact on home prices, which, given the large portion of the household budget allocated to housing, would have a far bigger impact on the overall economy.

Going Global

Finally, in our increasingly globally interconnected world, investors need to be aware of the international picture. The vector of the global economy is the sum of individual country vectors, and in this case, size really does matter. That means focusing primarily on the four horsemen that drive more than 65 percent of global gross domestic product—the Eurozone, the United States, China, and Japan (see Table 4.7). We aren't dismissing the economies of the other 183 regions tracked by the International Monetary Fund, but to get a handle on where the global economy is going, it's the four horsemen that have the biggest impact and are therefore the ones to watch most closely.

From time to time, the economies of the top four can move in harmony, and when that happens to the positive side, global growth can be quite strong. But those economies don't have to be headed in the same direction. A recent example can be found in the second half of 2014—growth in the Eurozone was slowing at an accelerating pace (vector down, velocity increasing), prompting some to call for a triple-dip recession, while growth in China cooled as well. In the United States the industrial and manufacturing economy was on fire.

Investors should first identify which countries are poised to grow faster than the rest, and then dig deeper to find the industries and companies that are most likely to benefit from that growth. We can use history as a guide when determining where in the four stages of the economic cycle a particular country is at the time, but remember, that is merely a guide, and just as a good guidebook might help you get around New York, London, Paris, or Milan, be aware that conditions may change, roads may be closed for repairs, and new hotspots may have recently opened.

Table 4.7 Top 30 Countries Ranked by Gross Domestic Product According to the International Monetary Fund for 2014

Rank	Country/Region	GDP (Millions of US$)	Percentage
	World	77,868,768	
	European Union	18,527,115	23.8%
1	United States	17,348,075	22.3%
2	China	10,356,508	13.3%
3	Japan	4,602,367	5.9%
4	Germany	3,874,437	5.0%
5	United Kingdom	2,950,039	3.8%
6	France	2,833,687	3.6%
7	Brazil	2,346,583	3.0%
8	Italy	2,147,744	2.8%
9	India	2,051,228	2.6%
10	Russia	1,860,598	2.4%
11	Canada	1,785,387	2.3%
12	Australia	1,442,722	1.9%
13	Korea	1,410,383	1.8%
14	Spain	1,406,538	1.8%
15	Mexico	1,291,062	1.7%
16	Indonesia	888,648	1.1%
17	Netherlands	880,716	1.1%
18	Turkey	798,332	1.0%
19	Saudi Arabia	746,248	1.0%
20	Switzerland	703,852	0.9%
21	Nigeria	573,999	0.7%
22	Sweden	570,591	0.7%
23	Poland	547,894	0.7%
24	Argentina	543,061	0.7%
25	Belgium	534,230	0.7%
26	Taiwan Province of China	529,597	0.7%
27	Norway	499,817	0.6%
28	Austria	437,582	0.6%
29	Islamic Republic of Iran	416,490	0.5%
30	Thailand	404,824	0.5%

SOURCE: The International Monetary Fund

Data Corroboration

No particular data set can paint a complete picture. A single data point or set can, at times, be misleading. For example, despite the "official" statistic telling us there was little inflation in 2013 and 2014, prices for the protein complex—beef, pork, and shrimp—made significant moves during 2014.

But the U.S. government's data don't reflect that. Earlier, when we were discussing why you shouldn't trust the "experts," we mentioned that in the United States, those on Capitol Hill view the Consumer Price Index, excluding food and energy, as the true measure of inflation. We shake our heads in frustration while pacing, asking "How can the government and the Fed exclude food and energy when it accounts for 15 to 20 percent of the average weekly paycheck?" (Remember that fancy chart in Figure 4.13 showing where household spending goes?)

That's why we track a series of other indicators, including commodity prices, Department of Agriculture supply-and-demand reports, and several others, as well as a few informal indicators. Other signs also warrant watching when it comes to inflation. One example is the Bacon Cheeseburger Index by ConvergEx, which showed a very different picture. The average bacon cheeseburger cost 7.9 percent more in mid-2014 than it did at the same point in 2013. Lest you think the cheeseburger index is, well, full of it, a quick scan of Bureau of Labor Statistics (BLS) data confirmed its findings. BLS data showed that bacon prices were up 16.4 percent in mid-2014 from the prior year, while ground beef was up 10.5 percent and American cheese prices were up nearly 10 percent.[14]

The bacon cheeseburger index is but one example of alternative economic measures. There are others for how fast the economy is growing, what the job creation picture really looks like, and more. You can get details on these from this book's website at CocktailInvesting.com.

Data from the federal government are like any other data source, meaning relying on just one source can be misleading. That reality check doesn't even include the vast number of revisions the government conducts for how the data are collected and reported. Those revisions can make comparisons with historical data much less meaningful.

Trade associations are also fantastic sources of data that can help bring your economic and investing mosaic into focus. No matter what the industry, from trucks and railcars to wireless and telephony to a specific demographic group, there are associations and institutions with all sorts of useful data. On this book's website, we'll give you a helping head start on some of the more useful ones that we use.

Application Examples

In early December 2014, the markets were as giddy as a room full of journalists upon the start of the latest political sex scandal. At first blush, the Bureau of Labor Statistics' 2014 November Employment Report stood out for job creation numbers that were nearly 40 percent higher than expectations, but as the trading day wore on, gravity set in on the stock market, which closed the day off its morning highs.

Normally one would have anticipated that better-than-expected job growth would fuel a move higher in the market, but the November figure was met with skepticism because the BLS-supplied figure was inconsistent with the previously released November 2014 ADP private-sector-focused jobs report, which saw a month-over-month drop in the number of jobs created. Moreover, the employment data released by the Institute for Supply Management (ISM) for November 2014 showed slower job growth in November than in October for both the manufacturing and nonmanufacturing categories. Even the payroll-to-population data published by Gallup for November 2014 showed a decline to 44.2 percent from October's 44.4 percent.

With so many other data points running counter to the BLS report, the growing thought was that the BLS report was more of an anomaly than a true indicator of the job market. A similar phenomenon occurred with the 2014 Thanksgiving weekend holiday shopping tallies. Per the National Retail Federation (NRF) report for the 2014 Black Friday period, sales during the four-day Thanksgiving holiday period fell 11 percent to $50.9 billion from $57.4 billion, with shoppers spending an average of only $380.95, which was a decline of 6.4 percent from the prior year's $407.02. If you attempt to tie those two figures together, you may be wondering how the NRF reconciles shoppers spending 6.4 percent less with an 11 percent decline in total sales.[15] The explanation, according to the NRF's report for the period, was a 5.2 percent year-over-year drop in the number of people who shopped over the four-day weekend to 134 million.[16]

According to that same report, online shopping accounted for 42 percent of spending over the four-day period, which was a decline from 44 percent the prior year, with the average number of consumers spending online declining 10 percent from the prior year to $159.55. This is where we turned on our inner Sherlocks to pick apart the NRF's findings, because several other reports contradicted the trade group's findings.

First, over the Thanksgiving weekend, IBM (International Business Machines) reported that online sales for Black Friday in 2014 were up 9.5 percent over the same day in 2013.[17] Digital measurement company ComScore reported data that confirmed IBM's take.[18] Per ComScore, online shopping on Thanksgiving Day saw a 32 percent gain to $1.01 billion, marking the first time in its history that online shopping on that day surpassed the billion-dollar threshold. ComScore saw the online spending surge continue on Black Friday 2014, with $1.51 billion in desktop online sales, up 26 percent from Black Friday 2013.[19]

Our analysis led us to greatly discount the NRF's online data, just as employment data from ISM, Gallup, and ADP raise flags on the BLS's November Employment Report.

The bottom line is that there are many forecasts, but what separates the forecasts you pay attention to versus the ones you don't are the track record and corroborating factors. In the example we just gave, it looked increasingly like the NRF needed to overhaul its forecasting methodologies to better capture data and reflect shopper preferences. The same can be said for the BLS, as well as the methodology behind the unemployment rate calculation to better reflect the low labor force participation and shrinking labor force.

Cocktail Investing Bottom Line

Successful investing requires an awareness of both the reality of economic conditions and the prevailing narrative concerning those conditions.

- Don't trust the experts. Know what they are saying, but do your own homework.

- To understand an economy, you need to know the vector and velocity for the various factors affecting households, businesses, and government.
- Verify what you see using data from more than one source.
- Look for corroborating data when you think you've identified a trend. One or two data points doesn't make a trend. Be patient and diligent. Look for multiple data points over time from multiple sources to confirm a trend.

Endnotes

1. Laura Kusisto, "Number of First-Time Home Buyers Falls to Lowest Levels in Three Decades," www.wsj.com (November 5, 2015).

2. Odysseas Papadimitriou, "Average Credit Card Debt Statistics, Historical Balances & More," www.cardhub.com.

3. www.aar.org.

4. Association of American Railroads Weekly Rail Traffic Data at www.aar.org/Pages/Freight-Rail-Traffic-Data.aspx.

5. Ibid.

6. Ibid.

7. Ibid.

8. American Trucking Association, "Reports, Trends and Statistics," www.trucking.org.

9. American Trucking Association, "ATA Truck Tonnage Index Decreased 0.8% in June," www.trucking.org (July 22, 2014).

10. American Association of Railroads, "AAR Reports Weekly Rail Traffic for October and Week Ending October 31, 2015," www.aar.org (November 4, 2015).

11. American Trucking Association, "ATA Truck Tonnage Index Rose 0.7% in September," www.trucking.org (October 20, 2015).

12. Anna J. Schwartz, "Origins of the Financial Market Crisis of 2008," *Cato Journal* 29(1) (2009): 19–23.

13. Ibid.

14. Jeff Cox, "The Bacon Cheeseburger Index, and Other Cool Measures," www.cnbc.com (June 13, 2014).

15. Sarah Halzack, "Fewer Shoppers and a Decline in Spending During Black Friday Weekend," *Washington Post* (November 30, 2014), www.washingtonpost
.com/business/economy/black-friday-weekend-sees-fewer-shoppers-and-a-decline-in-spending/2014/11/30/dd69aa0e-78bf-11e4-9a27-6fdbc612bff8_
story.html.

16. Shelly Banjo, "'Black Friday' Fades as Weekend Retail Sales Sink," *Wall Street Journal* (November 30, 2014), www.wsj.com/articles/holiday-weekend-retail-sales-sink-11-1417376714.

17. www-01.ibm.com/software/marketing-solutions/benchmark-reports/black-friday-2014.html.

18. Adam Lelia, "Thanksgiving and Black Friday See Online Buying Bonanza as Both Surpass $1 Billion in Desktop Spending," *ComScore* (November 30, 2014), www.comscore.com/Insights/Press-Releases/2014/11/Thanksgiving-and-Black-Friday-See-Online-Buying-Bonanza-as-Both-Days-Surpass-1-Billion-in-Desktop-Spending.

19. Ibid.

Chapter 5

The Impact of Politics and Regulation on Investing

I don't make jokes. I just watch the government and report the facts.
— Will Rogers

If you have ten thousand regulations you destroy all respect for the law.
— Winston Churchill

Giving money and power to government is like giving whiskey and car keys to teenage boys.
— P.J. O'Rourke

Politics is the art of looking for trouble, finding it everywhere, diagnosing it incorrectly, and applying the wrong remedies.
— Groucho Marx

uccessful investing requires keeping a close eye on government, yours and any other nation in which you invest or that trades with a region in which you invest. You've probably heard the phrase, "Don't fight the Fed" while watching the news. The phrase speaks to the ability of central banks and politicians to impact the economy, an industry, and the stock market. All the business fundamentals in the world won't save your investment if a politician manages to alter the tax code in some way that dramatically alters its industry's economics, such as the deduction on mortgage interest payments we discussed in the prior chapter. On the other hand, great fortunes have been made by accurately guessing which way the political wind is going to shift and how it will affect a particular industry, commodity, or company. Just look at how much wealthier many politicians are when they leave office relative to when they enter—it's not from salaries.

In Chapter 4, we showed how the political decision to increase home ownership rates contributed to the unprecedented rise in home prices and the explosion in mortgage-backed securities. Many of those that didn't see what was happening experienced painful losses. For those that did, such as Dr. Michael Burry of Scion Capital (featured in *The Big Short* by Michael Lewis, which we highly recommend), once-in-a-lifetime-type returns were possible.

In this chapter, we are going to focus further on how government actions and the prevailing narrative, what everyone simply *knows* to be true, affect investing. Government actions can have a tsunami effect on your investments, overwhelming a fundamentally sound ship by either drowning her or propelling her beyond that which she could do on her own.

We hear a lot of talk about which government policies help or harm the economy from both sides of the aisle. How do these actions and beliefs in turn affect the investing landscape? **We've already discussed the different schools of economic thought, so here is how those theories are implemented**, at least in the United States. Just in case you weren't convinced that this is something you need to understand, Figure 5.1 shows the year-over-year percent change in the S&P 500 index. The shaded regions represent recessions according to the National Bureau of Economic Research.

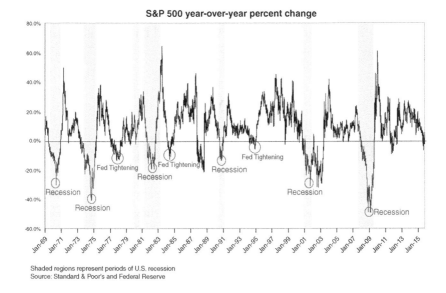

Figure 5.1 Percentage change in S&P 500 index, 1969–2015

You can see that declines in the index are not random; they occur either during a recession or when the Federal Reserve has tightened the money supply, thinking this will help to cool an overheated economy and stave off inflation.

Figure 5.2 shows the three primary levers that any government has to affect its economy: monetary, fiscal, and regulatory policy. When you hear *monetary policy*, think Federal Reserve, European Central Bank, Bank of Japan, or Bank of England. When you hear *fiscal policy*, think IRS and government spending. When you hear the term *regulation*, think

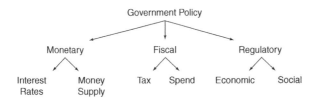

Figure 5.2 Primary government policy levers

antitrust, SEC (Securities and Exchange Commission), EPA (Environmental Protection Agency), and FDA (Food and Drug Administration), just to name a few.

Monetary Policy

In the United States, monetary policy is under the control of the Federal Reserve, which has historically had two levers to affect the economy: the Federal Funds rate and the money supply.

The *Federal Funds target rate* is the interest rate at which private depository institutions, mostly banks, lend the funds they hold at the Federal Reserve to each other, generally overnight. It can be thought of as the rate banks charge each other. This target rate is identified in a meeting of the members of the Federal Open Market Committee (FOMC), which usually meets eight times a year. For years, Wall Street considered this a yawn-inducing event that was rarely even acknowledged in the media. When Alan Greenspan took over the Fed in 1987, ears started perking up. Under Greenspan, the Fed was much more active in trying to manage the economy and prevent downturns, which gave investors more confidence than they otherwise would have had that things were going to never get all that bad. They believed that if things got wobbly, the Fed would do everything it could to right the ship, which many have argued led to excessive risk-taking thanks to the perception that downside risk had been minimized.

These days, when the FOMC meeting notes are released, the analysis that each and every word receives from economists, analysts, and other pundits, ourselves included, is akin to E! Entertainment commentary of starlet attire on the red carpet. A few words here and there from this group are now able to materially move markets. That means the "Street's" interpretation of meeting notes can have a material impact on your portfolio, at least in the near to medium term.

The Federal Reserve historically has altered the *money supply* by increasing or decreasing required bank reserves. When the Fed increases the amount of reserves banks are required to hold it is referred to as tightening the money supply. This is typically done when the government is concerned that the economy is "overheating" (vector up and rapid velocity), which many believe leads to inflation. To understand how that works, you need to understand our banking system.

The United States, along with much of the world, has a *fractional reserve* banking system, the understanding of which is vital to appreciate the 2008 financial crisis. If you want to understand how fractional reserve banking works, which will undoubtedly make you the center of attention at your next dinner party, whiten your teeth, and take inches off your waist, we recommend reading this next section. You can skip it if you'd like, although you won't understand why is it that the money you deposit into your checking account is no longer yours! Got your attention, didn't we?

Fractional Reserve Banking

The earliest forms of banking consisted primarily of money warehouses, where a depositor received a "receipt" stating the amount of "money," typically gold, that had been deposited. These receipts could be used as a form of currency. The bank could not touch the actual deposits. The money was simply stored like any other good, similar to the way today you store those itchy sweaters Aunt Betty knitted along with your 1970s record collection at a self-storage facility. Banks, like a storage facility, would charge a fee for holding the depositor's funds. However, some banks attempted to use the funds deposited with them for other purposes and proposed that the funds in fact belonged to the banks and were an implied loan rather than a deposit. The legal basis for this was established through a series of court cases in England from *Can vs. Can* in 1811 to *Foley vs. Hill and Other* in 1848 (we told you Lenore seriously geeks out on this).

In fractional reserve banking, the bank owns the depositors' funds. Yep, you read that right—funny what you find when you read the fine print when opening an account. Bank of America, Citibank, Wells Fargo, and U.S. Bank all own the money in your checking account. The money you deposited is a loan to the bank, which can then be loaned to another party, or invested, as long as the bank conforms to regulations. Banks generate revenue through the difference between the fee charged to the borrower and the interest paid to the depositor or through investment returns. The term *fractional* refers to the practice of keeping some *fraction* of the deposits in a "reserve" in order to meet any foreseeable demand for deposits.

In this form of banking, a bank is literally inherently bankrupt; the bank's short-term liabilities are in excess of its short-term assets. All depositors can demand immediate payment of their deposits; however, no bank under the fractional reserve system could actually honor this demand because it simply doesn't have that much cash available. Thus comes the term *bank runs,* whereby a bank is immediately bankrupt when a sufficient portion of its depositors attempt to withdraw their funds. This is partly why most countries have some form of depository insurance such as the FDIC (Federal Deposit Insurance Corporation) in the United States, which guarantees some portion of deposits in an attempt to prevent bank runs. And what about online and mobile banking? We'll talk about that in the next chapter.

The central bank (in the United States the Federal Reserve, in Europe the European Central Bank, and in Japan the Bank of Japan) defines the reserve requirement, which is the minimum fraction of the deposits that must be held in reserves. If the reserve requirement is 20 percent and the bank has $100 in deposits, it must place $20 in reserves.

The simplest explanation for the banking crisis in 2007 that precipitated the 2008 financial crisis is that the banks placed deposits in investments that declined significantly in value. In the previous example, the $80 that the bank was free to use was invested in activities that left it worth, say, $25. The bank has "loans" from depositors (your checking account balance) for $100 that can be called at a moment's notice, and only $45 to meet those demands ($20 reserves + $25 current value of investments). As of the beginning of 2015, the FDIC attempts to limit this risk by guaranteeing that up to $250,000 in deposits will be guaranteed by the FDIC.

According to a series of regulations and legislative acts, banks were given "extra bonus points" for holding government or quasi-government bonds, such as mortgage-backed securities issued by the government-sponsored enterprises Fannie Mae and Freddie Mac. These "extra special bonus points" meant that if they held these bonds, their reserve requirements were reduced. Using the example above with the 20 percent reserve requirement, this meant that if banks held these types of assets, rather than having to keep 20 percent in reserve, they could keep 10 percent. Please note that these aren't the exact numbers; we're using simplified math as it is the concept that is important here, not the actual figures. This meant that rather than only being able to loan out $80, they could now loan out $90, which meant they make more money! The same general system is in place in many other countries, including in Europe, where banks get "extra bonus points" for specified types of bonds, primarily those which are government or quasi-government issued.

Now you're probably scratching your head and asking yourself, "How does this relate to inflation?" Or perhaps we've lost your attention a bit and you're thinking about what to have for dinner tonight. Hang in there; you'll thank us later!

Using our first example where depositors put $100 into the bank, the bank can then lend $80 out to a business. There is now $180 in our simple economy. The original depositors can write checks against the $100 they deposited and the borrower can spend the $80 the bank loaned him. That means the supply of money increased by 80 percent. But we aren't done yet. The $80 that the first bank loaned out is then used to purchase a piece of equipment. The vendor deposits this $80 into his bank. This bank places $16 (20 percent of $80) in reserves and loans out the remaining $64. The supply of money has now increased to $244 ($100 + $80 + $64), which is a 144 percent increase. This process can continue again and again and is referred to as the "multiplier effect." Under a 20 percent reserve requirement, the multiplier effect would cause the initial $100 money supply to increase to $500 ($100/0.20), a 5× effect.

The Monetary Control Act (MCA) of 1980 authorized the Fed to impose a reserve requirement of 8 to 14 percent. As of December 2006, the reserve requirement in the United States was 10 percent on transaction deposits over $55.2 million, 3 percent for $10.7 to 55.2 million, and 0 percent is required for the first $10.7 million in deposits, effective December 31, 2009. The resulting multiplier has, until recently, been estimated at 7.7× to 8.5× for M2.[1] The Fed stopped publishing M3 in March 2006; thus, we are only able to estimate the multiplier effect on M3 at around 10×.

What happens when the supply of something go up? Prices go down.

For money, this means loss of purchasing power, which means that each dollar buys you less stuff. If the quantity of goods available for purchase remains constant, and the supply of money to purchase those goods increases, the price of the goods will rise. You need more dollars to buy the same amount of stuff. The supply of money available in the market then can be altered by increasing or decreasing the reserve requirements, by giving banks credit in their reserves, or by adjusting the interest rate paid to banks for the funds in their reserves.

When the money supply is increased, its impact is not felt immediately. Thus, the first to use these dollars created out of "thin air" get the benefit of pre-inflation prices. Over time, the prices of goods adjust upward from the increased supply of money. Typically, inflation most hurts those on fixed incomes (prices go up while their income stays the same) and least affects the government, whose income, namely tax receipts, is generated from personal and business income, which adjust quickly to inflationary pressures. Debt holders with fixed interest rates and incomes that adjust well to inflation will fare quite well during inflationary periods as the ratio of their loan payment to their current income drops.

For example, Bob borrows $400 at a flat 6 percent interest rate and his annual income is $80. His annual loan payment would be $24. His annual loan payment is 30 percent of his income. If inflation suddenly jumps to 8 percent annually and his income adjusts in line with inflation, by the fourth year his income would have increased to $109 and his loan payment would have dropped to 22 percent of his income. This is why we hear talk of countries using inflation to cope with their ballooning debt.

Now we're getting to the stuff that'll make you look oh-so-smart at your next cocktail party. So what's all this QE'ing?

After the financial crisis of 2008, the Federal Reserve implemented a new strategy for affecting both the money supply and interest rates called *quantitative easing (QE)*, but to understand how that works, we first need to talk a little bit about a four-letter word that has gotten a whole lot of the world into trouble since the dawn of mankind: *debt*.

First, governments around the world typically spend more money than they take in every year through taxes. It is really just human nature. Desiring to keep their jobs, politicians want to get reelected, which means they have a vested interest in providing more to the electorate than they take in through taxes. This difference between tax receipts and government spending is referred to as the *annual deficit*. The *national debt* is the accumulation of all those years of deficits. In order to spend more money than it takes in, the government has to borrow. The U.S. government does this by issuing *Treasury bills* (loan of 1 year or less), *Treasury notes* (loan of 1 to 10 years), *Treasury bonds* (loan of 20 to 30 years), or *Treasury inflation-protected securities* (TIPS inflation-indexed borrowing for 5, 10, or 30 years).

The interest rate the federal government pays on the borrowed money depends on what the lenders are willing to accept. This rate changes over time and is based in part on expectations around inflation. (If you are willing to loan money at 5 percent for one year when you believe there will be no inflation, you will demand 8 percent if you think that there will be 3 percent inflation so as to still get the same effective interest rate on the loan.) Figure 5.3 shows how interest rates on *Treasuries* (a generic term for anything issued by the Treasury) for various lengths of borrowing from 1 month to 30 years have changed from November 10, 2006, to November 10, 2015.

This is called the *yield curve*. An upward-sloping curve means that interest rates are less for short-term borrowing than long-term. An inverted yield curve means that interest rates for longer-term borrowing are lower than short-term, which is typically a sign that a

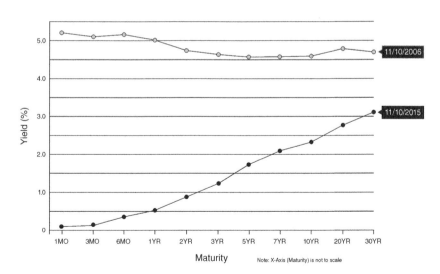

Figure 5.3 Yield curve of Treasuries as of November 10, 2006, and November 10, 2015
SOURCE: U.S. Department of Treasury

recession is on its way. As you can see, in 2006, we had an inverted yield curve.

U.S. banks, as well as foreign governments, foreign banks, corporations, investment funds, and individuals, purchase Treasuries. Quantitative easing refers to the process shown in Figure 5.4 wherein the Treasury Department sells Treasuries to banks in return for cash to fund the annual deficit or to pay off Treasury bonds that are coming due (maturing). Banks then turn around and sell the Treasuries to the Federal Reserve in return for cash. This cash is typically in the form of a credit in the bank's reserve account with the Federal Reserve, but for all practical purposes it can be thought of as cash since these reserves can then be used to loan money to businesses and individuals, who then effectively have cash in hand.

So how much does monetary policy affect investing?

Well, for most of the history of the Federal Reserve there was very little relationship between the central bank and the stock market, but then Federal Reserve Chairman Alan Greenspan came along, and the concept of the Greenspan "put" evolved. The theory was that any time the economy or the markets got a bit wobbly, Chairman Greenspan would loosen monetary policy, which was viewed as stimulative to the economy—thus, the term *Greenspan put,* which referred to the belief that Greenspan could take actions that would successfully limit any downturn in the economy and the markets. (This is a reference to "put options," which give the holder the right to sell at a specific price. Greenspan effectively had a put for the market, which meant there was a point at which he'd act so that the market would never go below that put price level.)

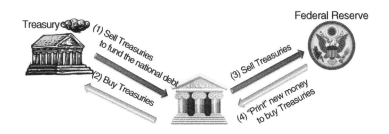

Figure 5.4   Quantitative easing

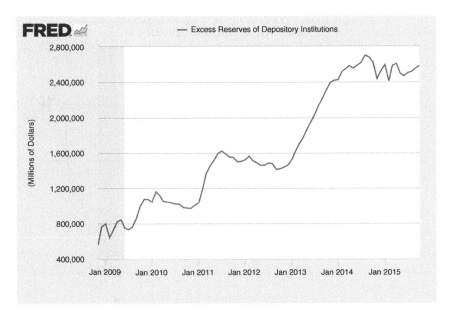

Figure 5.5 Excess reserves held by banks at the Federal Reserve and the S&P Index, November 1, 2008, to November 1, 2015
SOURCE: U.S. Federal Reserve

Then the financial crisis hit and we had the birth of quantitative easing. Figure 5.5, from the St. Louis Federal Reserve, shows the excess reserves held by banks at the Federal Reserve and the S&P 500 index from November 2008 to October 2014, which is the start of the first round of quantitative easing (QE 1) to the termination of the final round of quantitative easing (QE 3). During this time, the two have a correlation of 96.4 percent, when measured on a monthly basis. A correlation of 100 percent would mean they moved perfectly with each other. So yes, Fed policy impacts the stock market.

Prior to the financial crisis the two were not related in any material way as is evident in Figure 5.6 using data from the Federal Reserve and Standard & Poor's.

You can see how up until quantitative easing (QE) began after the financial crisis, there was no relationship between the two, yet from the inception of quantitative easing until it was terminated in October 2014, the S&P 500 index and the excess reserves at the Federal Reserve were almost perfectly correlated.

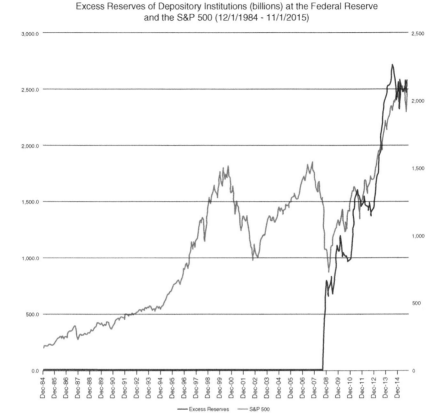

Figure 5.6 Excess reserves held by banks at the Federal Reserve and the S&P Index, January 1, 1980, to November 1, 2015
SOURCE: Federal Reserve

Fiscal Policy

Tax and spend—that about sums it up! Fiscal policy involves the level of taxation the government places on the private sector and the amount of money it spends. The government can affect companies and industries by either making it more expensive or less expensive for them to operate by increasing or decreasing taxes on an activity or by providing a subsidy (government spending) for it.

Fiscal Policy Example: Wind Energy

In the fourth quarter of 2014, the International Energy Agency cut its forecasts for oil demand growth. Meanwhile, production in North America was exploding, led by the shale oil boom. The United States had become the world's largest producer of oil and natural gas.

For products like oil and natural gas, excess production results in lower prices for consumers. Lower prices have their own consequences for the industry as well. Analysts at Sanford C. Bernstein & Co. released a report[2] in late 2014 revealing that at the then-prevailing prices, which had fallen more than 20 percent since June, as much as one-third of U.S. shale oil production would be too expensive to harvest. Lower prices mean a reduction in production—makes sense, right?

For government-backed industries such as wind energy, the relationship is directly the opposite; the more they produce, the more it costs ratepayers and taxpayers because they have to pay to subsidize production. It's not exactly intuitive that as supply increases, the prices go up. But this is an industry that is driven not by market forces but by policy. Whenever you see that, be careful, because the normal rules don't apply. Remember how badly things ended in our example on the pre–financial-crisis housing boom.

In late 2014, analysis showed that states with the largest use of wind power had the highest electricity bills. Bet you didn't see that coming! This led private investors to largely bypass wind companies, leaving them heavily dependent on the government for their survival.

Looking at the *International Journal of Sustainable Manufacturing*, researchers concluded, "A wind turbine with a working life of 20 years will offer a net benefit within five to eight months of being brought online." This raises the question as to why any tax credit for wind energy would span more than just a few years at most, let alone 10 years after the facility is up and running.

Congressional support for the Production Tax Credit (PTC) was in late 2014 largely split along party lines. Fifty-five members of the House of Representatives led by Mike Pompeo (R-Kan.) wrote a letter

to the tax-writing committee demanding an end to the wind energy
subsidies:

> We offer our full support of the current process undertaken by
> the House Committee on Ways and Means that will allow the
> most anti-competitive and economically harmful tax provisions,
> specifically the wind energy production tax credit (PTC), to
> expire. Ensuring that our nation's patchwork tax code under-
> goes significant reform is a noble goal and, as part of this process,
> we believe Congress should stop picking winners and losers and
> finally end the wind PTC.

It was presumed that a GOP-controlled Congress would see the
PTC on the chopping block in 2015 and a Democrat-controlled
Congress would fight for renewal; thus, the outcome of the 2014
mid-term elections was incredibly important for wind energy producers. Government policy was having an enormous impact on the
potential investment returns for the industry.

In an effort to help make sure that the PTC-friendly Harry Reid
(D-Nev.), the Senate majority leader, remained in office, the wind industry turned the League of Conservation Voters (LCV) into their own
personal Trojan horse. The organization bragged that it would spend
over $25 million supporting pro-PTC candidates and attacking their
opponents before November 2014 elections. If LCV's campaign were
to fail, the loss of the PTC could prove fatal to some wind companies,
something of which many investors in these companies may not have
been aware.

During the run-up to the 2014 mid-term election, one of the most
famous and successful investors in the world, Warren Buffett, told his
clients, "I will do anything that is basically covered by the law to reduce
Berkshire's tax rate. For example, on wind energy, we get a tax credit if
we build a lot of wind farms. That's the only reason to build them. They
don't make sense without the tax credit." If that tax credit were to go
away, Berkshire's investors would be hurt.

For investors, the power of cronyism should never be underesti-
mated. Political decisions that are incredibly difficult to predict can

seriously affect investing decisions. Investors need to always make sure they understand the political side of their investing choices.

Regulatory Policy

There are two types of regulation: economic and social. Economic regulation refers to those regulations concerning pricing, such as regulations affecting monopolies or potential monopolies in areas such as utilities, or to prohibit practices or mergers that would limit competition. Government may also use regulation to enforce social goals such as clean air and water.

Generally speaking, regulation is viewed as a positive, but it can also be burdensome. It all depends on how much is being layered on and whether the rules serve to improve the business landscape or hurt it. That's Chris's take on it and he has seen regulation mandates pull forward demand time and time again, which can be hugely profitable for the investor if he or she recognizes what's happening. Lenore, however, is a bit more wary of the entire concept of regulation for two reasons. First, regulation forces all players in an industry to behave in a similar manner, which is akin to having an entire population with similar genetic strengths and weaknesses. All it takes is some new threat, something unexpected, and the entire industry, much like a biological population, can be decimated.

Second, regulation assumes that those regulating are wiser and have more foresight than those within the industry, thus are better able to see what dangers are on the horizon and instruct industry players how to best behave. The history of regulation gives little evidence to support this assumption, with regulation typically addressing the crisis of the past with debatable ability to prevent future ones. Chris agrees with Lenore on this.

Investors ought to objectively look at how regulation impacts incentives and the cost structure of an industry, as well as assessing what systemic risks it might generate and invest accordingly. Remember our example in Chapter 3 concerning how regulation pushed banks to all behave in a similar manner, which made them all vulnerable to the same risks. When it turned out that the assumptions they all were instructed to abide by were faulty, the damage was widespread and brutal for the economy.

Regulatory Example: Banking

In 2013, we attended the Cato Institute's Monetary Policy conference and, as you can imagine, a lot was said about the Federal Reserve, stimulus tapering, the U.S. dollar, and more. There was no shortage of policy wonks both in the audience and at the podium, but the presentation that most caught our attention was from the retired chairman and CEO of BB&T Bank (BBT) and current president and CEO of Cato, John Allison.

During his watch at BB&T between 1989 and 2008, Allison grew the company from $4.5 billion to $152 billion in assets. That's an average increase of over $8 billion a year, or $682 million a month. With a track record like that, our ears perked up when he spoke, because it stands to reason that he knows at least a few things about banking and dealing with the Fed.

Allison spoke about the economy, issues with current monetary policy, and the risk to the dollar in the longer-term. However, what drew the most attention was his prediction about one aspect of Dodd-Frank. For anyone who's unfamiliar, the Dodd-Frank Wall Street Reform and Consumer Protection Act was signed into federal law by President Barack Obama on July 21, 2010. It brought the most significant changes to financial regulation in the United States since the regulatory reform that followed the Great Depression.

Dodd-Frank has produced a number of fallout effects, but the one that Allison highlighted was the impact on small- to medium-sized banks, as well as community banks, given the ballooning regulations. Dodd-Frank authorized more than 400 new bank rules and mandated the creation of the Consumer Financial Protection Bureau, which oversees more than 5,000 pages of regulations.

Large increases in regulation, such as the Dodd-Frank-mandated ones, result in increased costs that often place smaller companies at a significant disadvantage to larger firms.

> *Naturally, existing businesses generally prefer to keep out competitors in other ways. That is why the business community, despite its rhetoric, has so often been a major enemy of truly free enterprise.*
>
> Milton Friedman

Existing businesses are often in favor of regulations that increase costs to such an extent that they make it very difficult for new or small companies to compete. This can have a material effect on the nature of an industry, effectively reducing competition from new entrants, which can also slow the rate of innovation and reduce the rate at which companies are pressured to reduce costs and/or prices.

That was precisely Allison's point. According to the Kansas City Fed, 91 percent of the 322 small banks surveyed are laboring under higher training and software costs due to Dodd-Frank.[3] That suggests to us that we are in for yet another wave of consolidation and potential bank failures. Over the last few years, hundreds of community and small banks closed up shop due to the financial crisis and the early stages of Dodd-Frank compliance.

According to a study by the St. Louis Federal Reserve,[4] since at the least the 1980s, progressive consolidation has seen the overall number of banks continually decline while the size of banks has been increasing with the largest banks getting larger. A report issued at the end of 2014 by *SNL Financial* found that in the United States, the five largest banks controlled 44 percent of the industry's total assets.[5] In 1990, the top five held just 9.67 percent. The cost of doing business has changed so much that by 2014, the median return on average assets for the top five institutions was nearly 50 percent higher than that of the overall industry. In 1990, the return for the largest trailed the sector by 0.33 percent. With such a discrepancy in cost structure, consolidation will likely continue, with some forecasts suggesting that, over the coming years, fewer than 5,000 banks will remain, as compared with 6,891 at the end of September 2014. Those too-big-to-fail banks? Well, they just keep getting bigger.

Regulatory Example: Music Industry

If that doesn't have you convinced, maybe this tune will do it for you. When it comes to the content industry, the world is a-changing.

No matter what the industry—publishing, music, television, movies, comic books, and more—there has already been a significant shift in how and where people consume this content thanks to broadband, the Internet, and, more recently, mobile technologies.

According to Nielsen Soundscan[6] numbers, total consumption of music rose 15 percent over 2014 levels, but that growth came more from streaming than from purchases of tracks or albums. Per Nielsen, more than 317 billion songs were streamed on-demand in 2015 through audio and video platforms, an increase of 93 percent compared with 2014. Album sales continued to fall, dropping 6 percent in 2015 to 241.4 million units following an 11 percent decline in 2014. Digital track sales fells 12 percent in 2015 to 964.8 million, while CD sales declined 10.8 percent to 125.6 million in 2015 from 140.8 million in 2014. Pandora's application has been among the most-downloaded free apps for iPhones and iPads, demonstrating that streaming is becoming a mainstream way to listen to music. At the end of September 2015 the company had 78.1 million active listeners and during the three months ending September 2015, those millions and millions of people listened to 5.14 billion hours of Pandora programming. Hammering the point home about Pandora's app, Pandora derived 82 percent of its revenue during those three months from the mobile and other connected devices, with the balance from computer-based usage.[7]

Even third-party research firm Nielsen, the company that measures the ratings of television shows, updated its ratings measurement system to capture data about television viewing not simply through broadcast, but through streaming. Given Nielsen's acquisition of radio ratings giant Arbitron, one has to wonder how long until Nielsen Audio expands its measuring scope to include services like Pandora, Spotify, Apple's recently acquired Beats service and subsequent Apple Music subscription service, and Amazon's Prime Music offering.

As these changes have taken place, copyright law has failed to keep pace. Recent tweaks have been specifically targeted and usually at the behest of one sector of the content industry seeking advantage. Current copyright laws have not seen a comprehensive review since long before the existence of Netflix, Hulu, Pandora, or Spotify, which means the system as a whole is geared toward the content industry of yesteryear.

There is little debate that the current copyright laws need to be comprehensively reviewed and updated to reflect current market realities. Congress is in the process of doing just that. In mid-2014, the House Judiciary Committee held hearings to examine music licensing specifically, which sounds like a really forward-looking approach, but as is always the case when we are talking about regulatory power, there are some that will seek to rig the system in their own favor. In this example, the future of steaming music services could be at stake.

As a result of copyright law, power is highly concentrated in the music licensing business. Songwriters rightly control their work product. However, when songwriters and music publishers collectively assign control to Performance Rights Organizations (PROs) like the American Society of Composers, Authors and Publishers, the aggregation of control becomes absolute. Three PROs effectively control 100 percent of all musical compositions. There is no competition or marketplace for those wishing to license and use compositions, much like the domination of the three ratings agencies, Standard & Poor's, Moody's, and Fitch.

In the past, these organizations abused their power by colluding to push up rates. As a result, ASCAP and Broadcast Music Inc. have been deemed a monopoly and forced to operate under a federal consent decree since 1941 that gives licensees the right to seek federal court intervention when PROs' demands begin to cross the line of propriety. The third organization, The Society of European Stage Authors and Composers, was, as of the writing of this book, in the midst of a federal antitrust suit.

In addition to Congress's review of copyright laws, the Department of Justice announced in mid-2014 that it would review the consent decrees for ASCAP and BMI with a view of updating them as well. Not surprisingly, the music publishers and PROs advocated for a full repeal.

Pandora was forced in 2014 to petition the federal court to intervene in negotiations between it and ASCAP. In the decision, it was revealed that the major publishers intentionally withheld vital information about the details of their catalogs, giving Pandora three choices: Pay whatever amount the publishers wanted, not pay and face infringement claims that would wreck its business, or stop playing music altogether. In what other market could a seller of a product legally not tell the buyer what it is purchasing and then sue the buyer to oblivion if it refused to pay the ransom?

In addition to ASCAP's antics with Pandora, a Pennsylvania court in 2014 found that SESAC, which controls approximately 5 percent of the market, likely exercises monopoly power, and thereby might be destined for antitrust constraints. The major publishers, currently under consent decree, control market shares multiple times greater than SESAC.

The manner in which Congress views the answers to these questions will have significant implications for the growing streaming marketplace. Removal of the only check on the publishers' vast power would leave publishers completely unimpeded to raise rates.

It is clear that the publishers' main goal is to drive up rates paid by licensees. In addition to ridding themselves of the consent decrees, they are seeking legislation that would reconfigure the formula federal courts currently use, thus requiring the court to set higher rates.

Either of these policy changes would be devastating to streaming music providers.

In mid-December 2015, the federal Copyright Royalty Board ruled to raise Internet radio royalty rates, meaning companies like Pandora and iHeartMedia that offer ad-supported services will have to pay out increased per-stream fees in 2016. These companies will pay what equates to 17 cents per 100 streams of a given song on free, ad-supported services and 22 cents per 100 listens logged by paying subscribers. By comparison, in 2015 Pandora paid out 14 cents for every 100 free listens, or a 25 percent slice revenue, whichever was greater. Despite services like Pandora paying over 55 percent of their revenue in licensing fees in 2015, SoundExchange, which collects royalties for labels and individual artists, was pushing for higher rates between 25 cents and 29 cents for every 100 plays, or 55 percent of a streaming service's revenue.[8] With these new rates valid through 2020, profitability at Pandora and other streaming music services as well as their viability remain in question.

Cocktail Investing Bottom Line

Successful investing requires keeping a close eye on government and changes in its policies, be it your government or that of any other nation in which you invest or that trades with a region in which you invest. Changes in policies can alter, sometimes drastically, the industry playing field:

- Government impacts the economy through monetary policy, fiscal policy, and regulatory policy.
- Always be aware of the latest interest rate guidance from the Federal Reserve, as changes in guidance often have a material effect on markets.
- An inverted yield curve, one in which long-term rates are lower than short-term rates, is typically a sign of a recession, so keep an eye on changes in interest rates at various maturities.
- Be aware of central bank policy announcements from the four geographic horsemen we talked about in Chapter 4: the U.S. Federal Reserve, European Central Bank, Bank of China, and Bank of Japan. Commentary from these central banks and select others can have a material impact on the markets if it does not live up to Wall Street expectations. Be aware of what Wall Street expects from these organizations versus what was actually decided by their ruling bodies. Be prepared for overreactions from Wall Street, both good and bad, when these organizations or their officials publicly discuss their policies and views on their respective economies.
- Pay attention to discussions about changes in the tax code and regulation, as such changes can make previously attractive investments unattractive, and vice versa.
- Be aware of changing industry dynamics and which groups have control over delivery of products and/or services. Industry structures that worked in the past may no longer work and cause serious problems going forward as technological advancements change the way we buy or receive the goods and services we want.

Endnotes

1. M0, M1, M2, and M3 are different measures of money supply. M0 and M1 are also called narrow money and normally include coins and notes in circulation and other money equivalents that are easily convertible into cash. M2 includes M1 plus short-term time deposits in banks and 24-hour money market funds. M3 includes M2 plus longer-term time deposits and money market funds with more than 24-hour maturity. These are general definitions, as the exact definitions of the three measures depend on the country.

2. Brad Plumer, "How Far Do Oil Prices Have to Fall to Throttle the U.S. Shale Boom?" www.vox.com (December 3, 2014).

3. "Dodd-Frank Rules Strangle Small Banks," Investors.com (December 4, 2013), finance.yahoo.com/news/dodd-frank-rules-strangle-small-232900296.html.

4. Silvio Contessi, "The Evolving Size Distribution of Banks," *Economic Synopses*, 1 (2010).

5. Steve Schaefer, "Five Biggest U.S. Banks Control Nearly Half Industry's $15 Trillion in Assets," *Forbes* (December 3, 2014), www.forbes.com/sites/steveschaefer/2014/12/03/five-biggest-banks-trillion-jpmorgan-citi-bankamerica/.

6. http://www.nielsen.com/us/en/insights/reports/2016/2015-music-us-year-end-report.html.

7. http://phx.corporate-ir.net/External.File?item=UGFyZW50SUQ9NTk4Nz UyfENoaWxkSUQ9MzA5MjQwfFR5cGU9MQ==&t=1.

8. http://appleinsider.com/articles/15/12/16/pandora-others-must-raise-streaming-payouts-after-copyright-royalty-board-ruling.

Chapter 6

Enabling and Disruptive Technologies

It is not the strongest of the species that survives, nor the most intelligent that survives. It is the one that is the most adaptable to change.

— *Charles Darwin*

If you want something new, you have to stop doing something old.

— *Peter Drucker*

Creativity is thinking up new things. Innovation is doing new things.

— *Theodore Levitt*

I n this chapter, we will be looking at the enabling and disruptive effects technology can have on industries, companies, and consumers and how that creates investment opportunities. Some companies have risen to the challenges and adapted their business models around those enabling technologies, while others struggled with and in some cases denied the very changes that were happening around them.

Disruptive and enabling technologies aren't something that you can easily define in a noncontextual way, but the impacts of them are often the very things you might muse over when sharing a cocktail with friends. We will walk through some examples to show you what was changing and who benefited from it by providing enabling technologies so that you can practice seeing the world this way yourselves. It's all about detecting the shift in the way people do things, keeping your eyes open for the beginning of that change and patiently watching to see which companies take advantage of it best.

From an investor's perspective, disruptive and enabling technologies dramatically shift the playing field, altering the competitive dynamic so that today's winning company is tomorrow's has-been and the company you've never heard of becomes tomorrow's hottest topic. In this chapter, we'll walk you through what the change meant and point out companies that stood to benefit and those that, failing to adapt, fell behind. Enabling technologies are dynamic and, like a snowball rolling downhill, the longer they go, the bigger and more damage they do to the existing landscape.

> Two of the most powerful technological trends in the modern era are the unrelenting progress toward virtually unlimited data storage at costs nearing zero coupled with transmission of data, at incredibly high speeds around the globe, at costs nearing zero.

Combined, these two forces would have a massive impact on the creation, consumption, usage, and storage of information in ways that have and will continue to change almost every aspect of life in nearly every corner of the planet. Anything that could be turned into digital data would be affected. Cocktail Investing is about being aware of these tectonic forces, looking for the ways in which they can be implemented to improve our lives, and searches for those companies that best enable the technologies that arise along the way.

The Evolution into Mobile

As the cost of data transmission and storage moves toward zero, the desire and ability to have access to that data from anywhere, at any time, has evolved rapidly. In the 1980s, companies communicated by fax and company filings with the SEC had to be ordered from the library. There was actual physical mail. Businesses had huge copy rooms, used messenger services, and had even more people performing all sorts of manual, typically paper-based tasks that don't even exist today.

Think of just how relatively useless bits of data are on a piece of paper compared to an article online. The writing on the piece of paper exists in isolation, useful only to those in close physical proximity—and even then, it has limited features. The piece of paper isn't searchable, linkable, easily shared, or editable in any way that compares to the utility of online.

During the 1990s, computing was done primarily on desktops, with laptops so heavy they could barely be considered portable and were painfully slow. Computing technology was evolving from the earlier server-based systems (where all the data and applications were stored on a central server with "dumb" terminals that could do very little other than access the server) into client–server, where more of the applications were on the desktop, with just the data stored centrally. Here we see relatively costly and clunky data storage and transmission, but still a vast improvement over paper-based information storage and transmission.

In 1993, there were only 16 million cellphone subscribers[1] in the United States and those phones were "only" capable of making and receiving calls. Imagine that! Around that time, email and the Internet became more widespread. These changed the way people worked and how many people were needed to accomplish that work. For personal use, access to the Internet was exceedingly limited relative to today, with access primarily through such services as Earthlink or America Online (AOL), with excruciatingly slow speeds that allowed one to watch nearly an entire sitcom episode while waiting for a download. Over the coming years, mobile networks became faster, and eventually limited data could be transmitted across mobile networks, but mostly just basic text. Nokia was the undisputed global leader in mobile phone sales. Before too long, those mobile networks would evolve into ones that would enable BlackBerry devices, which allowed access to email, contacts, and calendars on-the-go as *more and more data was transmitted via mobile networks at more functional speeds.*

Earthlink and America Online were once the darlings of Wall Street, but today are just two among many, and by no means command any sort of leadership roles. What they got right in the beginning was people's desire to connect to one another and information via the newly evolving Internet, which was incredibly difficult for the average person to connect to, let alone use in the early 1990s. Both offered user-friendly ways to connect to and use the Internet. Cocktail Investing readers would have noticed that more and more retailers were advertising their web presence in store or in print ads, that more consumer goods manufacturers were directing customers to their online presences and would have likely been well aware of the growing use of email for personal use well before the 1998 movie, *You've Got Mail,* made that AOL voice part of pop culture vernacular. Spotting the shift into the online world early would have alerted them to look for those companies that best delivered this new world to customers.

But the trend didn't stop here and eventually getting online became a simple commodity service and more importantly, people didn't want to have access to the evolving magic of the Internet limited to their homes, offices, or the walled-in garden offered by most service providers. As consumers shifted to higher speed forms of online access and surfing the Internet directly via a web browser, Earthlink and AOL would soon see their role in the industry diminish significantly.

BlackBerry and Palm were the early winners in the smartphone and PDA (personal digital assistant) market, giving users the ability to carry around and/or access significant amounts of data through a handheld device, loosening the ties to the desktop. Next, Apple unwrapped its first iPhone in June 2007. Compared to today's model, the original iPhone had far weaker data transmission performance, with no wifi or 3G connectivity and less memory than many of today's models. Even so, the original iPhone marked a sea change in mobile technology that Nokia, Motorola, and Ericsson, once the biggest mobile phone companies in the world, utterly missed. Thus, they were unprepared for the smartphone boom and today look nothing like they did back then. Eventually, the iPhone would combine the Internet access of the desktop with the functionality of a PDA and the email utility of a BlackBerry, but it would not stop there. Apple created tools that had all the functionality of iTunes combined with Sirius and more, as well as your cable TV and DVR! These shifts would rock the very core of not just the mobile phone industry but also the music, television, and movie industries. Lest we forget, yet one more enormous change was in store that would affect yet another entire industry and would see the death of one of America's most successful companies.

The ability to store and transmit data at increasingly faster rates and lower costs also impacted the way in which everyone wanted to take, share, and store pictures. In 1995, the Fujix Nikon 1.3 megapixel camera, which used a removable 131 megabyte hard drive, capable of storing 70 photos, sold for $20,000, which would be roughly $31,000 in 2015 dollars.[2] By 2000, 10.34 million digital cameras were shipped worldwide, and that number would grow to 121.5 by 2010.[3] Digital cameras would come to dominate the camera market at the expense of many film camera manufacturers and film suppliers. In the second decade of the twenty-first century, however, mobile phone sales would explode, as manufacturers enticed customers to buy the latest with color displays and increasingly impressive in-phone cameras; the latter all but put the final nail in the film camera coffin. *Once again this was a shift in data as the limited usability of film images gave way to the superior storage, transmittal, and sharing of digital images.*

The observant Cocktail Investor would have seen these trends and looked for those technologies that would further enable it and would have been on guard against those that were blind to it and its ramifications. Advancements in digital cameras also led to the merging of the "point-and-click" camera with the smartphone, not only enabling the generation of beautiful digital content without the limitations of film but also for immediate transmittal of those imagines globally. The enabling technology of digital cameras and smartphones was a phenomenally disruptive technology that the once-veritable titan of photography, Kodak, completely missed and ended up filing for bankruptcy in 2012. Meanwhile, companies that provided mobile phone manufacturers with the ability to add camera functionality benefited from explosive growth in camera-enabled mobile phones and then smartphones that featured even more sophisticated cameras.

These changes were made possible by broadband and rapidly expanding mobile networks, *enabled by increasingly powerful semiconductors* (processing as well as graphics chips), new and more powerful storage formats, and ever-improving mobile technology. The companies leading the frontiers of these developments would offer the astute investor opportunities to benefit from such enormous changes in our everyday lives. In Chapter 10, you'll hear from one of Lenore's friends, Emmy Sobieski, about how she spots trends to help her identify which companies are most likely to next benefit from the ever-changing technological landscape.

Another part of the mobile evolution involved the speed of data transmission in order to make the growing amount of online data accessible from anywhere. Today, most of us have smartphones that are connected to mobile networks with broadband-like speeds or wifi. Smartphones and tablets are challenging the PC industry. A Pew Research Center survey of more than 1,000 teens published in April 2015 found that 92 percent of them go online daily and 24 percent of them go online "almost constantly."[4] Ninety-one percent of teens went online at least occasionally using smartphones.[5] In 2011, research firm IDC predicted that more people in the United States would access the Internet via mobile devices than through desktop computers or other wired devices by 2015.[6] That was considered a bold statement back then.[7] They were wrong—the shift occurred a year earlier, in 2014.[8]

With more and more accessing the Internet through mobile devices, the demand for mobile-accessible content and the ability to deliver that content in a reasonable time frame proved yet another game-changer that, by 2015, had completely altered the music industry and was on its way to having a similar impact on movies and television as consumers shift to demanding the ability to watch what they want, when they want, and where they want. Netflix, which once was exclusively in the business of shipping DVDs, was able to successfully, albeit not without some pain, adjust its business as the disruptive technology of increased data transmission, both wired and mobile, made video-on-demand as well as streaming possible. This also opened up a new offering for Amazon, which eventually offered not only music but movies for download or streaming.

One of the companies providing enabling technology in this mobile revolution is Skyworks Solutions, Inc., an RF semiconductor solutions provider that in 2015 enjoyed companies like Apple and Samsung as its customers for the smartphones, tablets, and other emerging wireless applications. Chris enjoyed a Cocktail Investing chat with David Aldrich, chairman of the board and chief executive officer of Skyworks. Figure 6.1 shows the company's stock price starting January 1, 2000. For much of the decade from 2000 to 2010, the stock was unremarkable, warranting little investor attention. However, for those investors who were paying attention to the shift into mobile, this was clearly a company whose fortunes were going to change.

This illustrates how investors can benefit from identifying disruptive technology shifts and hunting for those companies that provide the enabling technologies. If you had just looked at the company's stock performance from 2000 to the end of 2011, you would likely have not thought it was poised to take off. As you look at that chart, always remember the most important phrase in investing is *Past performance is not an indicator of future results.*

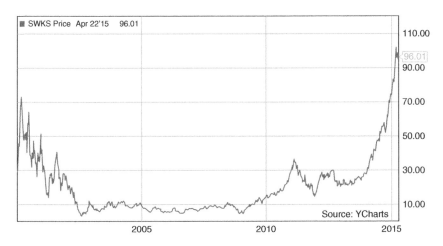

Figure 6.1 Skyworks Solution stock price
SOURCE: YCharts

Cocktail Investing Chat with Skyworks Solution Chairman and CEO

Chris Versace: Mobility has enabled one of the greatest transformations of our time. When you look at the world of smartphones and tablets, is there much more to go?

David Aldrich: We believe the industry is in the early stages of the connectivity revolution. Consumer demand for wireless ubiquity and the trend toward linking people, places, and things in ways previously not imagined is driving connectivity across a growing number of new markets and applications.

CV: How do you see mobility moving above and beyond those types of devices?

DA: In addition to smartphones and tablets, there is an entirely new generation of devices being developed spanning the connected home and car, medical and industrial applications, smart energy, and a variety of fitness and wellness products. While some of these are still in the early stages of deployment, they are gaining market traction quickly. In fact, a recent report by Morgan Stanley estimates that by 2020, the total number of connected devices could reach a staggering 75 billion units. General Electric, for example, has announced it will incorporate machine-to-machine communications across its entire industrial portfolio, including jet engines, locomotives, turbines, and medical devices. This is just one example of how analog end-markets are incorporating connectivity—in many cases for the first time.

CV: Where do you look to identify trends before they become obvious?

DA: Our priority is providing custom solutions that help our broad customer base navigate increasingly complex analog design challenges. We partner with OEMs and listen closely to gain insight into their product challenges and needs. Having said that, we focus our efforts on high-growth markets where we can leverage our comprehensive portfolio of technologies and leading-edge integration capabilities to deliver differentiated, best-in-class solutions.

CV: What do you envision when it comes to the connected car or the connected home? How real is it, and how could it change the way people interact with their homes and cars? Is there something else "connected" that you see out there that isn't getting any attention yet?

DA: The trend is very real. In the connected home, Skyworks is enabling everything from smart thermostats and smoke detectors, to home security systems, media gateways, and lighting platforms. As a result, consumers can turn lights off and on, set household temperatures, and secure their home from their smartphone or tablet. And this trend is just beginning. According to some estimates, the connected home market is expected to grow at a 67 percent compounded annual growth rate from 2014 to 2018, with well over a billion units shipped by 2017.

In the connected car, today we are enabling navigational assist solutions, delivering backlight drivers for in-dash displays and analog control ICs for collision avoidance systems and keyless entry. And once again, this market has tremendous growth potential with some estimates expecting it to grow at a 39 percent compounded annual growth rate over the next four years.

CV: There is much talk on the Internet of Things. Does Skyworks see it as the mobilization and sensorization of the industrial world, or is it something more?

DA: It's more than connecting the industrial world. It's about linking people, places, and things and is being driven by consumers' desire to always be connected. The global proliferation of wireless across a host of new markets and applications is proof that this is not a singular event tied to one region. For example, in some countries we are seeing people being connected for the very first time. In others, it's enabling mobile payments, streaming music/video, and the connected home.

CV: Do you see mobile connectivity transforming healthcare and payments? Do you see it disrupting any other industries in the next few years?

DA: Mobile connectivity is enabling both healthcare, as well as payment options. Many patients' medical records are now online and facilitating the sharing of information as well as doctor–patient communication. Mobile payment options are also beginning to soar. Suffice it to say, we will see a whole host of new and previously unimagined applications enabled by mobile connectivity.

CV: What do you think are the biggest risks the mobility trend will bring that wouldn't be there without it? We hear a lot about privacy and the ability to intercept data going to and from mobile devices, but is there something else we should be thinking about?

DA: Privacy is certainly a challenge, but an issue for which many are already seeking solutions. Most would agree, however, that the benefits of mobility and connectivity far outweigh some of the potential risks. There are likely to be other concerns, but these will be addressed as the Internet of Things market unfolds.

CV: Who are the winners and losers in this new brave new world?

DA: The winners are clearly those who have a broad product portfolio, can solve complex RF semiconductor and analog design challenges (for example, the tight space requirements inside these devices as more and more functionally is added), and have systems integration expertise as well as the scale to meet demand. Those companies selling discrete devices will find it difficult to succeed, even if they have the best-performing single-function device. Customers are looking for a company that can provide the best-performing overall system solution at a competitive price.

Hopefully, this conversation has shown that as you look for disruptive technologies, remember that company management teams can provide valuable information as well as insights, and they usually love to share. You can also get an awful lot by reading through management's discussion in the company's annual report, by hunting down interviews with industry experts or articles they've written, or by attending industry conferences. We'll talk more about this in Chapter 10 when we go over how to pick the specific securities in which you'll invest.

With all these mobile trends, you might be thinking that the PC industry, which is stuck sitting on your desk, is on the wane as consumers and users shift toward tablets and smartphones. We agree, largely because we have also shifted how we work and communicate to those devices as well.

How many of us use an iPad to check email and text messages right when we wake up, catch up on the day's news over morning coffee, take notes on projects, play a favorite TV show while logging miles on a treadmill at the gym, and entertain the kids with endless games while traveling? It can even be used as a sound machine and nightstand clock at the end of the day. Talk about change—a device that didn't even exist a few years ago is now a vital part of daily life. We wonder what will be the next new thing we can't imagine living without. Between an iPad and laptop, do we need or want a desktop?

Taking a step back, however, we can see that the computing industry has gone through an evolution as different technologies became mainstream, adding greater functionality along the way. Devices like the PC, which were once the hub of activity, have been replaced with smaller, lighter, connected ones, like our beloved iPads and Macbooks, that have ample storage capabilities on their own and are now able to connect to cloud storage from anywhere. As computing power increases, mobile connectivity improves and storage capacity grows, all while the associated costs continue to fall.

Data Proliferation

As the cost of data storage and transmission moves toward zero, we are becoming increasingly intense consumers and producers of data, pushing mobile carriers like AT&T, Verizon Wireless, and others around the globe to continually upgrade their networks to give us content faster and with wider network coverage. We've become so used to high broadband speeds that it sends both of us into a mini-tirade when faced with slow-to-no connectivity.

Cocktail Investing looks at all the data being created and sent around the world and anticipates the congestion it will cause for carriers like AT&T and Verizon. We then look at where are the greatest pain points for this congestion and which companies are poised to solve it in the most cost-effective manner, looking at network solutions from suppliers such as Alcatel Lucent, Nokia Networks, Ericsson, Cisco Systems, and Huawei, as well as semiconductor companies like Cavium Networks, Qorvo, and others.

Cocktail Investing also looks at how the falling costs of data storage and transmission spur the creation of new types data to improve our lives, affecting, for example, the way we interact with two of most families' biggest expenses, homes and cars. As of 2015, we were seeing the emergence of the connected home, which, for example, gives Lenore the ability to watch live video from inside and outside her home in San Diego when she's working over 7,000 miles away in Italy. From Italy, she can turn her San Diego home's water heater or lights on and off and adjust the temperature, either manually or programmatically, and even lock and unlock doors. She's not the only one who thinks this is a pretty profound change. In January 2014, Google paid a mind-boggling $3.2 billion to buy Nest, which at the time had wifi-enabled thermostats, smoke and carbon monoxide alarms, and webcams through which you can even tell your dog to get off the couch while watching him from your iPad at work!

Cocktail Investing looks not only at the obvious technological advancement such as Nest, but more importantly, at those companies that enable the technology offered by Nest. Chris refers to this as "buy the bullets, not the gun." Buried inside the Nest thermostat are a variety of sensors (temperature, motion), communication semiconductors, and software that allow it to "talk" over the network to your smartphone or tablet. You'll be reading more about these enabling technologies in just a few pages, but for now, it isn't just our homes that are evolving.

With the gains in wireless networks, the ways in which we interact with, operate, and even maintain our cars are evolving. We are seeing the evolution of satellite-based in-vehicle security systems that allow for tracking of location, speed, and direction of movement in case of theft. We've seen profound improvements in turn-by-turn navigation systems that can provide pinpoint accuracy. **We are witnessing the emergence**

of remote diagnostic systems that connect drivers with repair and maintenance providers when that increasingly smart car doesn't behave itself. We're also seeing ones that continually monitor the vehicles' systems and alert the driver as to when regular maintenance is needed or if a problem is just starting to emerge.

These technologies use semiconductors and sensors in the vehicle combined with GPS and cellular connectivity to provide a range of services only imagined in James Bond movies. In the event of an accident or other collision, sensors can deploy airbags and activate services that will automatically send information about the vehicle's condition and GPS location to call centers.

The proliferation of mobile data has impacted the way we interact with vehicles in yet another way, thanks to Uber. A user simply presses the app on his or her smartphone, punches in the desired destination, and requests service. In a few seconds, Uber sends an alert a driver in a particular car is en route, along with reviews of that driver. The driver's arrival time is not only displayed on a map in the app, but it's updated to the minute should the driver encounter some traffic. Even better, Uber has its customer's credit card information on file, so no money ever changes hands.

Here we have an application of expanded data production and improving data transmission manifesting outside the virtual world in a way that is disrupting the taxi and limousine industry, which for decades has been relatively stagnant. Cocktail Investing sees these trends, but is also aware of the impact of government on innovation, and those paying attention to all this were not surprised to see a push from the old-school taxi and limo world to get government to block this change and to keep things the way they were.

Even internationally, Lenore has seen where Uber is making a powerful impact. Taxi fares in Genoa, Italy, can easily run two to three times the fare price you'd expect in Milan, but with Uber she was enjoying a comfortable ride in a noticeably clean and well-kept car with a young and attentive driver, versus the usual excruciating drive in a smelly hunk of junk with no suspension system driven by a cranky and bitter Genovese for four to five times the price! Obviously, the cab companies there, like in many U.S. cities, did everything possible to ban Uber. Eventually, they had some success and Uber is having to regroup, but history is full of evidence that you cannot stop change—slow it perhaps, but never prevent it.

This highlights the need, however, in Cocktail Investing to always be aware of the potential impact of government through regulation and/or taxation. Disruptive and enabling technologies are all about innovation, which is, by definition, a threat to existing players in an industry, and those players can often wield political power in order to protect themselves, so always keep in mind the potential reaction of the status-quo team.

The ability to quickly and easily send and share data is making our lives not only more convenient, but safer, more enjoyable. With the enormous proliferation in data devices, let's talk to someone who is deep in it for their insights into what could be next. Here is a Cocktail Investing talk Chris had with Mike Canevaro, president and founder, Digital2Go Media Networks. Prior to Digital2Go, Mike was a vice president at CSR plc, a leading fabless provider of end-to-end semiconductor and software solutions for the Internet of Everything and automotive segments, which was acquired by Qualcomm in 2015 for $2.4 billion.

Cocktail Investing Chat with President of Digital2Go Media Networks

Chris Versace: We've seen the intersection of connectivity, processing power, and the Internet drive substantial changes in behavior for businesses and consumers. What could be the next one that changes or shifts that behavior even further?

Mike Canevaro: Certainly, sensors are driving a new wave of innovation in everything from wearables, to thermostats, to location-based beacons. I think processing power, and even battery power, are becoming less and less critical in many of these connected devices.

I can understand the need to pack tremendous processing power in a gaming chip or application processor powering a new generation of phones, tablets, or game consoles. But the idea that these small battery-powered, almost disposable devices can be

sprinkled everywhere (think Smart Dust) while providing consumers, marketers, healthcare providers, even big enterprise and
industry with real-time contextual data is going to be a tremendous boon for established technology companies, as well as new
start-ups with ideas we haven't imagined yet.

**CV: There is a lot of talk about the Internet of
Things, the Connected Car, the Connected Home, and
eHealth, but from your vantage point are they real? If
so, how much of a transformational effect do you think
they will have?**

MC: Well I think you used the right term there: *transformational*. This is truly a transformational period in technology, in
investment in technology, in innovation. We are in perhaps the
biggest investment phase for technology and innovation since
the inception of the Internet, so I don't foresee stagnation for
some time. The challenge I see is that companies that wish to
take advantage of these "connected" trends must transform, but
many simply can't, due to size, culture, people, or any number
of reasons.

I'm not sure if this will stifle innovation in big firms, or drive
a new wave of start-ups, but we are already seeing some pretty
interesting products and services. I am seeing companies like Feit
Electric, a privately owned manufacturer of light bulbs, maybe
the largest LED manufacturer in the world, enter the space with
"smart bulbs."

These are essentially computers with bulbs attached that
can turn on/off when a homeowner enters the space, save electricity, and drive other functions. We are also seeing companies
band together to drive whole ecosystems of products (Samsung,
Qualcomm, Apple, Intel, and others) that will interoperate
things like your lights and your thermostat, your TV and your
lights, your thermostat and your phone, all working seamlessly
for the consumer. I do, however, see several obstacles that
could affect how successful these products, companies, and

markets will be: consumer acceptance and user experience (UX). Companies that nail the execution here will succeed.

CV: What other technologies are you watching, and what kind of an impact do you think they could have?

MC: I'm personally very excited about what's happening with contextual-based technologies. These include beacons, indoor location, proximity sensors, even Google Glass, which is really just a manifestation of all of these technologies. Watching this space has me excited about how we as consumers will interact with the world around us—at bus stops, convenience stores, museums, hospitals, airports, everywhere.

There may be some apprehension to this type of technology, this type of constant connection, but I believe that the usefulness will outweigh the concerns. The release of the Apple Watch is an example, and will certainly be well received by the time of this publication. However, to me, it's the innovation and use of these sensor-based technologies that will drive and enable context-based experiences that consumers will embrace. This is the reason we formed Digital2Go, to build a network of these connected contextual devices that will interact with consumers in physical locations. The almost utilitarian functionality, and seamless user experience, will be far more rewarding than most people think.

CV: What industries do you see being impacted by these technologies and shifts in behavior (both enterprise and individual)?

MC: I can see use cases in healthcare, retail, enterprise, commercial, hospitality, logistics, and nearly any industry. Being able to provide context-based data, wherever a user is, no matter what he or she is doing, will prove powerful in these and many other vertical markets. And it's already happening in 2015 based on what companies like Verizon are reporting. In October 2015, Verizon was reporting nearly US$500 million in revenue from the Internet of Things—that's double-digit growth year over year. That's a powerful statement and commentary on how fast and big this new paradigm will become.

CV: Where do you look to identify trends before they become obvious?

MC: Having spent nearly 20 years in the wireless, mobile, semiconductor, and consumer electronics space, I get a chance to see products and services before they are released to the public. I have been involved in hundreds of product launches, from countless companies, so I get to see what works and what doesn't firsthand.

This also serves as an opportunity to be involved with some of the most talented engineering and product teams in the world. I'm a great watcher of people, of consumers, and I'm a bit of a gadget collector as well. I also like to watch smaller companies that may not have the best execution, but have some of the best products, even if just small pieces of a larger consumer product.

Watching these companies has been a great key in identifying what's next. Lastly, I have four boys, and these kids and their peers provide an incredible barometer for what a whole new generation expects from their technology. They have been born with an iPad in one hand and an Xbox One remote in the other, so their view provides compelling feedback outside the norm.

Cocktail Investing isn't something you do in a silo, separate from the rest of life. This discussion illustrates that we are surrounded by inspirations for investing every day. Being fully conscious as we go through the day, and paying attention to the way life and those around us are changing, helps us spot a great new potential area for investment and stay ahead of the curve. We regularly chat, often over a great Barolo or dirty martini, about the latest and greatest technology coming out, and usually at least one of us gets so giddy we end up buying some gadget just to experience first-hand how it can improve life. That's the Cocktail Investing way of life.

The App Revolution

The software world was once dominated by a small number of enormous companies that kicked out one-size-fits-all software on a global scale with distribution via CDs and DVDs managed primarily by other, very large organizations. This structure created enormous barriers for young startup software companies, so the best and brightest software designers were often better off joining one of the existing giants.

The continual progress toward unlimited data storage and high-speed data transmission at negligible cost, coupled with the proliferation of smartphones with essentially their own software store installed, has led to the democratization of software and data. Now almost anyone, almost anywhere, with very few resources can develop software that is available for immediate purchase to individuals all over the globe. The level of innovation that will promote is breathtaking. No longer is the world limited by the decisions of a few people at enormous software companies, but rather, almost anyone with an idea, sufficient passion, and commitment can offer their creativity on the global stage … and these ideas feed off one another. All those creative minds means many more experiments and many more chances to develop the "killer" apps that can truly change the world.

In 2011, 22.9 billion apps were downloaded worldwide, and in just two years that number grew almost fivefold to see 101.1 billion apps downloaded in 2013.[9] By the end of 2015, that number was expected to have reached around 180 billion.[10] With all these downloads, countless new companies have been created, and with them, thousands and thousands of jobs.

Cocktail Investing is about being aware of how this revolution in apps is affecting you and those around you. What are the new ways you find you are using your connected devices? What frustrates you? What do you love? What do your friends rave about, rant about, wish they had? Then even better, if you can find an app or a type of apps that address the need, try to take a step further into what makes the solution possible and where else that technology might be applicable.

The disruptive technologies we've been describing aren't anywhere near a finished story and are working their same magic in other industries and companies as the costs of storage and transmission continue to drop and as the capabilities of smartphones, tablets, and other devices continue to increase. The result will be more changes in how we conduct business across the globe, bringing ever-more changes in how we communicate, transaction, consume, travel, and more.

Think about all the disruptive technologies that you may encounter in your daily life. Perhaps you've used mobile payments, maybe seen some applications of 3D printing, or purchased one of the robotic devices that clean your home, like the Roomba from iRobot—Lenore can't imagine living without hers! Maybe you have or someone you know has benefited from the medical advancements that utilize robots to perform intricate surgical procedures that are not feasible with the human hand, or maybe you've enjoyed room service courtesy of a robot at a Starwood hotel. Maybe you've read about the trend for police officers, doctors, and other care providers to wear body cameras or about the beacons that will push coupons and other alerts to your smartphone as you shop up and down the aisles of your favorite store. There are countless applications for these emerging technologies to improve our lives, and for investors to spot that next can't-live-without solution.

Rules of Thumb

Like anything in life, one of the best ways to get a grasp on a topic is to do a little research. When it comes to disruptive technologies, there is a lot of insightful information on the web, just a few keystrokes and clicks away—yet another life-changing improvement, thanks to the data revolution. McKinsey and Company, for example, has produced some exceptionally high-quality reports on disruptive technologies and the Internet of Things, which are readily accessible to anyone. Just go to its website and type "Disruptive technologies" or "Internet of Things" into the site's search tool and you'll find a wealth of information. In late November 2015, the *Financial Times* produced a special report on "The Connected Business," in which it discussed payment platforms and how the convergence between physical and virtual online shopping was altering the relationship between retailers and customers. There is a plethora of information available at your fingertips.

To be successful today, investors need to see those disruptors that will alter the business landscape, paying attention to the way everyday lives are changing in sometimes big, sometimes little ways. Even if you have never been on Facebook or used a smartphone, it doesn't mean you can't profit from it by watching the changes that follow. If you are able to be up to date and utilize the (within reason) latest or greatest products and services, you'll be even better able to see where things are headed.

One of the most common questions we're asked is, how do we identify new disruptors or what markets, industries, and applications are likely to be disrupted next? We'd love to give you the secret codes, but unfortunately, it just isn't that easy, so we'll walk through an example.

The company that best symbolizes how we think about upcoming technologies and other disruptors is Apple. Although many see Apple as a technology innovator, the reality is that the company keeps abreast of technology developments, but only brings them to market in its devices when it sees the tipping point for consumer adoption is at hand.

Think back to what we shared with you about the first iPhone. It lacked a number of features that other competing smartphone models included, largely because of power consumption parameters and subsequent battery life issues. The mobile payment service it launched in 2014, Apple Pay, isn't the first. Similar services from PayPal and Google had been around for a few years. The same can be said for TV. We've had a number of new set-top boxes hit the market, with competing services from Google and Hulu. For Chris, Apple TV had, as of the writing of this book, fallen short of disrupting the way he consumes video programming at home. Lenore has a different perspective, as it allows her to watch the American TV shows she likes, either via Apple or Netflix, movies, and most importantly, lets her watch NFL games from Italy either live or anytime she wants after the game's been aired—providing, of course, that none of her friends blab the score!

When Apple does make its move, more often than not it integrates a number of technologies in an easy-to-use device that often requires few instructions. It is the master of coming in after the concept has already become familiar. By comparison, other companies have introduced new features, functions, and other capabilities when either the technology is still early in its lifecycle or the market, for one reason or another, simply isn't ready yet. Like a cake that isn't fully baked, those products tend to fall flat. Just look at Nokia's N-Gage mobile phone/gaming device, Palm's Foleo laptop, or Microsoft's Zune music player. When it comes to technology, being the very first is often a financial disaster. That company spends a fortune educating society and cajoling people into trying something new. The second wave of entrants doesn't have to shoulder that expense; it just benefits from it.

As to how we keep tabs on upcoming technologies and potential disruptions, we pay close attention to corporate events, such as Apple's World Wide Developer Conference, Facebook's F8 developer conference, and Google's own developer conference, better known as Google I/O. We scour for research like the McKinsey reports we mentioned earlier. We also think watching what the teens are jumping into is frighteningly insightful, annoyingly humbling, but important. In Chapter 10, we talk to a very successful technology stock analyst who does just that—watches the teens and tweens to see what new tech is going to be the latest and greatest.

In various parts of this chapter you've heard us reference the Consumer Electronics Show, a must-pay-attention-to each January, that is followed by the annual CeBIT tradeshow in Germany. Other such conferences and tradeshows that are on our radar screens include the annual North American mobile industry conference put on by CTIA, as well as its European counterpart, the annual Mobile World Congress. Frankly, industry conferences or publications are often more useful than ones intended for investors, a sentiment you'll hear repeated in Chapter 10.

In terms of reading, we do a lot of it, but when it comes to this we'd recommend perusing websites like TechCrunch and CNET, magazines such as *Wired* and *MIT Technology Review*, and the technology sections in the *Wall Street Journal* and the *New York Times*. We also like to look at new products as they hit the shelves, and we think about what's different, what brings about those new features or performance characteristics. There has to be something behind the ever-improving dryness of Pampers, the state-of-art 4K LED TV, or the next smartphone model with an even more scratch-resistant cover that consumers can't live without for investors to understand.

As we read, we like to jot down the companies, technologies, and markets that are mentioned to help us grasp the magnitude of potential change. The more these new disruptors are mentioned and the more companies that are introducing products or services that incorporate these disruptors, the more real and impactful they are about to become.

Cocktail Investing Bottom Line

You will need to learn a bit as you come to understand not only the new disruptors but also the markets, companies, and products they will forever alter and we are all too aware that the technobabble and parade of acronyms can be formidable. Frankly, our eyes tend to glaze over sometimes when we face them. We would suggest you try to KISS it (Keep It Simple, Stupid). You're not being asked to take a piece of hardware apart and reassemble it. Rather, try to have a basic understanding of what it does, how it does it differently, and why consumers or businesses would find it valuable. If you can answer those questions, you are well on your way.

- Disruptive technologies are nothing new. We can trace them back to the wheel, the printing press, the first train, car, radio, TV, and so on. Each has altered the way industries operate, companies compete, and consumers go about their daily lives.
- The digital disruption that began a few decades ago is being augmented by mobile connectivity, the Internet, social media, apps, and sensors. We've already seen how connectivity and computing power in your hand has dramatically changed how people communicate, shop, transact, and more.
- Falling prices in computing power, sensors, and connectivity are coming together with new business models to disrupt more aspects of our everyday life—the car, the home, healthcare, payments, robotics, law enforcement, and many more. Think about how things will change as the cost of storing and transmitting data becomes negligible and how much of life can and has become digital data.
- As an investor, disruptive technologies can bring big opportunities to your investment portfolio. You don't want to be too early or too late to identify disruptive changes and the companies that will benefit from them. Instead, we want to identify the beneficiaries early on, but wait to invest in them as disruptive technologies hit their tipping point. Waiting for the tipping point helps avoid limited adoption and other factors that cause a potential disruptor to flame out rather than burn bright. Remember it takes more than an incredible new technology to be a successful disruptor; it takes an irresistible delivery

of that technology for success. Investing too late means the bulk of the returns to be had have already been made.

- Finally, never forget that past performance is not an indicator of future results—disruptive technologies change the rules of the game, which usually means different winners and losers than in the past.

In the next chapter, we'll tackle what some would consider the flipside of disruption and the opportunities it can bring. While no one likes to feel pain, we can tell you from experience that pain points can lead to some very successful investing.

Endnotes

1. "Cell Phone Subscribers in the U.S., 1985–2010," www.infoplease.com/ipa/A0933563.html.

2. Michael Zhang, "Back in 1995, a 1 MP Pro Digital Camera Cost $20,000," Petapixel (July 17, 2015), petapixel.com/2015/07/17/back-in-1995-a-1mp-pro-digital-camera-cost-20000/.

3. "CIPA* Companies' Shipments of Digital Still Cameras Worldwide from 1999 to 2014 (in million units)," www.statista.com/statistics/264337/cipa-companies-shipments-of-digital-cameras-since-1999/.

4. Amanda Lenhart, "Teens, Social Media & Technology Overview 2015," Pew Research Center (April 9, 2015), www.pewinternet.org/2015/04/09/teens-social-media-technology-2015/.

5. Ibid.

6. Matt Hamblen, "Most Will Access Internet via Mobile Devices by 2015, IDC Says," Computerworld (September 12, 2011), www.computerworld.com/article/2511093/mobile-wireless/most-will-access-internet-via-mobile-devices-by-2015--idc-says.html.

7. Ibid.

8. Rebecca Mertagh, "Mobile Now Exceeds PC: The Biggest Shift Since the Internet Began," Search Engine Watch (July 8, 2014), searchenginewatch.com/sew/opinion/2353616/mobile-now-exceeds-pc-the-biggest-shift-since-the-internet-began#.

9. "Number of Free and Paid Mobil App Store Downloads Worldwide from 2011 to 2017 (in billions)," www.statista.com/statistics/271644/worldwide-free-and-paid-mobile-app-store-downloads/.

10. Ibid.

Chapter 7

Profiting from Pain

Problems are just businesses waiting for the right entrepreneur to unlock the value.

— Jay Samit

If you want something new, you have to stop doing something old.
— Peter Drucker

Each problem has hidden in it an opportunity so powerful that it literally dwarfs the problem. The greatest success stories were created by people who recognized a problem and turned it into an opportunity.

— Joseph Sugarman

When we call this chapter "Profiting from Pain," we're talking about how solutions for pain points pricking consumers and businesses can generate investing opportunities.

It's crucial to be an outside-the-box kind of thinker, recognizing the opportunities that pain points can offer. So just what do we mean by pain point? In this chapter we'll walk through a series of ongoing pain points and show you how to look for the investing opportunities hidden within them.

Over the course of our investing years, many a problem has confounded businesses, consumers, and governments. Much like the ones you face in your everyday lives, they come in all shapes, sizes, and degrees. Some are seen well in advance, some are off the radar but still eventually hit between the eyes, while there are ones that are never seen for what they are or could be until it's too late. There are the minor annoyances that lead to a minor grimace, but there are also those that really hurt.

We refer to them as pain points, and they tend to alter the very course of human behavior. For example, coming out of the Great Recession, job growth was lackluster, wages were stagnant, and consumers as well as businesses were faced with higher energy costs. In particular, gas prices, which hit a low of $1.77 per gallon in early 2009, climbed like a rocket launched from Cape Canaveral to more than $4 per gallon in April 2011. Even though gas prices would oscillate lower and higher over the ensuing quarters, it wasn't until late 2014 that they once again fell below $3 per gallon, according to Energy Information Administration data. Gas prices continued to drop in 2015 as oil prices continued to fall due to combination of the slowing global economy (remember Figures 4.13 and 4.14 in Chapter 4?) and greater supply, particularly from the United States.

That pronounced gas price increase between 2009 and 2011 came at a time when more and more people were leaving the workforce while the number of people on entitlement programs (disability and food stamps as well as Social Security) mushroomed, with wage growth practically nonexistent (on an inflation-adjusted basis), and many consumers were forced to alter where and how they spent their money.

This led Chris to focus on what he called the *cash-strapped consumer* to identify companies that would benefit as consumers became more mindful of what and where they spent their hard-earned dollars, as well as those who were likely to see their business struggle to grow sales in the increasingly frugal environment. As consumers traded down, it meant lost revenue for some companies, and the ability to identify those vulnerable companies meant sidestepping potential problem investments. Remember, too, in Chapter 1 that we talked about the need for many to deal with the savings and retirement shortfall that they are facing, which we suspect will continue to weigh on not only how much consumers spend, but also where they spend and on what. It comes as no surprise to us that consumers continue to increasingly shift spending online at the expense of department stores and other brick-and-mortar-based retailers. We saw that in spades in late 2015 during the holiday shopping season and, yes, Chris and Lenore can attest first hand to a far greater number of Amazon packages at their respective doors in 2015 compared to 2014 and 2013.

Now you might get the notion that when we say *pain point,* we're talking about extracting punitive prices or some other loan-shark-like practice; we're not. The intersection of the economy and its shifting demographics, with psychographics, technology, and other key influencers, can reveal a number of up-and-coming problems or pain points. If you're a fan of detective stories, the intersection of those moving pieces makes for an interesting detective story, and as any ardent reader of the genre knows, one of the first questions to ask is, "Who benefits?"

Pain points are those vexing issues that a company or a person contends with regularly. When Chris was an equity analyst, he would post the following questions when meeting with a company's management team: *Is there anything going on—today or on the horizon—that could force the company to change or impact its way of doing business? Is that a potential opportunity or a threat?* In a similar vein, Lenore tends to look at every company using Porter's Five Forces,[1] which we'll talk about more in Chapter 10.

Often, these talks with management lead to a conversation filled with, "If this ... then that," and show not only how well the management team knows its business but whether it is forward thinking in its strategy. There have been times, however, that the executives had blinders on when it came to their business. Not everyone follows the famous mantra of former Intel CEO Andy Grove, "Only the paranoid survive." Plenty of companies weren't paranoid enough.

Newspapers

A now-classic example of this deadly lack of paranoia from Chapter 6 was the impact that the Internet has had on newspapers and publishers, which were initially dismissive of this new medium—something that would eventually disrupt and alter their business to the very core.

The pain point for newspaper publishers became an opportunity for the Internet industry and the companies it comprised (Yahoo!, AOL, and others at the time). Some overcame it while some like the *New York Times* and the *Wall Street Journal* continue to flirt with different business models. However, the availability of content elsewhere, mixed with the loss of advertising revenue, has put more than a few newspapers in serious financial distress, and many have outright failed. The stock price movement of Gannett, McClatchy, and Lee Enterprises over 10 years (Figure 7.1) shows just how challenging this industry has become.

We'll walk through several other pain points that are vexing consumers, businesses, government, and other entities. With each, we'll show you how hidden within lie a variety of opportunities for you, the investor. As we go through these, think about how to shift your thought

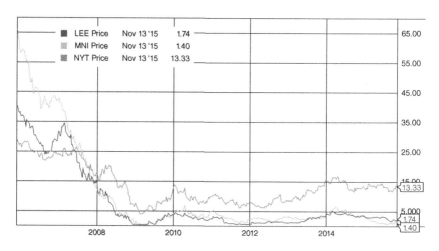

Figure 7.1   Percent change in stock price of the *New York Times* (NYT), McClatchy (MNI), and Lee Enterprises (LEE), November 13, 2005, to November 13, 2015
SOURCE: YCharts

process in your everyday life to see your frustrations as opportunities. That's the *Cocktail Investing* way. Our next pain point is in the headlines almost every week and potentially affects all of us.

Cybersecurity

Over the last few years, headlines have been near rampant with the growing number of cyberattacks that have hit both private-sector companies and governments. Cyberattacks, hacks, and identity theft are just one of the dark sides of the ever-increasing digital transformation society is going through: email; messaging through Apple's iMessage, Facebook's Messenger, or on Microsoft's Skype; sharing photos through email, messaging, or posting them on Instagram or SnapChat; using social media such as Facebook or Pinterest to keep up with friends and family; banking and conducting other transactions on your laptop, smartphone, or tablet; storing documents, photos, or other key need-to-have-within-a-moment's-notice files in the Cloud for easy usage anywhere, anytime; and downloading or streaming music, movies, and television shows to your connected digital device of choice.

There is even more to come, as the companies leverage the intersection of connectivity, sensors, and semiconductors as we discussed in the last chapter to bring new products and services to market. When we talked about AT&T (T), Verizon (VZ), and other mobile carriers spending billions on their networks in the last chapter, you can imagine that they won't be content with only connecting smartphones and tablets. Now they are tackling home security services and other connected home applications, the connected car, eHealth, and others, which naturally concerns anyone who travels extensively and ponders the complexities that come along with managing life when you're hundreds or thousands of miles away.

Whether you're reading this on a Kindle, tablet, smartphone, or an "old-fashioned" printed book, we're pretty sure you're taking part in, or at least recognizing, the digital transformation taking place around you. There was a time when you had to, *gasp,* get up from the couch to change the TV station to one of the only four options, but now you can watch a mindboggling number of programs and movies anywhere, anytime on your Apple TV, iPad, or laptop. Before broadband access was the norm, you would've heard a squawk and static-like noise as your dialup modem connected to your Internet service provider, like America Online. As a pair whose livelihoods rely on access to information and data, we both thank God for the proliferation of high-speed broadband, mobile, and wifi networks.

In 2012, as this digital shift reached critical mass, we started to hear about companies like American Express, Visa, Honda, MasterCard, Google, Yahoo!, LinkedIn, and Facebook being hacked. Those attacks and others prompted then–U.S. Defense Secretary Leon Panetta to warn in late 2012 that the United States would likely face a "cyber-Pearl Harbor" and that the country was increasingly vulnerable to foreign computer hackers.

Toward the end of 2013, Target was hacked over the Christmas holiday shopping season, later disclosing that more than 70 million credit cards and other customer data were "compromised." That's a pretty sour way to close out the year, particularly if you were Gregg Steinhafel, the chairman and CEO of Target. But Target wasn't the only company to get hacked in 2013. Soon afterward, retailer Neiman Marcus admitted that it, too, had been cyberattacked, and the thieves made off with customers' payment card information. As we moved through 2014, the high-profile attacks continued at companies like Sony (SNE) and the Home Depot (HD), as well as those at Staples, Healthcare.gov, and more. According to Symantec's annual Internet Security Threat Report, the number of cyberattacks against large companies rose by 40 percent last year, with five out of six companies employing more than 2,500 people targeted in 2014.[2] Needless to say, those attacks have continued into 2015.

Cyberattacks and hacking aren't just hitting corporate America, and identity thieves don't only target individuals. Government institutions are also in the crosshairs. Unknown hackers broke into more than two-dozen servers at the U.S. Postal Service in 2014, including one containing names, Social Security numbers, birthdates, and other personally identifiable information on about 800,000 workers and 2.9 million customers.[3] Other cyber-victims included the Washington State Administrative Office of the Courts and one of the internal websites of the Federal Reserve.

In a January 2014 Senate Judiciary Committee hearing, U.S. Attorney General Eric Holder said that the United States had not done enough to prepare for cyberattacks and that the Justice Department needed to "take very seriously" the creation of a multiyear plan to deal with the threat. Holder said he expected the threats to increase, although the United States hasn't devoted enough resources to the problem. Over a year after Leon Panetta raised his concerns, the government still hadn't done enough. Our ears perk right up when we see this; it is a big problem, and no easily implemented solution means opportunity.

Holder and others were correct, as evidenced by the November 2014 cyberattack on Sony Pictures Entertainment. This was one of the most high-profile hacks, and we eventually learned that the intrusion had been occurring for more than a year prior to its discovery.

The hackers involved claimed to have taken over 100 terabytes of data from Sony that included personal data, contract details, private email messages, and details of behind-the-scenes politics; they also leaked several upcoming films. In December 2014, former Sony Pictures Entertainment employees filed four lawsuits against the company for not protecting their data that was released in the hack, which included Social Security numbers and medical information. When it presented its first-quarter 2015 financial results, Sony Pictures set aside $15 million to deal with ongoing damages from the hack. Sony bolstered its cybersecurity infrastructure as a result, using redundant solutions to prevent similar hacks or data loss in the future, and Sony co-chairperson, Amy Pascal, announced her resignation effective May 2015.

In hindsight, it was pretty clear that Sony had not invested adequately in its cybersecurity, even though top management knew full well that nothing can turn a potential box office dynamo into a dud better than spoilers and leaks.

We'd like to say that was it for 2014, but there were dozens and dozens of other high-profile attacks and hundreds more that fell below the headline news cycle. Officials in President Barack Obama's administration confirmed that there had even been a cyberattack on White House computer networks in 2014.

We are avid readers of policy papers, studies, polls, and reports. On the topic of cybersecurity, we unearthed several key points in Cisco System's 2015 Annual Security Report. The report explores the ongoing race between attackers and defenders, and how users (that would be you and us) are becoming ever-weaker links in the security chain. Some of the key findings from the Cisco report follow.

Attackers have become more proficient at taking advantage of gaps in security to evade detection and conceal malicious activity. This means attackers are increasingly savvy concerning how, where, and when they are launching attacks. Through the first 11 months of 2014, spam volume increased 250 percent year-over-year, according to Cisco's data. Another strategy that is increasingly being used is *malvertising* (malicious advertising), which works through web browser add-ons to distribute malware and unwanted applications. Cisco notes that the use of malvertising also means that attackers are buying advertising to deliver malware—a very different strategy than what has been done before, which means more opportunities to offer protection.

The malvertising-focused strategy was part of a larger shift in the nature of attacks from the corporate entity, meaning networks, servers, and the like, to the user of a computer, tablet, or smartphone. Why attack the user? Because he or she is the entry point into a company or other institutional assets through tactics such as sending a fake request for a password reset that leaves one open to identity theft and other subsequent attacks. This is particularly true given the adoption of bring your own device (BYOD), the cloud, and desktop virtualization clients.

Just as attackers have upped their game, companies will need to respond, but in a more holistic and strategic way rather than simply addressing each attack as it happens. According to the "Cisco Security Capabilities Benchmark Study," 91 percent of organizations have an executive with direct responsibility for security, but what's really needed is a shift in thinking about security at the business unit and board level that includes understanding cybersecurity's role in the business and as a differentiator when it comes to competitors, customers, and partners. Businesses need to look at managing security well as a potential competitive advantage, rather than just a cost of doing business.

Society has always had crime. The criminals learn to take advantage of new technologies alongside the rest of society; thus, their methods become more sophisticated, and that forces institutions and individuals to get smarter in order to fend them off. The same is true with cybersecurity.

Cybercrime is an exploding pain point for many, and it has not only given rise to privacy concerns but also boosted demand for cybersecurity. By 2016, the global business community is forecasted to spend $86 billion on information security, up from $62 billion in 2012, according to market research firm Gartner Group.[4] *Ta-da!* Pain point meets opportunity.

As an investor, we love investing in companies that address pain points, and in this instance that means companies like Symantec Corp., the aforementioned Cisco Systems, FireEye, Palo Alto Networks, Fortinet, and a number of others. We'd also point out that cybersecurity companies are bulking up and acquiring other companies to round out their offering or fill a product gap for the challenges that lie ahead. In 2014, FireEye made a $1 billion offer to acquire Mandiant with the rationale that FireEye's cyberattack protection solutions would mesh well with Mandiant's ability to respond to cyber-espionage. Palo Alto Networks acquired Morta Security, a company founded by former National Security Agency officials.

As hackers become more resourceful and target newer digital lifestyle applications—the connected home, the connected car, eHealth, wearables, and those applications that will no doubt become popular in the next few years that no one has named yet—we expect cybersecurity spending and strategic M&A activity to continue.

As mentioned in Chapter 6, one of the best ways to better understand the dynamics of an industry is to talk with an expert in the field, so we headed out for some Cocktail-Investing-style chats with Andrew Braunberg, Research Vice President, and Mike Spanbauer, Vice President of Security Test & Advisory at NSS Labs, the world's leading information security research and advisory firm.

Talking Cyber Security with NSS Labs

Chris Versace: Over the years, people have become nonplussed by PC-led viruses and phishing. Given the shift from PCs to smartphones and tablets, are we on the cusp of seeing a wave of cyberattacks on these device types?

Andrew Braunberg: There is nothing new about malware targeting mobile devices. We are well into the wave.

CV: How protected are smartphones and tablets from viruses and other attacks?

AB: There are architectural features in most mobile devices that make them more secure than traditional PCs. These include: sandboxing of data between applications and restrictions on the ability to download applications from untrusted sources (if the device is not "jail-broken"[5]) in the first place, which is enabled through code-signing.

CV: With Android and Apple's iOS dominating smartphone operating systems, is one more secure than the other?

AB: Apple iOS, by far. Android has valued openness over security. Apple has been much more successful in maintaining a closed-app ecosystem and ensuring no malicious applications run on its devices. Android also suffers from fragmentation due to multiple hardware device manufacturers and a lack of update policies with carriers to push Android software updates to devices.

CV: We're starting to hear more about ransomware. What is it, and how prevalent could it become?

AB: Ransomware is malware that locks or encrypts someone's mobile device until they pay to have it unlocked/unencrypted. There are a lot of variants.[6] Ransomware is popular with Eastern European organized crime gangs this year [2015] and we do expect to see it continue to grow as a problem for the foreseeable future.

CV: Is there a danger as the connected home and connected car markets come about that a compromised smartphone could allow access to those connected devices?

AB: Internet of Things (IoT) devices will become their own attack surface for hackers without the need for attackers to go through mobile phones and tablets. "Connected" devices by definition are networked and therefore potentially vulnerable to attack. Securing the Internet of Things is a huge concern right now [early 2015]. Very big topic.

CV: What tools or services are being developed that business and consumers can use to fend off these attacks on their smartphones and tablets?

AB: The mobile operating system and device manufacturers, particularly Apple and Samsung, are all working on increasing the security of their technology. This is a natural maturing of products and also a shift from these vendors to create devices more appropriate for enterprise business use as opposed to just consumer-grade devices.

There is also a whole ecosystem of third-party enterprise mobility management (EMM) vendors that have grown up around these products over the last 10 years or so. Many started as mobile device management vendors, but they have moved into mobile application management, secure workspaces/containers, application wrapping, secure document management, etc. [These are] very vibrant markets today [2015].

CV: Are there any particular companies that are further along with these protective solutions?

AB: There are dozens, but a couple of the bigger players are Airwatch (acquired by VMware), Mobile Iron, Citrix, and Good Technologies (acquired by BlackBerry).

Next up, Chris Morales, practice manager, architecture and infrastructure, gives us his insights.

CV: What is the next wave in mobile threats that is not yet talked about in the media?

Chris Morales: The next wave, I think, is that the phone is becoming "our everything." Phones and other handheld devices are becoming our personal controller and the hub of each person's own "Internet of Everything." At the same time, these connections are increasingly being made over public resources, in particular with cloud computing. This will generate a multitude of inputs and outputs with server and application connections that cybercriminals (and others) will continue to go after.

CV: How does your company go about identifying the risk that has not yet arisen? How do you stay ahead of the "bad guys"?

CM: NSS Labs, Inc., was founded as an independent, hands-on testing laboratory of leading IT security products and today is the world's security intelligence authority. As part of its efforts to help clients be more cyber-resilient, NSS has launched the Cyber Advanced Warning System (CAWS), a suite of services to help enterprises manage their cyber-risk. This first-of-its-kind offering will allow CIOs [chief information officers] and CISOs [chief information security officers] to continually evaluate their security posture, identify which threats target their applications, and bypass their security controls, as well as plan and model responses. NSS's Research & Testing is the security industry's most comprehensive library of independent test results for leading security products as well as in-depth vendor, product, and market research. The NSS analyst team conducts ongoing research on cybersecurity and advises enterprise clients on how best to address today's cybersecurity threats.

Andrew and Mike are some seriously in-the-know guys. This is why we prefer meeting with industry experts to understand where the pain points and opportunities lie and which firms are most likely to take the lead on addressing the pain. Yet despite all that is being done, it looks like the cybersecurity industry is, at least in 2015, still in its infancy both in terms of defining the source of the pain and the possible solutions. There are a few companies that have a clear lead in specific applications, but overall, there is a lot that still needs to shake out.

We'll discuss in Chapter 10 the different ways to invest in pain point solutions, depending on the nature and age of the industry or sector. For now, we'll just say that sometimes it pays to pick a specific company;

other times, you may be better off investing in a broader manner within a sector or industry.

It isn't just new technologies that can cause pain; sometimes the simplest thing in the world, like water, can be in need of innovation.

Water

Did you know that those ears of fresh summer corn you slather with butter, salt, and maybe hot sauce take up to four gallons of water a week to mature? To produce an acre of corn, 350,000 gallons of water are needed over a 100-day growing season. And you thought your water bill was steep!

To produce a pound of wood, hardwood trees use about 120 gallons of water. An average-sized birch tree has about 200,000 leaves. More than 90 percent of the water that enters a plant passes directly through and evaporates into the atmosphere. If a human had a circulatory system like that, an adult would need to drink more than 20 gallons of water each day just to survive!

Given the astounding proliferation of bottled water, you'd think we had infinite supply, but while nearly 70 percent of the world is covered by water, only 2.5 percent of it is fresh, and just 1 percent of that is easily accessible.[7]

As the global population continues to grow, it means that over time, there will be greater competition for that 1 percent. We've seen the impact of short supply and rising global demand for beef, coffee, and other commodities, and it tends to lead to higher prices. As families in emerging economies have more and more disposable income and trade up in their purchase decisions, there will be greater demand for resources such as fossil fuels, oil and natural gas, mineral resources (such as copper), and others—including water and the more water-intensive products like beef.

Even without population growth, data from the United Nations points out that in the last century, water usage grew at more than twice the rate of population increase. By 2025, an estimated 1.8 billion people will live in areas plagued by water scarcity, with two-thirds of the world's population living in water-stressed regions as a result of usage, growth, and climate change.[8]

Now think of the implications on food, manufacturing, and what your own water bill could look like in the coming years.

Sadly, there is a second part to the growing water problem, and it has to do with the delivery mechanism for the water we consume. When something is out of sight, it tends to be out of mind, but if you've driven much across the United States in recent years you know firsthand the need for highway, bridge, and pothole repairs. When it comes to water, because most of it is out of sight, we aren't aware of the age and growing needs of our nation's water infrastructure. In a report to Congress released in 2009 and based on data collected from utilities in 2007, the Environmental Protection Agency (EPA) found that the nation's 53,000-community water systems and 21,400 not-for-profit non-community water systems need to invest an estimated $334.8 billion between 2007 and 2027.[9]

Like most problems that go unresolved, they tend to get bigger and bigger. According to the American Society of Civil Engineers (ASCE) most recent report card published in 2013, America's drinking water received a grade of D. Per the ASCE, there are 240,000 water main breaks every year, and trillions of gallons of water are lost each year due to "leaky pipes, broken water mains, and faulty meters." Leaking pipes lose an estimated 7 billion gallons of clean drinking water a day and projections are that 45 percent of the country's pipes will be rated poor, very poor, or beyond repair by 2020.[10]

Cities throughout the nation, including Toledo and Philadelphia, are dealing with water main breaks and struggling to pay for the upkeep and improvements of their water infrastructure. In the past 30 years, Philadelphia has had between 439 and 1,316 water main breaks per year.[11] In January 2016 the governor of Michigan declared a state of emergency for the city of Flint, Michigan, because of widespread lead poisoning caused by aging pipes in the city's water system. Shortly thereafter President Obama declared the crisis to be a federal state emergency. As of the writing of this book somewhere between 6,000 and 12,000 residents had been diagnosed with severely high levels of lead in their blood and 10 people were suspected to have died as a result of the contamination. This crisis is bound to push other municipalities to take a closer look at the state of their own water supplies.

It is estimated that more than one million miles of water mains are in place in the United States. In 2012, the American Water Works Association (AWWA) calculated the aggregate replacement value for these pipes was approximately $2.1 trillion[12] if all were to be replaced at once. The good news is that like most home repairs, not all pipes need to be replaced immediately or all at once. Making some modest adjustments, the AWWA estimated that the most urgent investments could be spread over 25 years at a cost of approximately $1 trillion.

While that sounds better, fixing the water infrastructure problem in the United States will take time. According to the ASCE Report Card:

> The need will double from roughly $13 billion a year today to almost $30 billion (in 2010 dollars) annually by the 2040s, and the cost will be met primarily through higher water bills and local fees.
>
> Delaying the investment can result in degrading water service, increasing water service disruptions, and increasing expenditures for emergency repairs. Ultimately we will have to face the need to "catch up" with past deferred investments, and the more we delay the harder the job will be when the day of reckoning comes.[13]

By 2050, the AWWA indicates the aggregate investment needs would total more than $1.7 trillion. For perspective, in 2015 GDP for the entire United States was just shy of $18 trillion.

Figure 7.2 shows the ever-widening gap in water spending needs, which for Cocktail Investors is evidence of profound possibilities.

While this has been a quietly festering problem, thanks to the near-persistent drought conditions in California, now in its third year, water problems have come into the limelight. How bad are the drought conditions? In April 2015, California Governor Jerry Brown issued a statewide order to cut water consumption. Included in California's preliminary recommendation by the State Water Resources Control Board, 135 communities faced a 35 percent reduction in urban water usage, another 18 communities, including San Francisco, faced reductions of just 10 percent, while the remainder of the 400 California water agencies covered by the executive order had to make cuts of 20 to 25 percent.[14]

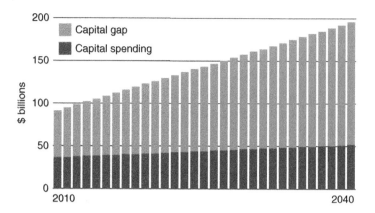

Figure 7.2 Projected water infrastructure spending needs vs. spending gaps
SOURCE: Downstream Strategies, EDR Group and the American Society of Civil Engineers

Taking the microscope off California and looking at data from the U.S. Drought Monitor shown in Figure 7.3, which looks at drought conditions for all 50 states, we find the situation is far more dire. As of mid-November 2015, more than 45 percent of the contiguous United States was in some state of drought.[15]

As you pay your monthly bills, you've probably noticed you've been paying more to your water utility. Water utility bills have been increasing pretty steadily, up almost 5 percent per year between 1996 and 2012 according to AWWA, but as the current drought situation worsened, the price of water rose 6 percent in 30 major U.S. cities during 2014.[16]

When we talked about reading the economy like a pro we told you that when we think we see a trend, we always look for confirming data points. That's applies not only for the economy, but also to trends like pain points.

Another confirming point that it's more than just California dealing with rising water costs, between 2010 and 2015 water prices in 30 major U.S. cities rose 41 percent on average,[17] which is the equivalent of adding roughly $20 per month to what was a monthly $50 water bill in 2010!

This situation has the potential to be a long-term pain point, which in our view is always appealing when it comes to making investment decisions. Like most problems there are layers, and that holds true for this water-related pain point. The supply–demand imbalance bodes well

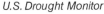
U.S. Drought Monitor

November 10, 2015

Drought Conditions (Percent Area)

	None	D0-D4	D1-D4	D2-D4	D3-D4	D4
Current	54.90	45.10	25.18	15.24	8.46	2.70
Last Week *11/3/2015*	51.84	48.16	26.17	15.46	8.84	2.72
3 Months Ago *8/11/2015*	56.13	43.87	28.92	17.87	9.18	3.00
Start of Calendar Year *12/30/2014*	53.20	46.80	28.68	16.93	8.96	2.54
Start of Water Year *9/29/2015*	44.91	55.09	31.36	20.09	11.45	3.00
One Year Ago *11/11/2014*	53.21	46.79	29.59	17.27	8.82	3.79

Intensity:

D0 Abnormally Dry   D3 Extreme Drought
D1 Moderate Drought   D4 Exp=ceptional
D2 Severe Drought   Drought

The Drought Monitor Focuses on broad-scale conditions. Loval conditions may vary. See accompanying text summary for forecast statements.

The U.S. Drought Monitor is produced through a partnership between the National Drought Mitigation Center at the University of Nebraska-Lincoln, the United States Department of Agriculture, and the National Oceanic and Atmospheric Administration

Figure 7.3   U.S. Drought Monitor
SOURCE: U.S. Department of Agriculture

for water utilities that are able to push through price increases that benefit revenues, margins, and earnings. Most publicly traded water utilities are also dividend-paying companies, which makes them an even sweeter investment at a time when suppressed interest rates are making decent income-generating investments more scarce.

We've looked at pain points arising from changing technology as well as limitations with natural resources, but pain points can also arise from changes in society.

Changing Demographics

Merriam Webster dictionary defines *demographic* as being of or relating to the study of changes that occur in large groups of people over a period of time. There is no shortage of collected data on the United States or even the global population broken down by any number of characteristics from age to income and many things in between.

Remember filling out those pesky Census forms? Well, it may take a while, but the U.S. government does indeed collect and eventually tabulate all that data and publishes much of it in one central repository known as Census.gov. Luckily for us, the U.S. Census Bureau now breaks down all that data into easily digestible topics, but so much data are available that the bureau also publishes summary findings, better known as QuickFacts.[18]

Notice we said "so much data" and not "so much information." The difference between the two is that data consist of raw and unorganized facts that need to be processed. When these data are processed, organized, structured, or presented in a given context so as to make them useful, they become information.

Many businesses collect and study demographic data because changes in the population, its preferences, and needs can have a big impact on an industry or a company's business. Strolling through the mall Chris has often wondered why it is that there are so many more clothing and footwear choices for women than for men (and no, he is not channeling his last name while doing so). The simple answer is that women are the world's most powerful consumers, and according to global strategic services firm EY, their global income will reach $18 trillion by 2018![19] With women driving 70-80% of all consumer purchasing, it stands to reason that retailers would target them first and foremost.

So, yes, demographic information can be very helpful, and the good news is that you don't need to spend a lot to get it. Unlike giant consumer products companies, you're not betting the farm on a few new products, but, rather, looking to see which industries and companies are poised to benefit from the demographic shift while sidestepping those that will be facing headwinds. We'll look at two different demographic shifts: the aging of the population and the plumper population.

Aging of the Population

Let's start with an issue that you've probably already noticed in your everyday life and one we touched on in Chapter 1. We are living longer, and the overall population is skewing older. We all know that the life expectancy for older Americans has continued to increase, given advances in medicine and the move toward a healthier lifestyle.

According to an NCHS report released in late 2014, in 2012, the most recent year for which data are available, people who reached age 65 can expect an average additional 19.3 years on the planet.[20] Women will like that they tend to average another 20.5 years, whereas men tend to average another 17.9 years. Those 19-plus years constitute a 34 percent increase from 1960, when a 65-year-old could expect to live another 14.4 years.[21]

By 2030, the Administration on Aging (AOA) estimates there will be about 72.1 million people aged 65 or older, more than twice their number in 2000. In 2010, the Baby Boom generation was between 46 and 64 years old. By 2030, all of the Baby Boomers will have moved into the senior generation, resulting in a major structural shift in demographics. From 2010 to 2030, the percent of the population over 65 will *increase* from 13 percent to 19 percent while the percent of the U.S. population aged 20–64, the primary working years, will *decrease* from 60 percent to 55 percent.[22]

We in the United States are hardly alone in this. In fact Canada, Japan, and most of Europe have an even higher percentage of their populations in the older age brackets. According to population projections from the United Nations published in its 2013 "World Population Ageing" report, the global population aged 65 and older will triple over the next 40 years, from 500 million in 2010 to 1.5 billion by 2050, thus increasing the share of this demographic across the world from 8 percent to 16 percent. There is a shift toward older age brackets in almost every country as people live longer and have fewer children. Digging into the specifics of that UN report one sees that:

- Roughly 26 percent of Japan's population is aged 65 or older, and 32.2 percent are expected to be senior citizens there by 2030.
- Germany has 17 million people who are aged 65 and older, and that number is expected to swell to 21 million by 2030.
- By 2030, there are projected to be nearly 16 million retirees in Italy with 25.5 percent of Italian citizens anticipated to be 65 or older.
- There are 8.4 million Spaniards age 65 or older, and they comprise 17.6 percent of Spain's population. Those numbers are estimated to

grow to 11.5 million in 2030, when this age group is expected make up 22 percent of the population.[23]

How does this stack up against what it used to be?

Per historical data from the UN, life expectancy was 65 years in 1950 in the more developed regions, as compared with 42 years in the less developed regions. (Note that the latter number was heavily skewed by higher child-mortality rates.) Between 2010 and 2015, these figures are estimated to be 78 years in the more developed regions and 68 years in the less developed regions. The gap is expected to narrow even further: By 2045 to 2050, life expectancy is projected to reach 83 years in the more developed regions, and 75 years in the less developed regions.

The number of people 65 and older was 841 million in 2013, four times higher than the 202 million seen in 1950. This population is expected to nearly triple by 2050, when its number is expected to surpass the two billion mark. Said another way, the proportion of the world's 65-or-older population is expected to increase to 21 percent, up from 12 percent in 2013 and 8 percent in 1950.

That's a lot of information, but the short of it is that money that was once dedicated to support a young and growing family is increasingly shifting toward aging lifestyle changes that can include dietary adjustments, physical constraints, medical considerations, and travel challenges.

To us there are a number of industries that will potentially benefit from that demand-induced spending shift, including healthcare, pharmaceutical, housing, travel, and leisure. Let's take a closer look at the healthcare industry. There is growing evidence that a significant portion of total healthcare costs is spent at or near the end of life. With the net population skewing older, it also stands to reason healthcare should be a booming business during the coming decade or two.

How big will this overall aging lifestyle-spending shift be? According to research firm A.T. Kearny, worldwide spending (remember the aging of the population is global) by mature consumers is forecasted to reach $15 trillion annually by 2020.[24]

Now, you're probably saying to yourself, "But all that data these two shared went out to 2030 and beyond." Absolutely correct, and that means much like a snowball that gets bigger as it rolls down a snow-covered hill, the size of this spending shift will grow even larger past the end of the decade. That's a huge opportunity for industries that are meeting the particular needs of consumers age 65 and older. It likely means that more companies will tailor products and services to meet this opportunity.

Cocktail Investing is all about recognizing opportunities like the ones mentioned above, ones that have yet to receive the attention they will one day get. When you look around in your everyday life you probably notice this aging population shift. When we do that, as investors, we do our best to connect the dots and look toward the cause and effect.

That means asking question like, "As the population ages, what are the effects on their lives and the lives of the people around them? How do their needs change, and what does this mean for industries and companies that serve them? Is this an opportunity or will the business slowly disappear as the number of people over 65 years old accounts for more and more of the population?"

It's a very subtle change to how you look at things, but it is one that can open your eyes to possibilities you may not have been aware of before. That's one of the advantages of Cocktail Investing.

With that lens now in place, let's take another look at the aging of the population.

Because we are living longer, the number of years after retirement has also grown longer. In 1950, the average length of retirement was eight years for men, but given the combination of earlier retirement ages and longer life expectancies, that retirement length grew to 19 years by 2010. In mid-2015, the U.S. Government Accountability Office (GAO) published its findings showing that as many as half of all households with Americans 55 and older have no retirement savings at all and about 29% have absolutely nothing: no pension plan, no savings, no 401(k), nothing.[25] To us this means there is a looming funding gap between the savings they do have socked away and what will be needed to one day retire.

That explains why nearly 6 in 10 Americans believe their financial planning needs improvement and 21 percent are "not at all confident" they'll be able to reach their financial goals, according to Northwestern Mutual's 2015 Planning & Progress Study. That report goes on to say that while a majority of people have taken steps to address that shortfall, 34 percent said they have taken no action at all.[26]

We always look for corroborating data points and in this case, sadly, there are too many:

- According to the Employment Benefit Research Institute's Retirement Readiness Ratings, 41 to 43 percent of Americans are at risk of running out of money in retirement.
- Aon PLC's (AON) Real Deal study is the most pessimistic, concluding that only 30 percent of workers at large employers (those with 50 or more employees) are on track to retire comfortably at age 65.[27]
- Boston College's Center for Retirement Research has found that 53 percent of Americans are at risk of not being able to sustain their current standard of living when they are in retirement.[28]
- Fidelity Investments' Retirement Preparedness Measure found that 55 percent of Americans are in fair or poor condition when being able to cover just the essential living expenses when in retirement.[29]

Ouch! That sounds like a pain point in the making, doesn't it?

Some may be tempted to look for quick fixes, like playing the lottery or heading to Vegas. Where would those people looking to take charge of their personal financial situations, rather than hoping the fates intervene, turn? Our answer would be to look for those companies in the financial services industry, particularly those that specialize in financial planning, wealth management, and asset management, that will best address these needs.

Plumper Population

There is another part of society that is growing, this one at the waistline. Obesity has been described as the fastest-growing public health challenge we've ever faced, and while there are a variety of causes, the most common ones cited include inadequate activity, unhealthy eating habits, and changing food alternatives. Figure 7.4 illustrates just how widespread the problem has become, and we have been closely tracking the costs associated with obesity for several years. All the data point to it being an epidemic that has both direct and indirect implications, on top of its staggering costs.

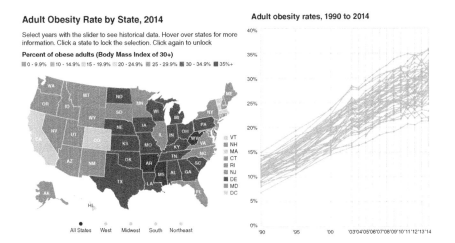

Figure 7.4 U.S. adult obesity by state, 2014
SOURCE: The State of Obesity, a project of the Trust for America's Health

The data are rather eye opening:

- The World Health Organization (WHO) estimates that two-thirds of the adult population in the United States is overweight.[30]
- According to the Centers for Disease Control and Prevention (CDC), during the past 20 years, there has been a dramatic increase in obesity in the United States. More than one-third of adults (34.9 percent) and approximately 17 percent (or 12.7 million) of children and adolescents aged 2 to 19 years are obese.[31]
- According to the American Medical Association, obesity rates in the country have doubled among adults in the past 20 years and tripled among children in a single generation. Nationwide, nearly 70 percent of Americans are overweight or obese,[32] and half of all Americans are projected to become obese by 2030.[33]

While those figures are not perfectly in sync, when taken together they present a pretty compelling argument, but the forward-looking view is even more disturbing.

Based on research by Emory University healthcare economist Ken Thorpe, Ph.D., executive director of the Partnership to Fight Chronic

Disease (PFCD), a report commissioned by UnitedHealth Foundation, Partnership for Prevention, and American Public Health Association showed that if current trends continue, 43 percent of U.S. adults will be obese, and spending on obesity-related medical problems will quadruple to $344 billion by 2018.[34]

According to the *Journal of Health Economics*, annual healthcare costs of obesity-related illnesses are a staggering $190.2 billion or nearly 21 percent of annual medical spending in the United States. Childhood obesity alone is responsible for $14 billion in direct medical costs.[35]

In 2010, the Congressional Budget Office (CBO) found that nearly 20 percent of the increase in healthcare spending was caused by obesity. Even the CBO recognizes that fighting obesity and related chronic conditions in the long run can help save money by reducing healthcare costs and obesity-related costs, such as absenteeism, that weigh on businesses.

Obesity costs so much because it leads to greater rates of heart disease, stroke, diabetes, cancer, hypertension, osteoarthritis, gallbladder disease, and disability. Now here's the real shocker—if obesity rates were to remain at 2010 levels, the projected savings for medical expenditures would be $549.5 billion over the next two decades.[36]

Don't let the U.S.-centric data make you think it is just a national problem; obesity is a global issue. The WHO estimated the global number of overweight adults increased 44 percent from 2005 to 2015 to 2.3 billion, while the number of obese adults was estimated to have increased 75 percent over the same period to 700 million.

In June 2013, the American Medical Association (AMA) voted to officially recognize obesity as a disease. That change meant doctors could change the way they treated the problem, and it could also mandate insurers to cover treatments. Clearly this was a signal from the AMA that we have to get a handle on obesity because of the long-term impacts it has not only our health but also on our healthcare costs.

Soon after the new AMA classification, "The Treat and Reduce Obesity Act" was introduced by Rep. Bill Cassidy (R., Louisiana) and Rep. Ron Kind (D., Wisconsin) in the U.S. House of Representatives and Sen. Tom Carper (D., Delaware) and Sen. Lisa Murkowski (R., Alaska) in the Senate. The bill, which was assigned to congressional committee in June 2015, aims to help lower healthcare costs and to prevent chronic diseases by addressing America's growing obesity crisis. It would allow Medicare patients access to weight-loss counseling and new prescription drugs for chronic weight management, among other provisions. In Chapter 5 we discussed how politics and regulation can impact investing. The AMA's decision started a process which is changing the economic dynamics of the weight management industry.

Think of this through your Cocktail Investing eyes:

- We know obesity is a growing problem with mounting costs associated with it.
- When obesity became recognized as a disease, that paved the way for treatment to be covered by Medicare. This means that tax dollars have been made available for treatment.
- That opened the door for new prescription drugs to treat obesity alongside or in addition to diet and eating better, exercise, and certain surgical procedures.

As awareness of a pain point rises, new solutions arise to address them, and that spells opportunity for new industries and companies, potentially at the expense of others.

So far in this chapter, we've talked about those kinds of pain points that cut across industries and affect a wide range of companies. We're not sure there isn't an industry that won't be impacted by cyberattacks. Maybe one that still uses a pencil and ledger to conduct their business, but as we saw in Chapter 6, those have probably gone the way of the dodo bird. Demographic shifts like the aging of the population ripple through a number of industries, bringing new opportunities and challenges along with them.

Not all pain points are as widely evident as cybersecurity, aging of the population, or the plumping population. Some are subtle, at least at the beginning. They start off small, but over time continue to grow until we wonder how we never saw them before. In some ways, it's like trying to imagine the world before the Internet, and we know how hard that can be at times. When we started talking about changing demographics, we shared how Colgate tracks demographic information to identify its target consumer—but what if those consumer preferences started to change?

Changing Consumer Preferences

If we watch evolving demographics over time, we can pick up on shifting patterns and preferences. Earlier we mentioned that some consumers are looking to eat "better." *Better* can mean different things to different people, but in this case we are defining "better" as higher-quality food, or what some have called "food with integrity." Many will quickly think of Whole Foods Market when they read that description, and while that would indeed be a good example, there is more going on than meets the eye.

You've probably noticed shifting square footage at the grocery store, with more and more of it being dedicated to natural, organic, non-GMO, gluten-free, and other healthy-lifestyle products. Even restaurant chains are focusing on gluten-free and low-calorie meals. Why? Because a growing number of consumers want those kinds of products.

According to the 2014 Market LOHAS (lifestyle of health and sustainability) MamboTrack annual consumer research study,[37] more than 80 percent of participants claim to seek out non-GMO products, and 70 percent of buyers searched for gluten-free products. Now "claiming to seek" out is a little nebulous, so here is some harder data from Nielsen's TDLinx and Progressive Grocer—the U.S. supermarket industry, which includes conventional supermarkets, supercenters, warehouse grocery stores, military commissaries, and limited-assortment and natural/gourmet-positioned supermarkets, had approximately $638.3 billion in sales in 2014, a 3 percent increase over the prior year.[38] Within that broader category, natural product sales through retail channels were approximately $98.6 billion, a 9 percent increase over the prior year, according to Natural Foods Merchandiser.

This trend is expected to continue. According to "United States Organic Food Market Forecast & Opportunities, 2018," the organic food market in the United States will grow at a compound annual growth rate near 14 percent from 2014 to 2018. The global gluten-free product market is projected to reach a value of $6.2 billion, growing at a CAGR of 10.2 percent by 2018. A 2015 report by TechNavio estimated the global organic food and drink market was $70.5 billion at the retail sales level in 2012, and the firm sees it growing to $223.5 billion at the retail sales level in 2016.[39]

Notice we used the word *trend*. A trend is a discernible shift in consumer behavior that has implications on tastes, preferences, and, yes, spending. Companies that fail to keep pace with those shifts run the risk of seeing their business come under pressure, potentially to the point where they could be no more.

This is a shift in consumer preference, which falls into the *psychographic* aspect of how we look at the world. If you've not heard of this term before, it refers to going beyond simpler *demographic* information to understand more about consumer lifestyle, behaviors, and habits. We just gave you two examples of shifting demographics; now we'll walk through two examples of shifting psychographics: fitter food and millennial mistrust.

Fitter Food

In Chapter 6, we talked about the impact of streaming on how we watch TV, movies, and other video programming. The one-time champ of what to do over the weekend—Blockbuster Video—did not keep pace with the changing consumer preference to stay home and download or stream a video that you wanted to watch right then and there, instead of trudging out, hoping to find something you may want to watch. Think about all those hours you spent walking the aisles of various Blockbuster stores only to walk out empty-handed.

It's that shift in behavior that differentiates a trend from a short-term phenomenon known as a *fad*. A fad is something that comes along and is fashionable for a short period of time before it disappears without a trace. Think of the Cabbage Patch Doll, the Furby, Silly Bandz, and, if you're in the 65+ camp, the one-time rage of flagpole sitting. Can you imagine sitting up on a flagpole for a few days? Especially in today's increasingly Connected Society?

With the difference between a fad and a trend in mind, let's take another look at this shifting consumer preference for food that is good for you.

It's not just a shift in the way we eat at home, but also at restaurants. The National Restaurant Association's Restaurant Trends Survey revealed that gluten-free items and healthier meals were some of the top menu trends for 2014.[40]

Now is it any surprise that soda sales have been hard hit? Total sales by volume of carbonated soft drinks fell 3 percent in 2013 to 8.9 billion cases, the lowest since 1995, before falling another 0.9 percent in 2014. Despite the drop for soda, sales volume across the entire beverage industry, which includes non-carbonated beverages and water, actually rose 1.7 percent in 2014.[41]

More often than not, examples are the best way to effectively communicate what we're talking about:

In September 2014, natural and organic food company Annie's announced that it was being acquired by General Mills. While the press release talked about how General Mills would expand the reach of Annie's business, which we don't doubt, it was the statement from Annie's CEO John Foraker that really caught our attention—"Powerful consumer shifts toward products with simple, organic and natural ingredients from companies that share consumers' core values show no signs of letting up."[42] Of course adding Annie's to its stable of products helps General Mills expand into the natural and organic foods market.

In early 2015, candy and confections manufacturer The Hershey Company announced it had acquired artisanal beef jerky company KRAVE, its first acquisition outside of candy. Over the years, Hershey has acquired a number of well-recognized candy brands, such as Reese's Peanut Butter Cups and Twizzlers to boutique chocolate businesses like Scharffen Berger, Joseph Schmidt Confections, and Dagoba Organic Chocolate, as well as international ones such as Chinese candy maker Shanghai Golden Monkey, to expand its sugary footprint. Acquiring KRAVE allowed Hershey to tackle the meat snack category, appeal to Paleo-friendly palates, and give Hershey a foot into the $5.9 billion "other sweet and savory snacks" category, which is defined by Euromonitor International as snacks other than chips, pretzels, nuts, popcorn, and dried fruit treats.

Those companies that best respond to the ever-growing desire for more health-conscious eating options are more likely to thrive, while those that continue to only offer only the unhealthy options, which are increasingly considered inferior products, are unlikely to maintain their share of the market. Investors need to pay attention to these shifts in preferences and look for companies that are responding to them, while avoiding those that maintain the status quo.

There's another subtler shift going on. A growing number of consumers, especially those in a certain demographic, are looking for new companies and brands as they increasingly distrust older, more established manufacturers.

Millennial Mistrust

If we were to tag one specific generation that is far more distrustful than other generations, data from Pew Research points us to the Millennials, or those people born between 1980 and 1999. Only 19 percent of Millennials felt that "most people can be trusted," with 31 percent of Gen Xers (born 1965-1979, the generation just before the Millennials) agreeing, 40 percent of Boomers (born 1945–1964), and 37 percent of Silents (born 1923–1944) also agreeing.[43]

Millennials are also the first modern generation to be saddled with student debt, poverty, and unemployment, as well as lower income levels than the two previous generations had at the same life-cycle stage. Consider some of what we've discussed in prior chapters—the Great Recession, median income levels, debt levels, and so on—and it's understandable that Pew Research finds that nearly 70 percent of Americans surveyed, spanning all generations, say that Millennials face more economic challenges than their elders did when they were first starting out.

A lot more can be said about the differences between Millennials and other generations, but one industry that touches many others is feeling the pain of what some would call the Millennial mindset. We're talking about the housing industry, which has recovered far slower coming out of the 2008 financial crisis than it has exiting prior recessions. There are several contributing factors, including the lack of wage growth, the kinds of jobs being created that favor part-time employment, and relatively low available inventory of homes that helped push housing prices up and up and up at a time when banks were far more stringent in approving mortgages and other loans.

Among those and other factors we can add what amounts to a lack of Millennial interest in housing. In a speech given by Federal Reserve Governor Lael Brainard in early 2015, he made the point that Millennials "see some risk that houses could become financial albatrosses due to events beyond their control." Brainard went on to say the percentage of renters in the 18-to-34 age group who thought housing was a safe investment dropped from 85 percent in 2003 to 59 percent in early 2015.[44] There are several implications to be had for housing and homeownership, and that has led some to conclude that property ownership could cease to be the norm.

We think that's a bit extreme, and we'd point out that while the housing market has been slow to recover, demand for apartments and rental properties boomed in 2014.[45] Findings from Marcus & Millichap Real Estate Investment Services showed new supply thus far has been well-matched by rising renter demand. Research commissioned by the National Multifamily Housing Council (NMHC) found the need for 300,000 to 400,000 new apartments each year[46] just to keep up with resident demand, even though "we've chronically under-built for years during and after the Great Recession," according to NHMC Chairman Daryl Carter.

Like many other examples we've shared, this ambivalent attitude over property ownership extends past the United States. In London during 2015, 82 percent of 20- to 45-year-olds say they will never be able to buy property, according to research firm Halifax.[47] More interesting was the six-point drop in the percentage of people even saving for a deposit, which fell to 43 percent—which gives at least the appearance of not even being interested in property ownership.

Housing is but one part of the economy—an important one, but still just one. As you might guess, there are other generational changes to be examined by comparing Millennials with prior generations—they set financial goals, saving is a top priority, and building an emergency fund was the number-1 objective, according to data from Northwestern Mutual and a 2014 survey of Millennials conducted by retirement research firm Hearts & Wallets[48]—that could help or hinder other industries.

Millennials are also much less likely than older generations to invest in the stock market, preferring to keep their savings in cash, according to a study by Bankrate.[49] What makes this all the more curious is the data turned up by E*Trade that showed the vast majority of Millennials recognize that in order to have a successful retirement, they have to go above and beyond their 401(k) with additional saving and investing.[50]

Perhaps the following findings help explain the discrepancy—a 2015 poll by Harvard University's Institute of Politics found 86 percent of Millennials expressed mistrust of Wall Street, which sounds pretty bad, but then again 88 percent reported that they only sometimes or never trust the press. Eighty-two percent mistrust Congress while 74 percent only sometimes or never trust the federal government to do the right thing and sixty-three percent have that same view of the president.[51] This level of mistrust represents a pain point that has wide-ranging impact on where and how this generation saves, invests, and spends.

Cocktail Investing Bottom Line

The central point that runs through many of the pain points we've shared throughout this chapter is that shifting demographics and psychographics shape and impact consumer behavior and preferences that can force companies to make fundamental changes to their businesses to succeed. Identifying the root cause of these shifts, be they the fallout from a disruptive technology, changing consumer preference, or other pain point, helps you, the investor, identify companies that will profit from the pain as they administer their soothing "medicine."

Are these all the pain points? Certainly not. Will there be new ones that come along in the coming years? Without a doubt, and that's why we encourage you to connect the dots you see in your daily life by thinking about the cause of what it is you are seeing and ponder the effect. One of our little secrets is to talk to others about it and see if they are seeing or hearing about it as well. The more confirmation you get, the more comfortable and confident you can be in that developing pain point or trend.

- Pain points are those vexing issues that a company or even a person may have to contend with in business or as part of his or her life.
- This chapter showcased several pain points (cybersecurity, aging of the population, fattening of the consumer, and changing consumer preferences), but those are just a handful, and there are many more.
- Pain points can offer investors fantastic opportunities, provided they identify those companies poised to benefit from the pain point and avoid those that will be the victim.

- When putting an industry or a company under the microscope, always ask the following questions: "Is there anything going on—today or on the horizon—that could force the company to change or impact its way of doing business? Is that a potential opportunity or a threat?"
- The more confirming data points you encounter from articles, studies, third-party research, or even anecdotally in your life or from people you know, the more comfortable and confident you can be in that developing pain point or trend.

In the next chapter, we will start to put the puzzle pieces that we've laid out over the last few chapters together to help you construct a cohesive view. Think of it as peering through a lot of noise to find an investable signal that you can follow as you get ready to identify investing prospects and whittle them down to companies you want to own.

Endnotes

1. Porter Five Forces analysis is a framework to analyze level of competition within an industry and business strategy development. It draws on industrial organization (IO) economics to derive five forces that determine the competitive intensity and therefore attractiveness of an industry.

2. Dan Kedmey, "Cyberattacks Against Big Companies Surged by 40% in 2104, Report Finds," *Time* (April 14, 2015), time.com/3820906/cyberattacks-companies-symantec/.

3. Jai Vijayan, "4 Worst Government Data Breaches of 2014," *Information Week* (December 11, 2014), www.informationweek.com/government/cybersecurity/4-worst-government-data-breaches-of-2014/d/d-id/1318061.

4. Chris Versace, "3 Takeaways from Cisco's Cyber Security Report," *Fox Business* (January 21, 2015), www.foxbusiness.com/technology/2015/01/21/3-takeaways-from-cisco-cyber-security-report/.

5. Luke Villapaz, "iOS 8.1 Jailbreak: Pangu Developers Release Tool for Apple iPhone 6 Plus, iPad Air 2 And iPod Touch," *International Business Times* (October 22, 2014), www.ibtimes.com/ios-81-jailbreak-pangu-developers-release-tool-apple-iphone-6-plus-ipad-air-2-ipod-touch-1709958.

6. For a good list of some variant examples see blog.fortinet.com/post/mobile-ransomware-status-quo.

7. Fred Foldvary, "The Coming Water Catastrophes," Progress.org (July 26, 2015), www.progress.org/article/the-coming-water-catastrophes.

8. "Water Scarcity," www.un.org/waterforlifedecade/scarcity.shtml.

9. U.S. EPA, "What Is the Drinking Water Infrastructure Needs Survey and Assessment?" water.epa.gov/infrastructure/drinkingwater/dwns/.

10. American Society of Civil Engineers, "Drinking Water," *2013 Report Card for America's Infrastructure* (March 2013), www.infrastructurereportcard.org/drinking-water/.

11. Dan McQuade, "We're Not Alone in Water Main Breaks," *Philadelphia* (March 8, 2015), www.phillymag.com/news/2015/03/08/water-main-breaks-philadelphia/.

12. American Water Works Association, "Buried No Longer: Confronting America's Water Infrastructure Challenge," www.circleofblue.org/waternews/wp-content/uploads/2012/02/AWWA_BuriedNoLonger.pdf.

13. American Society of Civil Engineers, *2013 Report Card for America's Infrastructure* (March 2013), www.infrastructurereportcard.org/wp-content/uploads/2013ReportCardforAmericasInfrastructure.pdf.

14. Adam Nagourney and Emma Fitzsimmons, "Under New Water Rules, Beverly Hills Must Turn Off Taps; Santa Cruz, Less So," *New York Times* (April 8, 2015), www.nytimes.com/2015/04/08/us/californias-water-conservation-slowed-in-february.html?_r=0.

15. "Drought Condition (Percent Area): United States," droughtmonitor.unl.edu/Home/TabularStatistics.aspx.

16. "Price of Water 2014: Up 6 Percent in 30 Major U.S. Cities, 33 Percent Rise Since 2010," Circle of Blue (May 7, 2014), www.circleofblue.org/waternews/2014/world/price-water-2014-6-percent-30-major-u-s-cities-33-percent-rise-since-2010/.

17. "Price of Water 2015: Up 6 Percent in 30 Major U.S. Cities, 41 Percent Rise Since 2010," Circle of Blue (April 22, 2015), www.circleofblue.org/waternews/2015/world/price-of-water-2015-up-6-percent-in-30-major-u-s-cities-41-percent-rise-since-2010/.

18. QuickFacts can be found at quickfacts.census.gov/qfd/faq.html.

19. Bridget Brennan, "Top 10 Things Everyone Should Know About Women Consumers," *Forbes* (January 21, 2015), www.forbes.com/sites/bridgetbrennan/2015/01/21/top-10-things-everyone-should-know-about-women-consumers/#127222602897

20. Ettinger Law Firm, "The Average Lifespan Continues to Increase," New York Elder Law Attorney Blog (October 20, 2014), www.newyorkelderlawattorneyblog.com/2014/10/the-average-lifespan-continues.html.

21. Ibid.

22. U.S. Census Bureau, "The Next Four Decades: The Older Population in the United States: 2010 to 2050" (May 2010), www.census.gov/prod/2010pubs/p25-1138.pdf

23. United Nations, Department of Economic and Social Affairs, *World Population Ageing 2013* (2013), www.un.org/en/development/desa/population/publications/pdf/ageing/WorldPopulationAgeing2013.pdf.

24. Martin Walker and Xavier Mesnard, *What Do Mature Consumers Want?* (A.T. Kearney, Inc., 2013), www.atkearney.at/documents/3709812/3710918/What_Do_Mature_Consumers_Want.pdf/2fab37a7-0c6a-4d9f-aba8-8cbd433f3920.

25. U.S. Government Accountability Office, "Retirement Security: Most Households Approaching Retirement Have Low Savings" (May 12, 2015), www.gao.gov/products/GAO-15-419.

26. "Planning and Progress Study 2015," www.northwesternmutual.com/about-us/studies/planning-and-progress-2015-study.

27. Steve Vernon, "How Big Is the U.S. Retirement Crisis?" CBS MoneyWatch (November 18, 2014), www.cbsnews.com/news/how-big-is-the-u-s-retirement-crisis/.

28. Alicia H. Munnell, Matthew S. Rutledge, and Anthony Webb, *Are Retirees Falling Short? Reconciling the Conflicting Evidence* (Chestnut Hills, MA: Center for Retirement Research at Boston College, 2013), crr.bc.edu/wp-content/uploads/2014/11/wp_2014-16.pdf.

29. Vernon.

30. Christopher Murray, Marie Ng, and Ali Mokdad, "The Vast Majority of Americans Are Overweight or Obese, and Weight Is a Growing Problem Among U.S. Children," Institute for Health Metrics and Evaluation, www.healthdata.org/news-release/vast-majority-american-adults-are-overweight-or-obese-and-weight-growing-problem-among.

31. "Adult Obesity Facts," Centers for Disease Control and Prevention, www.cdc.gov/obesity/data/adult.html.

32. "Obesity Information," American Heart Association, www.heart.org/HEARTORG/GettingHealthy/WeightManagement/Obesity/Obesity-Information_UCM_307908_Article.jsp#.Vkjp64SQGI8.

33. "Physical Activity," President's Council on Fitness, Sports, and Nutrition, www.fitness.gov/resource-center/facts-and-statistics/.

34. "New Data Shows Obesity Costs Will Grow to $344 Billion by 2018," Partnership to Fight Chronic Disease, www.fightchronicdisease.org/media-center/releases/new-data-shows-obesity-costs-will-grow-344-billion-2018.

35. "Childhood Obesity in the United States," National Collaborative on Childhood Obesity Research, www.nccor.org/downloads/ChildhoodObesity_020509.pdf.

36. Finkelstein et al., "Obesity and Severe Obesity Forecasts Through 2030," *Am J Prev Med* 42(6) (2012): 563–570.

37. Meg Major, "Non-GMO Trumps Organic in 2014," *Progressive Grocer* (March 4, 2014), www.marketlohas.com/uploads/7/2/5/4/7254872/www-progressivegrocer-com.pdf.

38. Whole Foods Annual Report (November 13, 2015), www.sec.gov/Archives/edgar/data/865436/000086543615000177/wfm10k2015.htm.

39. "United Natural Foods' CEO Discusses F2Q 2014 Results—Earnings Call Transcript" Seeking Alpha (March 20, 2014), seekingalpha.com/article/2079643-united-natural-foods-ceo-discusses-f2q-2014-results-earnings-call-transcript.

40. National Restaurant Association, *2014 Restaurant and Industry Forecast* (2013), www.restaurant.org/Downloads/PDFs/News-Research/research/2014Forecast-ExecSummary.pdf.

41. Anita Balakrishnan, "Soft Drink Sales Hit a Decade of Decline," CNBC (March 26, 2015), www.cnbc.com/id/102539254.

42. "Annie's to Be Acquired by General Mills for $46 Per Share in Cash" General Mills, Inc. (September 8, 2014).

43. Pew Research Center, *Millennials: A Portrait of Generation Next* (Pew Research Center, February 2010), www.pewsocialtrends.org/files/2010/10/millennials-confident-connected-open-to-change.pdf.

44. Jeffrey Sparshott, "Fed's Brainard: 'Great Recession' May Have Long-Lasting Financial Consequences for Younger Americans," *Wall Street Journal* (April 2, 2015), blogs.wsj.com/economics/2015/04/02/feds-brainard-great-recession-may-have-long-lasting-financial-consequences-for-younger-americans/.

45. Marcus and Millichap, *2014 National Apartment Research Report* (Phoenix, AZ: Marcus & Millichap, 2014), www.marcusmillichap.com/downloader/2014-National-Apartment-Research-Report-2120.file?ext=pdf.

46. "Apts. Add $1 Trillion-Plus to Economy: NMHC," Latitude 38 Group (April 8, 2015), l38group.com/l38_news/apts-add-1-trillion-plus-economy-nmhc.

47. Phillip Inman, "Young People in UK Increasingly Giving Up on Owning a Home—Halifax Study," *The Guardian* (April 7, 2015), www.theguardian.com/money/2015/apr/07/young-people-uk-increasingly-giving-up-owning-home-halifax-survey.

48. Kathy Lynch, "Cash Is Costing Millennials, Survey Says," *Financial Advisor* (October 2, 2014), www.fa-mag.com/news/cash-is-costing-millennials--survey-says-19385.html.

49. July 2014 BankRate Financial Security Index, www.bankrate.com/finance/consumer-index/financial-security-charts-0714.aspx.

50. Matthew Frankel, "Millennials Know They Should Be Investing. So Why Aren't They?" *The Motley Fool* (June 2, 2015), www.fool.com/investing/general/2015/06/02/millennials-know-they-should-be-investing-so-why-a.aspx.

51. Chris Cillizza, "Millennials Don't Trust Anyone. That's a Big Deal." *Wall Street Journal* (April 30, 2015), www.washingtonpost.com/news/the-fix/wp/2015/04/30/millennials-dont-trust-anyone-what-else-is-new/.

Chapter 8

Cocktail Thematic Investing

The signal is the truth. The noise is what distracts us from the truth.
— Nate Silver

We cannot solve our problems with the same level of thinking that created them.
— Albert Einstein

The key to investing is not assessing how much an industry is going to affect society, or how much it will grow, but rather, determining the competitive advantage of any given company and, above all, the durability of that advantage.
— Warren Buffett

At the end of this chapter you'll have an understanding how we put together the puzzle pieces that we've given you over the last few chapters. We aim to distill this noise of disparate data points into clear *investable signals* that cut across industries, as defined by Wall Street and others. We'll also give you a list of these investing

4g age bonds chemicals china cloud cnbc cnn cocoa confidence connected consumer copper corn cpi debt demographics dollar dow earnings economy election emerging eps equities euro europe exchange fat food fox gas gdp greece growth hours housing income india inflation interest italy jobs manufacturing margins mobile mortgage oil options orders os pmi politics population ppi profits recession retail reuters revenue sales scarce services spain steel stocks sugar uncertainty unemployment valuation votes wages water wheat wsj

Figure 8.1   Investing noise

signals, what we call Cocktail Thematics, as they stand today and then we're going to break down one of them into industries and companies that give rise to the investing contenders that we'll then put under the microscope in Chapter 10.

Over the last few chapters, we've thrown quite a bit at you, and at first it might feel like too much, as Figure 8.1, which Chris created based on what you've read so far, clearly shows. But from our experience, once you change your mindset from the Wall Street herd-think to one that connects the dots, and are able to really *see* the world around you, you won't be thinking that anymore.

Let's Go Online Shopping

Let's start with an example that ties together a number of things we've talked about—online shopping. Over the last few years, we've seen the gradual shift away from visiting brick-and-mortar retail stores in favor of those that are just a few clicks away on the Internet or an app. Online shopping has been growing since the late 1990s, but it really exploded with smartphone and tablet proliferation that allow shopping anywhere,

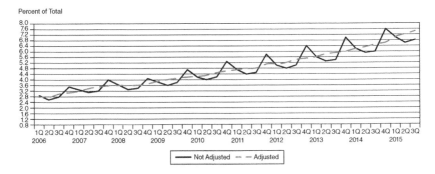

Figure 8.2 Estimated quarterly U.S. retail e-commerce sales as a percent of total quarterly retail sales, Q1 2006–Q3 2015
SOURCE: U.S. Census Bureau

anytime. Data from the Census Bureau in Figure 8.2 reveals the steady growth in online sales since 2005, but it was the smartphone explosion that took hold in 2011 with Apple's iPhone and app store that enabled retail e-commerce sales to break through the 5 percent threshold. In fact, according to IBM Digital Analytics, mobile traffic accounted for 46.5 percent of all online traffic for Valentine's Day in 2015 versus 26.5 percent in 2014.

Who doesn't love sitting all nestled up on the couch ordering all sorts of fun things from Amazon, Macy's, or most other retailers through a smartphone or tablet, only to have your selections show up on your doorstep a few days later? Aside from that convenience, the ability to find deals, sales, and use digital coupons to get better pricing has had wide appeal, given the lack of income growth in the United States, the overall shrinkage of the U.S. labor force since 2000, and the growing number of people over age 65 years looking to stretch their dollars as far as they can.

As Mike Canevaro pointed out in our Cocktail Conversation in Chapter 6, watching today's children who will soon be tweens, this method of shopping is natural for them. As they grow older, we'll see continued growth in the number of people who are digital shoppers. According to a report from Walker Sands Communications, some 68 percent of U.S. consumers admit to shopping online at least once per month. As children who have grown up in and around online shopping become tweens and beyond, we will see them readily adopt the digital shopping lifestyle.

You or someone you know is probably one of that 68 percent. Think about those companies and businesses that you, your family, or friends are digitally shopping in comparison with those brick-and-mortar retailers that you are shopping at far less frequently, or not at all. For us, Amazon has replaced a number of stores that we used to visit—particularly Best Buy and Staples. When we see a shift like that, we next ask, "Who benefits? Who gets hurt in the process?" That naturally leads to, "Which companies are benefiting from this shift to digital shopping? Which companies are getting hurt in the process?"

Which companies benefit? Online retailers and those companies that have a strong online presence as well as the shipping companies that get those packages to you or the intended recipients. Examples include Alibaba, Amazon, Apple, Staples, United Parcel Service, and FedEx.

Which companies are getting hurt? Those that are seeing their in-store sales decline as consumers shift their purchasing habits online. Past examples include companies like Blockbuster Video and Circuit City, which ultimately shut their doors, while those like Barnes & Noble, Books-A-Million, Best Buy, and hhgregg are struggling.

You can probably add a few others to both of those lists. As you build that mental list, you're recognizing part of what we call the Connected Society Cocktail Investing trend.

What do we mean by Cocktail Thematic investing? A Cocktail Thematic is a market shift that shapes and impacts consumer behavior, forcing companies to make fundamental changes to their businesses to succeed. As you've noticed over the last several chapters, there are a number of factors that can shape and influence a Cocktail Thematic such as evolving economics, shifting demographics, changing psychographics, shifting political winds, regulatory mandates, disruptive technologies, and pain points. Furthermore, sometimes we'll see a vodka-like trend, clear and easy. Other times we'll see something that is a more bourbon-like trend, a little bit murky but once you get it, it packs a serious kick.

Think back to the online and digital shopping example and let's put the Cocktail Thematic pieces together. The initial disruptive technology (the Internet) that originally drove online shopping has been augmented by mobile computing, apps, and new forms of payments that are making digital shopping more commonplace. Those companies that have embraced the consumer's shift toward online shopping are prospering while those that have lagged or missed the shift have seen their businesses flounder.

Shifting Perspectives

One key point that we have to make concerns the evolution of online shopping from desktop to mobile thanks to smartphones and tablets. If you focused solely on digital shopping from the desktop, you'd miss the next iteration of digital shopping.

To hammer this point home, let's consider the difference between a movie and a photograph. There are many aspects between the two that are very similar—getting the right positioning of the subject or subjects, making sure the lighting is just right, ensuring the wardrobe is appropriate, adjusting for weather conditions, and, oftentimes, wrestling with multiple takes from multiple angles. If you've ever taken family photos or videoed an event, you know that to do either well takes a lot of hard work.

Despite those similarities, the two are very different. A photograph is a snapshot of a moment in time, preserved for eternity. A movie, on the other hand, is a collection of photographs over time. Think about it: Movies may be digital today, but originally, they were a spool of thousands or millions of photographs that told a story over time. That's the biggest difference between a photo and a movie—one is a snapshot of a moment in time, while the other is a story that unfolds over time, often with twists and turns along the way.

Similar to movies, Cocktail Thematics evolve over time as those drivers we talked about—evolving economics, shifting demographics, changing psychographics, new technologies, regulatory mandates, and more—change, evolve, or are disrupted.

This sounds rather different from the industry-focused research used by many financial firms that is focused on identifying the best in, say, retail, semiconductors, or manufacturing. Our beef with it is that while there are very smart and talented people following certain industries, they are forced to pick the best companies that fall within that specific industry and its purview. We see that as maybe only identifying the best company or two in a small pond. What you really want are those companies poised to ride the next wave of demand and innovation irrespective of Wall Street categories like retail, tech, banks, and semiconductors.

In order to see these drivers, you have to change your perspective. It's not that hard to do, but we've found an example that helps to illustrate the idea. Chris was helping one of his students with some math homework, and she was having problems with the following question:

If $f(x) = 3x^2 + 2x + 9$ and $g(x)$
$= -x^2 - x - 3$, what are $f(x) + g(x)$ and $f(x) - g(x)$?

She took one look at that question and was genuinely stumped ... until Chris suggested she change her perspective on the question. To do that he simply rewrote the questions like this:

$$f(x) = 3x^2 + 2x + 9 \qquad\qquad f(x) = 3x^2 + 2x + 9$$
$$+g(x) = -x^2 - x - 3 \qquad\qquad -g(x) = -x^2 - x - 3$$

Once he did this, the student realized the vexing and convoluted question was really a simple addition and subtraction problem. Many times, a simple shift in perspective can reveal a whole world of possibilities.

Cocktail Thematics provide us with that different perspective, allowing us to collect data and then connect them into a cohesive view. Not all data points are useful or confirming, but as we've learned over the years, all we need is a few reinforcing data points to spot an emerging Cocktail Thematic or a different facet of an existing one. As more smartphones and shopping apps not only became available, but were actually being used, we could see the transformation in online shopping to mobile shopping. Chris will not only order things using the Amazon app, but when running low a few quick taps on the Nespresso app and great tasting coffee is soon on its way to him. During that mobile shopping expansion, we asked one of our favorite detective-like questions, "Which companies benefit and which ones are vulnerable?"

As a rule of thumb, we'll want those companies that sit at the intersection of one or more Cocktail Thematics. As you'll see when we roll up our sleeves in Chapter 10 and identify specific companies, we're going to want the ones that have meaningful operating profit exposure to each of the various Cocktail Thematics.

Multiple Cocktail Thematics

So what are some of the Cocktail Thematics that we've identified by canvasing the various shifting, changing, and evolving landscapes? What are the thematic tailwinds that are being shaped the world around us? Putting together the different puzzle pieces that we've introduced to you thus far in *Cocktail Investing* gives rise to the following nine Cocktail Thematics:

1. *Connected Society*. Talk about a perfect vodka-style Cocktail Thematic! This one you experience every day. As we've pieced together over the ensuing pages, the combination of always-on broadband networks and the growing plethora of connected devices is driving a sea change in consumer behavior. This has rippled across a number of industries—music, television, movies, news and publishing, mail, just to name a few—and has forever changed how individuals and businesses—pretty much all of us—consume content, communicate, collaborate, advertise, shop, bank, invest, share, and more.

   The key question for investors is which companies are leading this disruption? Which ones are benefiting from pain points associated with more and more data, not to mention the expansive growth in video traffic?

2. *The rise of the new middle class.* This refers to the improving socioeconomic landscape and better lifestyles in a number of emerging economies, like China and India. This is more of a margarita-style trend, deceptively subtle and tasty at first, but before you know it you've got something seriously powerful going on! As disposable incomes improve and quality of life rises, this new middle class spurs demand for goods and services that previously had not been there. This leads to consumers trading up with their purchasing dollars for more expensive clothing, cosmetics, food, transportation, indulging in affordable luxuries like an afternoon latte, and so on. Over the coming years, those economies are slated to experience significant population and disposable income growth, the combination of

which is slated to drive a measurable pickup in global consumption as well as result in greater competition for scarce or limited resources. According to the Organization for Economic Co-operation and Development, in 2009 the middle class included 1.8 billion people, but is expected to increase to 3.2 billion by 2020 and 4.9 billion by 2030, with the overwhelming portion of the new middle class coming from Asia Pacific.[1]

3. *The cash-strapped consumer.* We also call this the decline of the existing middle class. This one is a bit of a whiskey-style Cocktail Thematic; a bit painful to start, but once you get the hang of it, you can appreciate the possibilities ... or maybe more of a champagne taste on a beer budget. Either way, the concept behind the cash-strapped consumer reflects the economic backdrop in the United States and much of Europe since the 2008 financial crisis, which is looking more and more like the new normal. Lower levels of employment, increased savings rates, lack of available credit, and weak income growth have led to consumers saving where they can, trading down when possible, and seeking more value for each dollar that is actually spent. This affects not only what and when consumers will buy, but also where and how they buy. Will they shop at higher-end specialty stores or will they instead shop at discount stores and warehouse clubs? Are they buying private label and store brands or premium branded products? Will they dine out or eat in? Do they take a vacation or remain home for a "stay-cation"? Do they pay with cash, or with debit or credit cards?

Most aspire to the finer things in life, such as an expensive car, nice clothes, a lavish home filled with all the electronic doodads, and more. Sadly, fewer are able to attain these in the current economy or the one we're likely to face in the coming years.

One of the ways to bridge the gap between want and ability comes in the form of affordable luxury. Affordable luxuries are goods that can be considered luxury or premium goods according to the marketed image, but which cost less than truly luxury goods. As such, these goods are sold to a larger segment of the market— the mass affluent—usually defined by a household per-year income between US$100,000 and US$1,000,000.

Luxuries can take on many forms and may often be a centerpiece around something larger, be it jewelry, electronics, clothing, and so on. Affordable luxury capitalizes on companies that have premium products at affordable prices. Examples of such affordable luxuries include brands such as Michael Kors, Kate Spade, and Coach rather than Gucci, Prada, or Louis Vuitton.

4. *Scarce resources.* You got a flavor for this Cocktail Thematic in Chapter 7 when we talked about the long-term pain point that is water. Think of this as that rare champagne of Cocktail Thematics. There is only so much water on the planet that is presently drinkable, and with a rising middle class (see Cocktail Thematic #2), it means more people vying for that limited resource.

The scare resources Cocktail Thematic examines those goods and resources whose availability is increasingly less than the quantity desired. The rising global population and the awakening of third-world economies will continually increase the need for scarce resources such as oil, gas, water, and rare earth elements. That's the demand side of the equation, but we could also see disruptions on the supply side.

Everyone but vegans experienced an example of such supply-side disruptions during 2013–2015 with the sharp rise in animal and seafood proteins such as beef, pork, chicken, and shrimp. That protein cost explosion reflected several factors including herd supply constraints due in part to drought conditions (there's that water thing again), rising demand from the emerging economies (rise of the new middle class), and the shift in other parts of the globe to lower carb, higher protein diets (those psychographics we talked about in Chapter 7).

5. *New demand, new solutions.* This is the fusion mixed drink of Cocktail Thematic investing, taking something tried and true and putting a new twist on it that makes you see the classic in a whole new light. The new demand side examines the industries and companies that are positioned to benefit or be hurt, depending on where the global economy is or is heading in terms of the economic cycle. Are the domestic, foreign, or world economies strengthening and expanding or slowing and contracting? Are we in the early or late stage of that

expansion or contraction? The answers determine the industries and companies that warrant your focus.

New solutions look for growth applications fueled by a combination of new products and services to fill replacement demand that had been addressed by new products, services, or technologies. Examples we all know include how CDs and DVDs replaced audio- and videocassettes, LCD TVs and monitors replaced cathode-ray-tube models, and Bluetooth and wifi technologies replaced a number of wires and cords in homes, offices, and other locations. A similar transformation is underway in the lighting market as filament bulbs are being replaced by energy-saving emissive semiconductors called light-emitting diodes, or LEDs.

New solutions are more than just new technologies like those mentioned above. These solutions can include new materials as well as processes. One area we firmly believe has to change is the education system in the United States, and here's why: According to the most recent data published by the National Center for Education Statistics, based on the 2012 Program for International Student Assessment (PISA), U.S. students ranked below average in math among the world's most-developed countries and were close to average in science and reading. More specifically, in mathematics, 29 nations and other jurisdictions outperformed the United States by a statistically significant margin, up from 23 nations in 2009, despite the fact that the United States spends more per student than any other developed nation, according to the Organization for Economic Development.[2] In science, 22 education systems scored above the U.S. average, up from 18 systems in 2009. We're spending more and yet getting a lot less.

In our view, the current modality of education needs to be overhauled if the United States is to remain a competitive powerhouse and source of innovation. We believe that technology is poised to be a disruptive force in teaching, and we'd point to the massive open online courses (MOOCs): online programs from some of the best colleges and universities in the United States, such as Yale, Stanford, and others that can be accessed through Coursera and edX.org, and iTunes U on Apple's iTunes platform. We suspect we are in the early innings in this aspect of new solutions.

6. *Safety and security.* This is the hot-buttered rum on a cold winter's night of the Cocktail Thematics. The right to defend oneself and his or her property applies today just as it did more than 200 years ago. The threats that we are facing are changing, much like the ways we interact with people, data, and content are changing. As you saw in Chapter 7, cyberattacks are the latest form of warfare and corporate espionage.

As people, companies, and countries must be increasingly on guard, behaviors need to shift from those of reactionary defense to always prepared and secure. Our safety and security Cocktail Thematic targets companies from corporate security solutions to firearms and home-security systems to cybersecurity and more.

7. *Guilty pleasure.* The peach piña colada you never admit to enjoying zeroes in on the little vices that we as consumers like or, for some of us, need to have from time to time, even though there may be a form of guilt associated with indulging. Chocolate, beer, wine (a favorite of ours), coffee (another one!), spirits, cigarettes, junk and fast food (Lenore couldn't live without In-N-Out burgers while Chris has been more of Five Guys burger guy, but he has warmed up to eating his burgers animal sytle), and gambling are typical products that are characterized by inelastic demand. That means consumers will want to buy them no matter what is happening with their pocketbook. As a result, the companies that make them tend to have good cash flow generation and are dividend payers.

Guilty pleasures cut across several traditional Wall Street industry verticals, as the concept focuses on those companies that bring the kinds of products that consumers won't do without, regardless of the economic climate. With that in mind, it should come as little surprise that the guilty pleasure group of stocks held up well during the last two recessions and performed even better on a relative basis when compared to several stock market indices. A 2009 report by Merrill Lynch that examined the performance of tobacco, alcohol, and casino stocks during all of the recessions since 1970 found that while the broad S&P 500 fell by 1.5 percent on average, the guilty pleasure group of stocks rose on average 11 percent.[3] During the great tech meltdown, the broad market fell 20 percent between June 2001 and June 2002, but during that time tobacco stocks gained 8 percent and gambling-related stocks nearly 20 percent.

The inelastic nature for the products produced by these guilty pleasure companies has enabled them to weather price increases better than other products and services that are considered to be more of a commodity in nature. Perhaps the best example is in the tobacco industry. Consider that while the domestic tobacco business is in a decline as more people become aware of the health effects of smoking on their well-being and taxes are raised each year on cigarettes, the levels of price increases that cigarette makers generate more than offset the decline in consumption by customers. Despite the increasing concern over sugar as part of our diets, chocolate companies, like The Hershey Company, have been able to pass through price increases to offset any combination of higher raw material, fuel, utilities, and transportation costs.

8. *Cashless consumption.* This "cold beer after a hot day working in the yard" Cocktail Thematic is a little simple something that just makes the day better. As we alluded to in Chapter 6 in our Cocktail Conversation with Skyworks Solutions CEO David Aldrich and as pointed out by consulting firm McKinsey, tapping your smartphone or connected wearable device (Apple Watch or Samsung's latest smart watch) is one of the latest forms of payment.

Over the last several decades, there has been a shift away from hard cash transactions by consumers to other forms of payment, principally checks, credit cards, debit cards, and, more recently, online payments. With a new set of technologies, including near-field communication (NFC), and some older ones, including bar-code scanning, we have entered the next phase in that shift away from cash consumption. From apps that allow you to pay at the register to others that allow you to book online reservations and get the check when you're done—all on your smartphone—to services like PayPal and Apple Pay, the "Swiss-Army" smartphone started to encroach on cash, credit, and debit payments in 2015.

The first debit card was introduced in 1978, the first nationwide debit system was launched in 1984, but it wasn't until 1998 that debit card transactions outnumbered the use of checks around the world. Given the expectation for continued smartphone growth across the globe—wireless infrastructure company Ericsson forecasts there will be 6.4 billion smartphone subscriptions globally by the end of 2021, up from 3.4 billion in 2015[4]—we expect the adoption of mobile payments to grow significantly faster. This rapid growth will challenge existing payment companies as well as existing transaction infrastructure companies, particularly point-of-sale solution vendors. As you can rightly imagine, security and privacy will be key concerns.

All of this offers opportunity, however, for chip companies that will be the backbone of enabling mobile payments on your connected devices. In order for your device to connect to the payment terminal and complete the transaction, the two have to be able to communicate, and that's where solutions such as near-field communication (NFC) and other semiconductor chips come into play.

These new payment systems will also find ample opportunity in emerging markets, which will be able to leapfrog from the most primitive payment systems to the most advanced, without expending resources on the interim solutions developed nations have used over the years. Companies that see this opportunity and effectively take advantage of it will be able to greatly reward their investors.

9. *Living longer lives*. The fine aged wine of Cocktail Thematics. People all over the world are living longer. As investors, we're always on the lookout for opportunities characterized by an expanding addressable market, and the living longer lives Cocktail Thematic identifies and looks to invest in companies positioned to address the needs and demands of the expanding, older population. As with several of our Cocktail Thematics, there are a number of facets that include companies that participate in both a direct and indirect basis. From healthcare and investing to beauty products, medical aesthetic treatments, and nutrition to assisted living, dental services, and laboratories there are a number of traditional industry verticals that fit into living longer lives when viewed through the right lens.

These are just some of the Cocktail Thematics that you'll recognize as you open your eyes and look at the world as we do. As you get into the Cocktail Thematic mindset, we suggest you watch for signposts. These signposts act as either confirmation points or warning signs, depending on how things are progressing, because they identify the factors or tipping points that are driving a Cocktail Thematic. Often times, it means diving deep into the industries that are being impacted by the Cocktail Thematic to get a better understanding of the opportunities as well as the potential disruptions that could lie ahead.

Signposts

While today we have GPS navigation in many devices, this approach is much like the way many of us used to drive—by watching the road and checking a map for markers, or even asking for directions and looking for signposts along the way. Much like those driving experiences, as you see the markers and signposts, you have a growing confidence that you are on track. If you don't see those markers, after a while you're going to wonder where you are and how far you have gone off course.

Think of it this way: If you were to construct a map that sketches out directions for a friend, you would be sure to include the key sites they would see on their way, and these would let them know they were on course or signal them that a change in direction was nearing.

The same is true for Cocktail Thematic investing, except we have to develop our own markers and signposts that tell us whether a position is on track or if we are off course and need to get out of the investment. To the uninitiated, we admit this might sound a little daunting, but the reality is that it's far from impossible to do. All it takes is making sure you understand how the Cocktail Thematic is affecting an industry and what that means for the companies in that industry.

Here's an example: If you think the economy is picking up steam and that is a good thing for the shipping of goods (products, subassemblies, and components) from supplier to factory, factory to port, port to customer and their distribution facilities, and so on, you would be right. One industry you may want to invest in would be the trucking industry; after all, how else do those goods get to and fro? As you're reading up on the industry, you notice the average age of the heavy truck fleet (those 18 wheelers you see traveling down interstate) is rather high. Your next thought should be, "Wow, there is a real need to replace these trucks!"

Boom! Replacement demand.

Upon further reading, you learn that several truck manufacturers are starting to bring electric-powered trucks to market to replace diesel engine–powered ones (new demand, new solutions!). Some manufacturers also might be offering new driver collision avoidance technology or maybe even assisted driving (new demand, new solutions!).

After doing some preliminary research, you may realize there are several companies that manufacture medium- and heavy-duty trucks. You begin digesting all you can about the industry, how it works, who the key players are, who the competitors are, what key inputs go into building a heavy-duty truck, any pending regulatory mandates, and so on.

Along the way, you might read about several truck trends and data points—build rates, order rates, backlog levels, truck tonnage, and more—as well as sources for those data points. Some of those data points are easy to obtain, like monthly industrial production and purchasing managers data, as well as truck tonnage information, while others would require more diligence in collecting, such as monthly industry statistics for truck order and build levels.

Once you've identified these items, you have to watch the vector and velocity—what direction they are traveling and how fast. If the data are favorable, as when truck orders are rising faster than production while the economic data continues to improve, that's a good thing. If orders fall below build levels for a sustained period of time, it likely signals weaker production levels ahead. That's not a good sign, one that should have you thinking about trimming the position back or exiting altogether.

In the case of these new features, do they make the truck that much more expensive? Is there a regulatory mandate that will require them in new trucks past a certain date? At the same time, what are the trends in other input prices that could make a truck more expensive—steel, aluminum, plastics, rubber, engines, transmissions? What about new solutions that could make operating a truck less expensive? Those would make owners of those new solutions more competitive.

By building this list of items to watch—signposts, as we call them—you can keep tabs on the industry in a far easier fashion because you know what you're watching for. Here's the best part: Like any muscle that you exercise, the more you do this, the stronger your aptitude will become. Want some more good news? The more you do this, the more pitfalls you'll avoid, because your signposts will help keep you on course.

Now that's one example, but there are dozens, if not hundreds, of others out there. From our vantage point, the only thing better than one Cocktail Thematic is when two or more intersect, which is a bit like mixing various potent liquors together. In the end you have a Long Island iced tea, which we can both attest goes down deliciously, but oh, how it packs a surprising wallop! The more Cocktail Thematics you have working together, the stronger the mix that, as we've seen, can happen with a Long Island iced tea, which will change the behavior of consumers and businesses alike, which will force businesses to respond or see customers vote with their hands, feet, and wallets by going elsewhere.

One simple example (and you may have already thought of it) is found at the intersection of *Always On, Always Connected* + New Demand, New Solutions + Safety and Security:

Because of *always on, always connected,* we know consumers are increasingly turning to their smartphones and tablets for new ways to do things—shop, communicate, transact, work, and so on.

New demand, new solutions has seen the deployment of online banking and investing at both the desktop and increasingly smartphones and tablets.

One focus in *safety and security* is cybersecurity. As we execute more banking and investing either online or on mobile connected devices, commercial banks, investment banks, and brokerage companies will need to improve their cybersecurity offering to protect customers and their accounts, as well as the firms' own threat-detection capabilities and defenses.

Here's another Cocktail Thematic intersection. As you've probably deduced by now, water availability is one of the long-term scarce resource Cocktail Thematics that we've identified. The pain point of having sufficient fresh water available to businesses, farmers, and consumers is prompting the development of new solutions (new demand, new solutions), including desalination plants.

In 2015, after three years of drought conditions, California pushed seawater desalination into the spotlight as San Diego County, Santa Barbara, and other cities moved ahead with treatment plants that would turn the Pacific Ocean into a source of drinking water. Desalination has emerged as a newly promising technology in California in the face of a record dry spell that forced tough new conservation measures, depleted reservoirs, and raised the costs of importing fresh water from elsewhere.

As we like to say, Cocktail Thematics are happening all around you in your everyday life, and now that you've learned how to identify them, you'll start to realize the impact they are having, especially as you ask our two favorite questions—Who benefits, and who is vulnerable? It is much like your muscles—the more you use them, the stronger they become!

Cocktail Investing Bottom Line

In this chapter, we've tied together a number of puzzle pieces to help you see the world around you and recognize the various tailwinds that are changing the way we interact with the world around us. One of the really great aspects of Cocktail Investing is we can identify the companies that we might want to invest in while avoiding the potential pitfalls that are the ones being left behind. In the next chapter, we're going to look at the different types of securities you can choose from as you fine-tune your investment selection. Chapter 9 will have you looking at stocks, bonds, ETFs, mutual funds, and other securities in a new light.

- With Cocktail Thematic Investing, you're connecting economic, demographic, psychographic, technology, and regulatory dots to identify Cocktail Thematics that are taking place in and around your day-to-day life.
- A Cocktail Thematic is a market shift that shapes and impacts consumer behavior, forcing companies to make fundamental changes to succeed.
- Cocktail Thematics are not set in stone, but rather, evolve as do the underlying economic, demographic, psychographic, technology, and regulatory mandates.
- The more Cocktail Thematics intersect, the more powerful and sustainable the resulting punch.
- Asking, "Which industries and companies benefit?" as well as, "Which industries and companies are vulnerable?" will identify the companies you want to invest in and those you want to avoid.

Endnotes

1. Mario Pezzini, "An Emerging Middle Class," *OECD Observer* (2012), www
.oecdobserver.org/news/fullstory.php/aid/3681/An_emerging_middle_class
.html.

2. Organization for Economic Development, "Society at a Glance 2014"
(March 18, 2014), p. 106, www.oecd-ilibrary.org/docserver/download/
8113171e.pdf?expires=1430787039&id=id&accname=guest&checksum=
771CA032D4A3E9E80C0F4B5AB21C261D.

3. Rosemary Terpolilli, "Investing in Sin Stocks," *Examiner* (March 4, 2010), www
.examiner.com/article/investing-sin-stocks.

4. Olof Swahnberg, "Ericsson Sees Video Driving Tenfold Rise in Mobile Data
by 2021," Reuters (November 17, 2015), www.reuters.com/article/2015/11/
17/us-ericsson-mobilephone-idUSKCN0T624W20151117.

Chapter 9

Designing Your Portfolio

Where should I invest my money?
Put it in booze. Where else can you get a guaranteed 40 percent?
— *Anonymous*

I have spent most of my money on women and beer. The rest I just wasted . . . .
— *Steve Forde*

If we really did profit from our mistakes, I'd be extremely rich by now.
— *Anonymous*

W e've covered a lot of information to help you narrow down investment ideas, but now we are going to get personal. We've walked you all though how to read the economy like a pro, and the difference between the economy and the stock market; they often don't move together. We've walked you through how politics and regulations can have a big impact on industries, which can affect your investment choices. We've shown you how to notice those disruptive technologies that can create major investment opportunities along with the pain points and psychographic changes that can serve as catalysts, headwinds, or tailwinds. Finally, we just showed you how we go about putting all that together to identify investable Cocktail Thematics.

Now we are going show how you can go about designing a portfolio that suits your unique needs while using the Cocktail Thematics you've identified. Designing a portfolio can be thought of as similar to designing and building your dream home. First, you would learn about all the latest Cocktail Thematics and developments to give your fantasy home the latest technologies and design techniques that you like. You'd likely be flipping through and collecting ideas and images from publications like *Architectural Digest*, and *Dwell*. At the end of this process you would have a list of the Cocktail Thematics that most appeal to you to bring to an architect that might look something like this:

- Open space design
- Use of natural and renewable materials
- Multifunctional kitchen space
- Use of the latest "smart/connected home" technologies
- Tankless water heaters and highly energy-efficient furnaces and sensors that save on space and help with your monthly bills
- Built-ins to increase space utilization

This is akin to the Cocktail Thematics like the ones discussed in the prior chapters that you have selected to focus on in order to identify investments for your portfolio. For your dream home, an architect would ask you more detailed questions so that he or she can create a blueprint that combines the things you like and prefer with your specific wants and needs for the home:

- How many bedrooms do you want?
- What is your target square footage, and is this one, two, or three stories?
- Do you want the bedrooms to have en suite bathrooms?
- Do you want an island in your kitchen?

Back in Chapter 2, when we discussed "Investing Guidelines," we introduced you to the idea of your investing personality. At the website for this book, CocktailInvesting.com, you can find a checklist to make sure you know exactly what you need from your portfolio. The next step is to combine your "specs" with the list of Cocktail Thematics you've identified to create a portfolio blueprint. For your dream home, you would take the architect's blueprint and give it to a builder, who would ask you to get even more specific, selecting the exact flooring material, paint colors, and cabinetry for the home. For your portfolio, you will use your portfolio blueprint to help you identify specific securities in which you will invest.

By the end of this chapter, you will have a portfolio blueprint, meaning you will have combined the Cocktail Thematics with your specific wants and needs for your portfolio. You will be able to generate a list of 50 to 60 securities that interest you, which will then, in Chapter 10, narrow down to 10 to 25 in which you will invest. Finally, in Chapter 11, you will learn how to monitor your portfolio and when to sell.

There are four main areas you need to consider in order to understand what kind of portfolio best suits you:

1. Number of securities
2. Risk tolerance
3. Income today versus long-term growth
4. Tax considerations

Number of Securities

The first question is, "Just how many and what type of securities will you be able to manage successfully?" This is all about the amount of time you are willing and able to devote to your portfolio. While we are doing everything possible to help you be efficient, there are no shortcuts for doing the necessary homework. You need to spend time making sure you fully understand exactly what you are investing in and then monitor the investments within your portfolio. The good news is the more you do this, the easier and more natural it will become. Think of it like building your investing muscle—while it may be difficult at first, before too long your ability to not only digest data but distinguish usable information (signals) from noise will become stronger and stronger.

In the introduction to this book we mentioned that you should never have more than 3 to 5 percent of your portfolio invested in any one company, and no more than 8 to 10 percent in an exchange-traded fund or mutual fund. The less time you have to devote to your portfolio, the more you should rely on well-diversified and potentially actively managed funds. With this in mind, if you have very little time, you should focus on selecting 10 or more funds for your portfolio. On the other end of the spectrum, most people who don't work on their portfolios fulltime should have no more than 20 to 25 individual securities (meaning stocks, bonds, mutual funds, exchange-traded funds, etc.) so as to be able to adequately monitor their holdings. Depending on the amount of time and your desire to put in the time and effort, you can be anywhere between these two extremes.

Assume that each stock will take about 20 hours over several weeks to research fully before investing and will average around 10 minutes a week to monitor. Some weeks it will take less than a minute for a particular stock; another week it might take over an hour. Consider these numbers as you decide if you prefer all funds, all stocks, or some combination of the two. While the hours to get going probably sound a little daunting, as you'll learn in Chapter 11, you shouldn't buy all of the securities in your portfolio at one time and rarely do you buy 100 percent of all the shares of a company all at once. In other words, you can breathe a sigh of relief because all that time tends to be spread out over several months.

Risk Tolerance

You'll often hear investment-types talk about portfolio volatility and/or risk tolerance. This really just boils down to how much money you can stand to lose, both financially and emotionally, within a given period of time, because, frankly, how many people would get stressed out about having their investments gain a lot more than they expected? No one cares about volatility on the upside! The concern is, how would you react if a stock you owned dropped 10-15 percent? Would you feel a panicky need to immediately sell it, or would you happily purchase more, confident that your thesis for the stock will pan out?

In general, companies that are smaller, faster growing, in emerging industries, and don't pay out dividends have more volatile stock prices than large companies that have a consistent track record of delivering stable results. Those companies that have consistently paid out dividends, generally speaking, tend to have more stable stock prices. Keep in mind, however, that during times of extreme market stress, everything can get hit hard. We saw this at the end of 2000 into 2002, again in 2008 into early 2009, shown in Figure 9.1, and again in January 2016. The silver lining in those cases, however, was what came after that extreme market stress, particularly for those investors who had the risk tolerance and available cash on hand to buy those investments on their shopping lists at discounted prices.

Your time horizon also affects what types of risks you can take. The longer your time horizon, meaning the more time you have before you will need to start taking money out of your portfolio—for a down payment on a home, a dream vacation, a new car, or retirement—the more risk you can afford to take, still limited of course by what you can stomach, as there is no point in having a portfolio that gives you insomnia, an ulcer, or both!

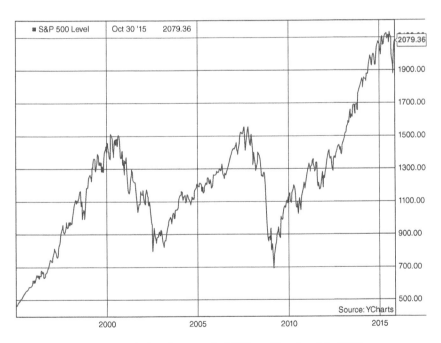

Figure 9.1   S&P 500 Index, January 1, 1995, to October 30, 2015
SOURCE: YCharts

You also need to consider what you are looking for from your portfolio with respect to the kind of long-term returns versus income generation. Generally speaking, the younger you are, the more growth you want versus investments that give you income (keep in mind that income from investments is taxed at a higher rate than long-term gains). Those who will depend on their portfolios to generate sufficient income to cover part or all of their living expenses need to have portfolios in which prices fluctuate less and that produce more reliable, consistent income streams.

This is a list of the most widely used types of securities:

- Stocks
- Bonds
- Real estate investment trusts (REIT)
- Master limited partnerships (MLP)
- Mutual funds
- Exchange-traded funds (ETF)
- Exchange-traded notes (ETN)
- Closed-end funds (CEF)

We are going to focus on stocks and on funds comprised of stocks, as those are the primary ways to express the Cocktail Thematics you've read about in Chapter 8 and have subsequently identified for yourself. Although REITs and MLPs are also useful investment vehicles, as you'll see later in this chapter, their structure, dividend policy, and tax implications are somewhat different from typical publicly traded companies or stock funds. Everything we teach you here applies to them as well, but they do have a few unique traits that we'll cover at a high level. If you are interested in investing in them, you'll find references and more information in the Appendix.

Stocks

Countless books have been written about stocks and there is a bounty of information on them on the Internet and you'll find a few of our favorite tomes on CocktailInvesting.com. In the interest of preserving everyone's sanity, we aren't going to repeat the basics of stocks here, things like the difference between common and preferred shares. Those of you who aren't familiar with stocks should review the references we cite in the Appendix. When it comes to just the basics, we can't add much value; instead, we focus here on where we can add value.

First off, we suggest that any stock you consider has a daily average minimum trading volume of 100,000 shares per day, but we prefer higher. Keep in mind that for every transaction, there are buyers and sellers, which means the actual number of shares traded is really half the reported amount. We also avoid stocks priced $10 or below. We avoid stocks with low trading volumes or that trade at low prices out of concern for getting into a position that we cannot quickly and easily exit—what we refer to as avoiding a roach-motel situation.

Most importantly, for any stock you absolutely must read the company's filings with the Securities and Exchange Commission (SEC). The documents can be found at www.sec.gov/edgar or most investing services such as Schwab and Fidelity. Research sites like Morningstar.com or YCharts have links to the documents as well. Of particular importance are the company's annual report (10-K), the quarterly reports (10-Q), and statements of changes in beneficial ownership (4), which tell you if the insiders are buying or selling.

For companies that only recently went public, we'd recommend reading the S-1 filing that breaks down the company's industry, business, products, potential risks, and historical financial performance. One other filing to be familiar with is a company's proxy statement (Def 14A) that can contain additional insight from the company's management team, as well as items to be voted on at the annual shareholder meeting. (If you've never attended one of those meetings, we highly recommend it. You'll come away with a better understanding of the company as well as its business.)

Price is the most important aspect of any investment decision. For almost everything you consider investing in, there is some price at which there is very little risk and a lot of potential upside and some price at which there is so little potential upside that it just isn't worth buying. There is no investment that is a good idea at any price. When we think of price, we often remember one of Warren Buffett's more well-known sayings, "Price is what you pay. Value is what you get." Which to us means getting the price right (or as right as possible) is crucial.

So how do you know if something is priced well to buy or to sell? Here come the metrics!

P/E Ratios

When you hear someone say Apple is trading at $130 or Exxon trading under $85, what does that mean?

Apple is trading at a higher price than Exxon, but we don't actually know from that if one is a better price than the other. The reality is that knowing that Apple trades at $130 doesn't tell you a darn thing!

It's important to get a second piece of data, the company's earnings per share (EPS), to have any sense of how to compare the price of Apple (AAPL) shares to Exxon (XOM) shares. Taking the price divided by earnings per share gives you the company's P/E (price-to-earnings) ratio.

There are many flavors of P/E ratios for a given company, so you always want to make sure you are clear on just which one people are talking about. Unfortunately, you'll often hear people on the major financial television shows talking about P/E ratios without specifying to which they are referring, which annoys us to no end.

The numerator is always the current market price, but the denominator can vary widely, from being the last four quarters of earnings-per-share (trailing P/E ratio, which is typically annotated as TTM), the expected earnings per share for the next four quarters (forward P/E ratio), and even the past two quarters combined with expectations for the next two quarters (blended P/E ratio).

Say that Apple's trailing 12-month earnings per share (EPS TTM) was $7.40 while Exxon's was $7.60. Now we can calculate the price-to-earnings ratio (P/E) (trailing 12 months) for these two stocks:

PE ratio (TTM), which is the price-to-earnings ratio, trailing 12 months:

$$\text{Apple's share price} = \$130/\$7.40(\text{EPS}) = 17.16$$

$$\text{Exxon's share price} = \$84.9/\$7.60(\text{EPS}) = 11.18$$

What this tells us is that investors are willing to pay $17.16 for every $1 of Apple's earnings versus $11.18 for every $1 of Exxon's earnings.

Now we have a way to better compare Apple's share price to Exxon's. From this, we can see that Apple is trading at a more expensive multiple than Exxon. Two other ways to say this are as follows: Apple shares are trading at a *premium* to Exxon shares or Exxon shares are trading at a *discount* to Apple shares. Generally, a higher P/E ratio means that investors are anticipating higher future growth. P/E ratios tend to be more consistent within an industry so we are not surprised to see a wide discrepancy between Apple and Exxon here. In Chapter 10, we'll show you how to use this metric to compare companies within the same industry or peer group.

We should also mention that the P/E ratio can be used for more than just an individual stock. It can be used for a fund or an index, which is simply the weighted average of the P/E ratios for all the companies in the fund or index. For example, the Shiller P/E ratio (named after economist Robert Shiller) is based on the average inflation-adjusted earnings from the previous 10 years for the S&P 500 index.

In November 2015, the Shiller P/E ratio had long-term average of around 16.6 with a peak of 44.19 in December 1999.[1] Let's assume that today the current Shiller P/E ratio is 27 and the S&P 500 trailing 12-month P/E ratio (current stock price divided by the training earnings per share for the past 12 months) is 20 versus 18 a year ago and its forward P/E (current stock price divided by the expected earnings per share over the coming year, which you can find from FactSet and other services) is 17. So:

Current Shiller P/E = 27

S&P 500 trailing 12-month P/E ratio = 20

S&P 500 trailing 12-month P/E ratio (one year ago) = 18

S&P 500 forward P/E ratio = 17

What does this mean? Stocks are more expensive today than a year ago.

Investors are paying more today for each dollar of earnings from the S&P 500 than they did a year ago and also more than the historical average, since the trailing 12-month P/E ratio rose from 18 to 20.

Earnings for the S&P 500 are expected to grow over the coming year, which is why the forward P/E ratio is lower than the trailing P/E ratio. Here's the math:

$100 share price today/$10 EPS for the past 12 months = $10.00

$100 share price today/$16 EPS forecast for the next 12 months

= $6.25

Most investing services provide P/E ratios for individual companies, funds, and indexes, often giving both the trailing and the forward, as P/E ratios are pretty much the standard for assessing where a stock is over-priced, underpriced, or fairly priced. However, there are some things you need to take into account when using the P/E ratio.

First of all, a company's net income (earnings per share equals a company's net income divided by its outstanding shares) can be manipulated in a variety of ways. For example, a company may take a one-time restructuring charge, which it could use as an excuse for having weak earnings, and will prefer to talk about pre-one-time-charge net income instead of the actual earnings. This could be legitimate if the one-time charge is truly a unique event and does not reflect typical operating expenses, but we've seen more than a few occasions where compa-nies have reported these "one-time restructuring charges" every few years. This looks to us like a great way to play with accounting in order to make typical operating expenses look less than they really are. There are so many accounting games that companies play in order to paint the best picture possible of their net income that countless books have been written on the topic of managing a company's bottom line. So investors ... beware!

Share Repurchases

Companies can reward shareholders in a number of ways, including through stock price appreciation and dividends. One way that has become increasingly popular is share repurchases (also called stock buybacks). This refers to when a company buys back their own shares. Generally, when companies buy back their own stock it is beneficial to shareholders, because with fewer shares outstanding, those shares that are in the public's hands are worth more.

However, with the exceptionally low interest rates after the financial crisis, we have been seeing a significant increase in the number of companies buying back their own shares, with a growing percentage of them issuing debt to do this, thanks in no small part to the various quantitative easing programs that have kept interest rates at exceptionally low levels. Figure 9.2 shows the increase in share repurchases in recent years.

For companies that issue debt (bonds) to fund share buybacks, the benefit to shareholders is more complicated than when the buybacks are funded through normal business profits. When the interest rate paid on the bonds is lower than the dividend yield on the shares being repurchased, this is a cash-flow-positive strategy. Here's the math, using small numbers to keep it simple.

A company's stock is trading at $100. The current stock dividend is 4 percent on an annual basis, which means it is paying $4.00 in dividends on every share per year.

The company issues $1,000 worth of bonds, yielding 2.5 percent. This means that if you bought $100 of this bond, you would receive $2.50 a year in interest payments. The company uses the proceeds of the bond issuance (the $1,000) to repurchase 10 shares of its own stock ($10 \times \$100/\text{share} = \$1,000$). Now the company is paying only $25 a

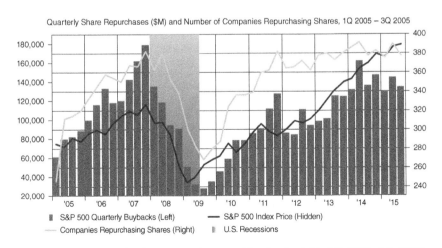

Figure 9.2   Quarterly share repurchases and buyback yield, 1Q 2005–3Q 2015
SOURCE: FactSet Fundamentals

year in interest versus the $40 it was paying previously in dividends on those shares, saving $15 a year.

Looking at those equations one can see how low interest rates (a la Federal Reserve quantitative easing) could make it more attractive for companies to buy back their shares and would put downward pressure on dividend yields. Let's look at the top 10 companies by dollar-value and their share returns in late 2015 as shown in Figure 9.3.

How could these share buybacks affect share prices and not just reduce the amount of money companies pay out in dividends?

The price of a stock on any given day is just a function of supply and demand. The greater the demand (buyers) the more the stock price is pushed up until no more buyers are interested at the higher price. The converse is also true; the more that want to sell, the lower the price will go until no more sellers are interested in selling. (Real-world example—when home prices are high, lots of people consider selling their homes, but when home prices fall, more people are happy to stay just where they are.)

So how big of an impact do these share buybacks have on demand? We can answer this by looking at fund flows, meaning money going into and coming out of the markets, shown in Figure 9.4.

The chart on net equity inflows shows that the single largest source of funds going into the equity markets came from corporations.

Company	Sector	TTM Buybacks ($M)	% Change in Shares (TTM)	Dividend Outflows	1 Year Total Return
Apple Inc.	Information Technology	$41,588	(4.7%)	$11,426	13.4%
Microsoft Corporation	Information Technology	$13,209	(2.6%)	$9,882	(4.4%)
Wells Fargo & Company	Financials	$10,271	(2.0%)	$8,572	(1.6%)
Intel Corporation	Information Technology	$9,996	(3.9%)	$4,447	(15.0%)
QUALCOMM Inc.	Information Technology	$9,210	(6.0%)	$2,844	(26.8%)
Exxon Mobil Corporation	Energy	$9,105	(2.2%)	$11,846	(22.3%)
Johnson & Johnson	Health Care	$8,301	(1.9%)	$7,948	(10.5%)
Pfizer Inc.	Health Care	$8,258	(3.3%)	$6,772	11.1%
Oracle Corporation	Information Technology	$8,091	(2.7%)	$2,255	(11.3%)
Gilead Sciences, Inc.	Health Care	$7,919	(3.5%)	$633	3.1%

Figure 9.3 Top 10 companies by dollar-value buybacks—trailing 12 months, September 2015
SOURCE: FactSet Fundamentals

Goldman Sachs forecast of 2015 U.S. net equity flows (in $ billions)
as of January 7, 2015; summary statistics through 3Q 2014

	Net Equity Inflow/(Outflow)			
Category	2012	2013	2014 Ann.	2015E
Corporations	$385	$389	$415	$450
ETFs	133	167	121	170
Foreign Investors	127	(79)	103	125
Mutual Funds	(38)	163	133	125
Life Insurance	15	13	33	50
Pension Funds	(69)	(147)	(169)	(175)
Households	(241)	(55)	(183)	(245)
Other	2	3	(5)	
less				
Foreign equities by U.S.	(51)	(212)	(231)	(250)
Credit ETF purchases	(52)	(12)	(39)	(30)
TOTAL	**$210**	**$229**	**$178**	**$220**

Figure 9.4 U.S. Net equity inflows, 2012–2015E
SOURCE: Federal Reserve Board and Goldman Sachs.

Households on the other hand were net sellers, as were pension funds, meaning that on a dollar basis, more households and pension funds were selling than buying stocks. Further, it shows that in 2014, households took $183 billion out of the stock market while corporations put $415 into the equities market. Doing some simple math we find that if no corporations had purchased equities, there would have been a net outflow of $237 billion! Talk about a reduction in overall demand. What this tells us is had it not been for companies buying back their own shares, stock prices in 2014 would have likely declined as there were overall more sellers than buyers.

Now let's go back to the company making the decision to issue bonds (borrow money) and use the proceeds to buy back shares of their own stock. There are a few things to keep in mind: This is not a sustainable process. Companies cannot endlessly issue debt and then use the proceeds to buy back shares—rather intuitive, but something to keep in mind, as it is not a long-term way for a company to generate returns for shareholders. As debt levels climb at a company, shareholders may become increasingly worried that the company will not be able to service its debt (meaning being able to make the required payments). This is akin to a homeowner repeatedly refinancing their home, with each successive mortgage borrowing even more than the one before. In a contracting economy or in a recession this problem can become even more worrisome.

If stock prices fall, then the entire equation we did above falls apart. How's that? Well, we left out the impact of share price and the company's balance sheet in that analysis. Tricky, aren't we? So let's revisit that equation taking share price into account.

The company issues $1,000 worth of bonds and immediately buys $1,000 worth of stock, or 10 shares since the stock was trading at $100/share. So on the company's balance sheet there is now a liability worth $1,000, but an asset, most likely cash, that is worth $1,000 counters it.

If the company's stock were to decline by, say, 15 percent, then those shares would be worth $850. The company now has a liability worth $1,000 that is countered by an asset worth only $850. This negative change in the company's net worth makes it less attractive than before the share price decline, so now it has a double hit. Its shares have been falling and now its balance sheet looks less attractive. That can put further downward pressure on the company's share price, which results in an even less attractive balance sheet, and so on. This is another example of how debt can exacerbate problems when asset prices fall.

One of the reasons that companies do this is the difference in tax treatments between debt and equity. Remember how we discussed earlier in this book the way fiscal policies (a.k.a. tax and spend) can affect investing? Companies are able to use the payments they make on loans to reduce their taxable income. Dividends paid to shareholders are completely different. Companies first have to pay taxes on their net income; then they can distribute what remains to shareholders. Shareholders then must pay taxes on the dividends they receive. This is referred to as *double-taxation*. The same income is taxed once at the company level, then again when received by shareholders. Companies may choose to use some level of debt to help reduce the amount of taxes they pay, leaving more money to give to shareholders.

Most importantly, these share buybacks affect earnings per share (EPS) as the fewer shares outstanding, the higher the earnings per share for the same net income. For example, if a company has 100 shares outstanding and buys back 20 shares, its earnings per share will look greatly improved, even though the company's actual performance is the same!

$$\$100 \text{ net income}/100 \text{ shares} = \$1.00 \text{ EPS}$$

$$\$100 \text{ net income}/80 \text{ shares} = \$1.25 \text{ EPS}$$

This makes comparing performance over time using P/E ratios rather convoluted as the P/E ratio is based on price and EPS.

As you can see, there are no quick answers when assessing the value of a company's stock. There are many things a company can do to manipulate its numbers, so you need to look at more than just one or two metrics to understand performance over time. In the next chapter, we will give you a checklist to help you get an understanding of the key data points as efficiently as possible.

Now that you better understand some of the ways that a company's earnings-per-share can be manipulated and how to calculate various price-to-earnings ratios, we'll walk you through a few other types of securities that you might be interested in using to execute on the investment Cocktail Thematics you have identified.

Real Estate Investment Trusts

A favorite for generating income, real estate investment trusts (REITs) invest in real estate either directly, by purchasing the actual property, or through mortgages. REITs allow the typical investor to invest in diversified real estate in a cost-effective manner that would otherwise be impossible for most.

An equity REIT buys, develops, manages, and sells real estate. Equity REITs can invest in various types of real estate such as corporate office buildings, medical facilities, shopping malls, apartments, warehouses, hotels, and senior care facilities or in particular regions such as a state or country. Shareholders of equity REITs are buying portions of a managed pool of real estate.

A mortgage REIT invests in property through mortgages by loaning money to the owners of real estate or by purchasing existing mortgages or mortgage-backed securities. For a mortgage REIT, income is generated from the interest earned on the mortgages rather than from operating the physical properties.

A REIT is just like a publicly traded company in that you want to read the annual report (10-K) and quarterly reports (10-Q), but unlike a company, in which you are buying the right to participate in the profits of the company, in a REIT you are buying not only a share of the profits but a portion of the real estate generating those profits as well.

The most important aspect of a REIT is its requirement to distribute nearly 90 percent of its yearly taxable income to shareholders. This amount is deductible to the company, unlike dividends, so there is only one level of taxation for the funds distributed to investors. Remember our earlier discussion of double-taxation for corporations. For common stockholders, the corporation's executive team and the board decide what, if any, of the cash generated by the business is distributed to the shareholders. Regardless of how much, if any, of the profits of a corporation are distributed to shareholders, a corporation pays corporate income tax on its entire net income.

If you want to know more about REITs, please see our recommended reading list in the Appendix. This isn't the only type of security that is focused primarily on generating cash for its investors. There is another type we want to discuss that typically invests in natural resources.

Master Limited Partnership (MLP)

A master limited partnership (MLP) is a type of limited partnership that is publicly traded. The limited partners (you, the investor) are those that provide the capital to the MLP, and the general partner is the party that runs the business and is compensated based on performance.

In order to qualify to be an MLP, the partnership must generate a minimum of around 90 percent of its income from real estate, natural resources, or commodities. Much like REITs, one of the main reasons MLPs are attractive is because of their tax treatment. Where REITs are able to reduce their taxable income by the amount that is given to shareholders, MLPs do not pay taxes on their income at all (as opposed to a corporation, which is subject to double taxation). The money is only taxed when distributed to unit holders of the partnership.

The downside of MLPs is that once a year, unit holders receive a K-1 statement detailing their share of the partnership's net income, which needs to be filed with the investor's taxes. However, typically investors pay taxes on less than the amount of cash they received from the MLP because unit holders are taxed on the partnerships income, not on its distributable cash flow that benefits from MLPs typically having rather high depreciation expenses. Eventually, an investor will pay taxes on everything received, but portions are deferred until the entire investment is sold.

This unique tax treatment makes MLPs potentially problematic in tax-exempt accounts such as an IRA, because the cash distributions are considered unrelated business taxable income (UBTI) and could create a tax liability for the investor. Therefore, typically it is better to hold an MLP in a regular, taxable brokerage account.

If you want to know more about MLPs, please see our recommended reading list in the Appendix.

Funds

We mentioned earlier that a lot has been written about stocks and bonds. That goes double for commentary on funds—and no wonder, given their proliferation. At the end of 2014, $33.4 trillion was invested in mutual funds and exchange-traded funds worldwide.[2] The United States represents the largest portion at $18.2 trillion, coming primarily from the more than 90 million U.S. retail investors, meaning individuals like all of us. Investors have increasingly relied on funds over the past few decades, with 24 percent of household financial assets held in investment companies at the end of 2014 versus just 2 percent in 1980.[3] Part of this increasing allocation has been due to the growth of individual retirement accounts (IRAs) and defined contribution plans such as 401(k) plans, as well as greater usage by financial advisors, as seen in Figure 9.5. One of the best places to get information on either mutual funds or ETFs is Morningstar, but we caution against blindly following its ratings as those tend to be based primarily on past performance. Always remember that things change and the past may not be indicative of the future, and frankly, last year's top performers are rarely this year's stars.

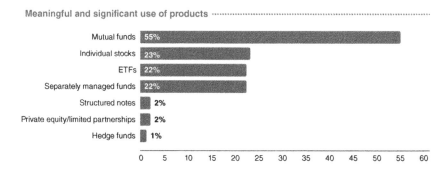

Figure 9.5   Use of products by financial advisors
SOURCE: WealthManagement.com 2015 Investment Trend Monitor Report: Advisor Use of Financial Products

As funds have become increasingly popular, the range of offerings has also grown considerably. We'll walk you through the different types and discuss why you may want to consider them for your own portfolio. As with the earlier types of securities we've discussed, we aren't going to replicate the great work that is available out there on funds, but will instead give you our take on them. In the Appendix you will find suggestions for further readings about funds, which we highly recommend if you decide to include funds in your portfolio.

First off, keep in mind that in some industries, particularly new and emerging ones, it may not be feasible for you to pick a specific company; thus, a fund that focuses on your area of interest may be a better choice, regardless of how much time you are willing to spend.

Given the number of cyberattacks launched on companies like Target and Sony and even the federal government, the need for security is a pretty obvious pain point. But unless you have very specific knowledge in this part of technology, it is incredibly difficult to identify which cybersecurity suppliers will end up winning. This type of situation is one where you might want to consider a fund. In this case, you could use the ETF PureFunds ISE Cyber Security™ (HACK). Some industries tend to be extremely volatile as well. Thus, even if you were willing and able to spend the time to select specific stocks, say in biotechnology, if you think the way stock prices in that sector tend to move around rather wildly is going to give you some sleepless nights, you may be better off using a fund rather than taking on the risks and volatility inherent with an individual company. In this case, you might want to consider a fund like the ETF iShares Nasdaq Biotechnology (IBB).

Funds mostly fall into one of two main categories: mutual funds or exchange-traded funds (ETFs). Right off the bat, the biggest difference you'll notice between the two as an investor is that an ETF is priced throughout the day and you are able to buy or sell any time during normal market hours just like you would a stock. In contrast, mutual funds are priced just once a day, after the market closes. If you want to buy or sell a mutual fund today, you will have to put your order in during the day before you know the actual price for shares of the fund for that day. This can make things a bit complicated if you would like to set it up to automatically buy or sell shares at a specific price, for example.

This can make it more challenging to stick to your guns with a planned buy or sell. It can become difficult to objectively "pull the trigger," so to speak, when you don't actually know if the price is going to hit your target when the transaction gets executed that afternoon. It can also be tempting to try and game it, for example, thinking, "Oh, the price is falling/rising … I'll just wait a bit longer … maybe a bit past my target for an even better entry/exit point." And then—you've missed your opportunity.

Exchange-Traded Funds versus Mutual Funds

The various structures of ETFs vary by country, but the fund itself is divided into shares, which are held by shareholders who then indirectly own the assets of the fund and are thus entitled to the profits, dividends, and interest generated by the assets of that fund.

ETFs differ from mutual funds in that investors do not buy or sell their share at the net asset value (NAV), which means essentially the value of the underlying assets.

For example, to calculate the NAV for shares representing one-tenth of a fund that owns 20 shares priced at $5.00 and 10 shares priced at $20 would be $1/10 \times [(20 \times \$5.00) + (10 \times \$20.00)] = 1/10 \times (\$100 + \$200) = \$30$. This is basically how the NAV for a mutual fund is calculated every day after the markets close, except it's done for every security the mutual fund owns.

Since an ETF is constantly traded throughout the day at the same time as its underlying assets, the price of shares of the ETF is determined the same way as prices for stocks, by the matching of buyers and sellers, which means that at any point in time, the ETF can be trading at a premium (priced above) or a discount (priced below) to its NAV. Using the previous example, this means the shares could be trading at, say, $31 (a premium) or $29 (a discount), even though the underlying assets are worth $30.

The difference between the fund's underlying NAV and the current share price is kept in check by the process by which the financial institutions (such as JP Morgan, Morgan Stanley, or Citibank, with whom you directly buy and sell ETF shares) purchase and sell the ETF shares directly from the ETF provider. This is done in large blocks of usually around 50,000 or so shares, which are called *creation units*. The ability to purchase or redeem creation units for an ETF gives these institutions arbitrage opportunities when the NAV of the bundle of securities is more or less than the market price of ETF, which in turn serves to minimize the potential difference between the two. They can make money taking advantage of the difference and, as they do, the difference shrinks.

ETFs can be bought only through a brokerage account, just like buying a stock. In contrast, investors can usually buy or sell mutual funds directly through the fund provider, such as Fidelity, Vanguard, PIMCO, and so on. Mutual funds also typically have a minimum investment, such as $1,000, whereas you can purchase just one share of an ETF, which is typically far less than $1,000.

Since ETFs trade on the market like stocks, investors can engage in many of the same types of trades that they can with a stock, such as selling short, buying on margin, and often times options in the form of calls and/or puts can be written against them. ETFs generally have lower costs than mutual funds for a variety of reasons and are more tax efficient for investors:

- ETFs that track an index have lower management fees because they are not actively managed.
- ETFs are insulated from the costs of having to buy and sell securities when shareholders purchase or redeem shares, which reduces costs and reduces potential tax liabilities for investors.

- ETFs usually have lower marketing, distribution, and accounting expenses than mutual funds.
- Most ETFs are not subject to 12b-1 fees, which are annual marketing or distribution fees associated with mutual funds.
- Index-style ETFs generate relatively low capital gains because they have low turnover of their portfolio securities.

In 2002, ETFs had a mere $100 billion under management. By 2006, that total had gone to $400 billion. By 2009, it was $800 billion, and by the end 2014, it had mushroomed to $2 trillion. To put that into perspective, $2 trillion equates to each of the estimated 322 million U.S. citizens holding more than $6,200.

That's impressive, but by the end of May 2015 the global exchange-traded products industry reached US$3 trillion in combined assets under management. At the time, Goldman Sachs saw that figure doubling by 2020 due to rapid adoption of ETFs and similar products by "registered investment advisors (RIAs), the roll-over of 401(k) into IRAs, increasing use of auto-allocation products, regulatory push into lower-cost products, geographic expansion, and innovation." As you'll read in the next section, not all ETFs are the same.

There is one other key difference between mutual funds and ETFs. Mutual funds typically only disclose their holdings on a quarterly basis, which means the fund manager can execute a strategy without the world seeing what he or she is doing and trying to take advantage of that information. Exchange-traded funds, in contrast, are required to disclose their holdings on a daily basis, which makes it more difficult to execute an active investment strategy as the world can watch the fund manager's every move.

Types of ETFs

Most ETFs are index funds that seek to replicate the performance of a particular index such as the S&P 500 or even a particular set of bond maturities like Treasury bonds with a maturity of 20 years or later with the iShares Barclays 20+ Year Treasury Bond ETF (TLT). These ETFs can either replicate the index by investing 100 percent of their assets proportionally in the securities underlying the index or engage in representative sampling where as little as 80 percent of their assets are invested in the securities and the rest is in options or futures or other securities not in the underlying index with the intent of helping the fund meet its investment objectives.

Stock index ETFs can be focused on a particular type of company, such as companies with large market capitalization such as Apple, or growth companies or high-dividend-paying companies. They can also focus on particular sectors such as biotechnology, banking, or even airlines.

Bond ETFs can be focused on particular types of bonds, such as U.S. government Treasury bonds, municipal bonds, corporate bonds, or international bonds with varying maturities.

There are also ETFs that track everything from the price of gold (such as ticker GLD) and silver (such as ticker SLV) to companies in the agricultural industry (such as ticker MOO) to even wind energy (such as ticker FAN). There are even ETFs that track relative values of currencies or baskets of currencies, and even volatility. ETFs also allow investors to take advantage of leveraged or inverse investment strategies, such as an ETF that seeks to generate two or three times the underlying index or to move opposite the index. Investors need to be aware that these funds can have considerable tracking error. Tracking error refers to just how far off a fund is relative to its underlying index. For example, a fund that seeks to generate two times its underlying index will likely diverge significantly because most all leveraged funds compound daily. If the index reverses direction, meaning up one day and down the next, the fund will be well off its underlying index. Here's the math:

Day 1:	Index up 2%	$100 × 1.02 = $102
	Fund up 4%	$100 × 1.04 = $104
Day 2:	Index down 3%	$102 × 0.97 = $98.94
	Fund down 6%	$104 × 0.94 = $97.76
Day 3:	Index up 2%	$98.94 × 1.02 = $100.92
	Fund up 4%	$97.76 × 1.04 = $101.67
Over three-day period		Index up 0.92%
		Fund up .67% = 1.8x index

As you can imagine, over time the difference between the two can grow, particularly if there are a lot of reversals of direction. So why does this "tracking" error occur? Because the fund rebalances its assets every day so that it can generate double the index's returns for that day. As long as the index moves in one direction, the fund will be able to track accurately, but once it changes direction, it starts to be off. If you want to leverage an investment over a longer period of time, a margin account, which allows you to purchase, say, $100 worth of shares for only $50, may be a better way to go, but of course you are risking more, too, so this is something to be considered carefully. We'll discuss this in later chapters. There are some funds that seek to compound on a monthly basis, but they will still have the same challenges over longer periods of time.

An inverse or "short" ETF seeks to give investors returns that are the opposite of the index's. For example, an inverse S&P 500 index would give you a positive 2 percent return on a day when the index itself fell 2 percent. However, these funds have a similar compounding problem. Both inverse and leveraged funds will perform as expected as long as the underlying index continues to move in the same direction; once it shifts, game over. Thus, these are particularly challenging funds to manage during volatile times when the index has large moves both up and down. There are also a few different types of ETF structures: exchange-traded open-end index mutual fund, exchange-traded unit investment trust, and exchange-traded grantor trust. Before purchasing an ETF, make sure you understand the details of its structure and the cost and tax implications it will have. Leveraged or inverse ETFs can be useful, but typically only for a short period of time, so make sure you understand exactly how they work.

Regardless of the type of structure, funds can be either actively managed or passive. Passive funds are typically index funds, meaning they attempt to as closely as possible track the performance of a particular index such as the S&P 500, or a specific commodity such as the price of gold, or a specific type of bond such as U.S. Treasury bonds with maturity greater than 20 years, a specific country index like the 50 largest companies in India, or a sector index such as healthcare, biotechnology, cybersecurity, utilities, or even water resources. Managers for actively managed funds buy and sell as they see fit in order to maximize returns and minimize losses. Typically, actively managed funds experience more turnover, meaning more securities are bought and sold, which translates into more expenses for the fund, and charge more because the manager is doing a lot of work. Index funds typically experience less turnover and their fees are notably lower because the manager is simply ensuring that the fund tracks its index as accurately as possible.

Cocktail Investing Bottom Line

Much like building your dream house, there are all sorts of decisions that you will have to make when constructing your investment portfolio now that you've identified the Cocktail Investing themes that will be the backbone of your portfolio. There are a variety of financial products, with different features that can make them appealing depending on one's investment risk tolerance, tax situation, and income needs.

- Investors need to be aware of how much time they will be able to devote to their portfolio and select securities accordingly. The more time available, the more stocks you can manage, the less time, the more you should consider diversified funds.
- Different types of securities are designed to meet different needs. Determine what you want from your portfolio, such as a target level of income generation and levels of volatility, then select candidate investments that can help you meet those goals.
- When comparing different investment products, you need to understand the various trade-offs between them (strategies, risks, fees, and other costs) as you refine your choices.
- When comparing individual stocks, be sure to compare companies within like industries, lest you fall victim to comparing apples and oranges when looking at various valuation and other metrics.
- The majority of investors have assets in funds, be they mutual funds or ETFs. Although both may offer diversification depending on the fund's investment strategy, mutual funds tend to have higher fees and expenses than ETFs, but may be more effective for actively managed strategies given the quarterly disclosures for holdings versus daily for ETFs.
- Investor dollars in ETFs have exploded over the last several years, which has led to the creation of many diverse and at times niche strategies that can offer exposure to various Cocktail Investing themes.

As we've discussed previously, investors can no longer rely on buy-and-hold investing, which is why in the next chapter we talk about proactively monitoring the investments in your portfolio.

Endnotes

1. "Shiller PE Ratio," www.multpl.com/shiller-pe/.

2. *2015 Investment Company Fact Book* (Investment Company Institute, 2015), p. 8, www.icifactbook.org.

3. Ibid., p. 11.

Chapter 10

Choosing Your Investments

Know what you own, and know why you own it.

— Peter Lynch

How many millionaires do you know who have become wealthy by investing in savings accounts? I rest my case.

— Robert G. Allen

The individual investor should act consistently as an investor and not as a speculator.

— Benjamin Graham

In Chapter 9, we discussed the different types of securities to choose from once you've formulated your thematic view of the world as we did in Chapter 8. Now it's time to pick a specific security and a price at which you are comfortable buying it. Much of the work has been done, but what lies ahead can make all the difference between picking a loser or a winner. A winner is pretty self-explanatory—it's a security that experiences an upward move in price. *Yippee!* Everyone loves a winner in the stock market. A loser—well, that's the one you end up wishing you'd never heard of. While you might feel like you are alone if you have picked one you wish you hadn't, we can tell you both first hand and from conversations with our colleagues, it happens. What's key is learning from it so you can minimize the odds of it happening again. We are going to start with stocks, so let's take the next steps to find those winners and avoid everything else.

12 Questions You Need to Answer When Looking to Buy a Stock

For any investor, whether new or experienced, it can be tempting to buy the latest hot stock without doing much homework, relying on all the wonderful things you've heard. Take it from us, we've seen this countless times before and even experienced it early on in our investing careers; it usually leads to nothing good. If you're tempted to do this, odds are after learning this the hard way, you'll understand it usually leads to trouble. As you get ready to make your portfolio selections, you will need to understand several key aspects of the company that is behind the shares you are contemplating adding to your holdings. How do you know how to gauge a company's business and the competitive landscape if you don't have a firm understanding of what the company does and how it makes money? The following 12 questions will help you assess which stocks you ought to avoid, which have the potential to be winners, and at what price you should consider adding them to your portfolio.

1. What Does the Company Do?

To determine what a company does means identifying which industries the company participates in and recognizing which one or ones drive a significant portion of the company's revenue stream. This requires digging into the company's financial statements, either the 10-K (annual) or 10-Q (quarterlies), which you can find at www.sec.gov. Examine the income statement, and potentially the business segment information that's found in the notes at the back of the filing to identify the different business lines the company may have. Some may only have one business segment, which can make this easier, but you should still read the company description to understand its products and services. Always read the notes in the filings, as that is often where you will find a lot more of the juicy details that investors need to know and companies may hope you overlook.

To give you an example of what we mean by understanding what the company does, let's take a look at Apple, a company almost everyone knows. While the company's history was one of personal computers, Apple today competes in the consumer electronics business with revenues coming from sales of iPhones, iPads, Mac desktop computers and laptops, Apple Watches, Apple TV, other products such as accessories, and services (Apple Care, iTunes, Apple Music, iCloud, and Apple Pay as well as the upcoming CarPlay and HomeKit). So now you know what it sells, but you don't know what brings in most of its revenue.

2. What Are Its Key Products or Services?

The answers to the first question—what does the company do?—gave you the big picture of the company. Here we're talking about those products or services that drive the bulk of the company's sales and profits. For Apple, iPhone sales were responsible for 63 percent of revenues generated in the quarter ending June 2015, which is Apple's third quarter as its year-end is September 30.[1] That's double the revenue contribution from all of Apple's other businesses (iPad, Mac, services, and other products) combined.[2] In fact the next-biggest product line—the Mac—accounted for only 12 percent of revenue during the quarter! The bottom line is that in 2015 Apple's business was highly dependent on the iPhone.[3]

If someone tried to convince you to buy Apple shares based on the Apple Watch or Apple TV, you would think twice. These new products may be sexy and may make headlines, but at least for a while, they won't be moving the revenue or profit lines in a meaningful way.

Figure 10.1 is a summary of the financials as reported by Apple for the third quarter of 2015, which ends June 30.

3. Which Business Unit or Units Make Most of the Profits?

Even after you break down the company's revenue stream, you still have to identify what really drives the company's profits. We tend to focus

Apple Inc.
Q3 2015 Unaudited Summary Data

(Units in thousands, Revenue in millions)

Operating Segments	Q3 2015 Revenue	Q2 2015 Revenue	Q3 2014 Revenue	Sequential Change Revenue	Year/Year Change Revenue
Americas	$20,209	$21,316	$17,574	-5%	15%
Europe	10,342	12,204	8,659	-15%	19%
Greater China	13,230	16,823	6,230	-21%	112%
Japan	2,872	3,457	2,627	-17%	9%
Rest of Asia Pacific	2,952	4,210	2,342	-30%	26%
Total Apple	$49,605	$58,010	$37,432	-14%	33%

Product Summary	Q3 2015 Units	Q3 2015 Revenue	Q2 2015 Units	Q2 2015 Revenue	Q3 2014 Units	Q3 2014 Revenue	Sequential Change Units	Sequential Change Revenue	Year/Year Change Units	Year/Year Change Revenue
iPhone (1)	47,534	$31,368	61,170	$40,282	35,203	$19,751	-22%	-22%	35%	59%
iPad (1)	10,931	4,538	12,623	5,428	13,276	5,889	-13%	-16%	-18%	-23%
Mac (1)	4,796	6,030	4,563	5,615	4,413	5,540	5%	7%	9%	9%
Services (2)		5,028		4,996		4,485		1%		12%
Other Products (1) (3)		2,641		1,689		1,767		56%		49%
Total Apple		$49,605		$58,010		$37,432		-14%		33%

(1) Includes deferrals and amortization of related non-software services and software upgrade rights.
(2) Includes revenue from iTunes, AppleCare, Apple Pay, licensing and other services.
(3) Includes sales of Apple TV, Apple Watch, Beats Electronics, iPod and Apple-branded and third-party accessories.

Figure 10.1 Apple Inc. 3Q 2015 data summary from Apple

on operating profit generation, because it factors in things like selling, general and administration costs, as well as research and development (R&D) spending for the company.

In this case, let's step away from Apple and turn to semiconductor chip company Qualcomm (QCOM), which derived 68 percent of its 2015 revenue from chip sales and 31 percent from its licensing business.[4] Digging into the notes found toward the back of the 2015 10-K revealed the chip business accounted for only 26.3 percent of operating profits in 2015, compared to 73.6 percent for the licensing business.[5] This told us that at the heart of things, the real driver of Qualcomm's business and earnings was the very profitable licensing business. As such, investors in Qualcomm would need to understand the dynamics of that business and prevailing trends (vector and velocity once again) in the royalty rate.

4. Who Are the Customers, and How Are They/Will They Be Changing?

Now that you know what the company sells, what generates the majority of sales, and where it makes the most profits, you need to look at to whom it is selling. Is the company focused on a customer base that is shrinking or growing? Are preferences evolving in favor of or away from the company's products and/or services? Looking to the future, will the customer base likely have more money to spend on the company's offerings or less? Is the customer base highly concentrated (e.g., the majority of sales are to a very small number of entities)?

For example, microchip producer Cirrus Logic reported in 2015 that Apple orders accounted for 72 percent of its sales.[6] As you can imagine, strong iPhones sales are a boon to Cirrus and weak sales a killer. An investor in this company would have to understand just how much Apple could affect it, both directly by demanding lower prices and indirectly through the success of Apple's products. Potential investors would have to recognize that shares of Cirrus Logic stock will likely react to the latest thoughts on how Apple's products (most of which are iPhones!) will fare in the future, which can make for a bumpy ride if there is a high degree of skepticism over how those Apple products will perform. Something to keep in mind as you consider your risk tolerance level for a particular company and its shares.

5. Who Are the Company's Suppliers, and What Are Its Key Inputs?

Whatever a company sells—goods, services, or both—it needs some sort of inputs, such as coffee beans for Starbucks, protein for Red Robin Gourmet Burgers, cotton for the Gap, and microchips for Apple. Investors need to understand what the key inputs are for the company and how they might be affected. Did this year's weather damage the coffee crop? Are beef and chicken prices skyrocketing, and if so, why? Have cotton prices tumbled and, if so, is that good for the Gap? (Yes it is!) Is there a trend among microchip manufacturers to merge, which might mean fewer suppliers to companies like Apple, resulting in perhaps an ability to demand higher prices for those microchips?

You also want to understand the market dynamics between the company and its suppliers. For example, Walmart has enormous purchasing power relative to many of its suppliers and has a reputation for placing significant pressure on its suppliers to cut costs.[7] On the other end of the spectrum, iron ore is used to produce steel, and there are three iron ore suppliers that significantly dominate the industry[8]—Vale, Rio Tinto, and BHP—while the largest steel company in the world, ArcelorMittal, controls less than 10 percent of the steel market.

6. Who Are the Key Competitors, and How Are They Impacting the Market?

Looking again at Apple, the key competitors to watch out for would be those in the smartphone industry where those devices accounted for the majority of Apple's sales in 2015, rather than, say, personal computers or iPads. Samsung is the primary competitor to Apple's iPhone business, given its sizable market share,[9] according to data from a market research firm, but an investor would still want to keep tabs on other players such as Lenovo, Huawei, LG, and HTC, as well as the once high-and-mighty BlackBerry.

Investors need to read competitor press releases and financial filings to develop a feel for how their products are doing. Watching new product introductions, feature sets, and promotional activity, as well as product pricing trends, can tell you if one of the competitors is aggressively targeting market share gains, which could reduce profit margins in the future.

7. *Who Is Running the Company, and What Do They Think?*

A rather well-known maxim in Silicon Valley is, "I'll take an A team with a B idea over an A idea with a B team any day." The greatest products or services in the world still need a talented management team. Investors need to understand who is running the company, what their track record is, and what the team dynamics are.

You want to compare what you think the company does to what the management team thinks it does. Are they in sync? To get your arms around this, you can listen to the management team give their quarterly or annual earnings review. You can also read management's views in the 10-Ks and 10-Qs, as well as listen to how they talk about the company, its business, and its opportunities at investor conferences that tend to be captured in the investor relations section of the company's website. This will also give you a feel for where management is focusing their energies: Are they focused on the primary revenue and profit areas, or do they seem distracted by areas that contribute little to the company's bottom line? If so, is there a good reason for this that isn't immediately obvious?

What's the track record of the team? How long has this particular one been together? Any recent changes to the team? Any upcoming ones? If so, why? You want to try and get a good feel for the dynamics within the group. Management teams that have too much internal friction can end up wasting time and energy that ought to be put into the company. On the other hand, too much camaraderie can lead to, shall we say, lethargic leadership. You want to make sure the team is hungry and that they push each other to bring their A game every day.

Investors also need to understand who is on the board of directors and what their relationship with the management team is like. Are they working well together? Are there productive or destructive tensions? Are there any activist investors, such as Elliot Management Corporation or David Einhorn's Greenlight Capital? Just Google "Top Activist Investors" to get a current list. If so, what are they saying about the company and the management team? Do they have plans to acquire or are they already involved in the company? To what end? Are they adding value or being a distraction?

It is always a good idea to check on insider buying and selling. If members of the management team have started to sell off a material portion of their ownership, it probably isn't a good time for you to be buying. You can find information on this from the SEC, as well as from the online sites of services like Morningstar and Insider-Monitor .com. At the SEC's site you'll want to look at Form 14A, the proxy statement, which gives a list of the directors and officers and the number of shares they each own, as well as Form 4, which reports changes in ownership.[10] You'll want to see if anyone has been buying or selling a material amount recently, but keep in mind that often, particularly with companies that have gone public more recently, executives set up a 10b5–1 plan that schedules to sell a specific number of shares at regular intervals regardless of the price. A very good overview on 10b5–1 plans can be found in "Rule 10b5–1 Plans: What You Need to Know" on the Harvard Law School Forum on Corporate Governance and Financial Regulation.[11]

8. What Is Driving Growth at the Company?

Again, let's stick with Apple and its June 2015 quarterly results. iPhone revenue soared 59 percent year-over-year, which was head and shoulders ahead of the company's overall revenue growth of 33 percent for the quarter compared to what it did the prior year.[12] Generally speaking, those businesses that are growing faster than the corporate average—in this case, that 33 percent revenue growth we mentioned for the June 2015 quarter—are the ones to watch.

When it comes to growth, size does matter. We see this in Apple's Other Products business, which houses Apple TV, Apple Watch, Beats Electronics iPods, and other accessories. During the June 2015 quarter, revenue from Other Products grew 49 percent year over year—impressive!—but the business only accounted for 5 percent of Apple's overall revenues. That's still pretty small potatoes, so when you hear about high rates of growth, make sure you understand just how much of a company's revenue and profits come from that growing area.

The bottom line with Apple is that it's a smartphone company that as of this writing is still growing faster than the overall industry, which means that its products continue to take customers away from Samsung and other competitors. Despite delivering fantabulous results, the longer-term concern is: What products will overtake Apple's revenue and profit generation? Longtime investors will remember that at one point it seemed PC and mobile phone sales would never slow, let alone contract, yet we are seeing the latter happen in both of those markets today.

9. What Is Driving the Company's Profit, and, If It's Not Improving, Why Is That?

We tend to look at a company's operating margin, which is simply operating profit divided by revenue. There are several parts of the income statement that we use to calculate a company's operating profit. Here's the formula we use:

Operating profit = Revenue − Costs of goods sold

$$- \text{ Selling, general \& administrative expenses (SG\&A)}$$

$$- \text{ Research \& development (R\&D)}$$

To calculate a company's Operating margin, use

$$\text{Operating margin} = \text{Operating profit}/\text{Revenue}$$

And just to be sure we have things crystal clear:

$$\text{Operating margin} = \frac{(\text{Revenue} - \text{Cost of goods sold} - \text{SG\&A} - \text{R\&D})}{\text{Revenue}}$$

Generally speaking, a company's profit picture can improve when it earns more per dollar of revenue. If Starbucks raises its prices on a cup of coffee or Apple's latest iPhone model is priced higher, then odds are that margins will be rising. If, however, Starbucks initiated that price increase to fend off the pain of higher coffee prices, the company's margins might improve, but maybe not as much because the benefit of the price increase is offset by higher costs to the company. Keep in mind, though, that any time a company raises prices, it risks losing customers. That means that while margins could be improving, which we like, total revenue could be falling, which we don't like.

Companies can also see margin improvement due to something called *economies of scale,* which means the more a company builds a product, the more efficient it will get and the lower its costs are per unit produced. Think of it this way: If you have a factory that can manufacture anywhere from 100 to 1,000 units in the same amount of time and with the same number of employees, the cost per unit of making 1,000 units is less than the cost per unit of making 100. Hand in hand with that robust product volume may go more favorable costs associated with key parts or ingredients that go into the product—the joys of buying in bulk. Also look for when a company initiates a new manufacturing technology or does something to reduce its production costs. There may be some short-term pain or disruptions as those new procedures are implemented, but before too long, the benefits should begin to kick in.

Another way a company can see its profitability improve is through lower costs. Take the Starbucks example above. If coffee prices drop and Starbucks doesn't lower its coffee drink prices, its operating margin would benefit from the fall in its coffee cost prices. Keep in mind though that Starbucks would run the risk of losing customers if other coffee shops, such as Peet's and Coffee Bean and Tea Leaf, lowered their prices and became more attractive to customers. In that case, while Starbucks margins would have improved, it may end up actually making less money because it has lost customers.

Of course, coffee is one input among many at Starbucks. But that's why you need to read the company's financial filings to determine which inputs are critical. The same goes for other companies and other parts and ingredients. We walk you through this with Starbucks in Chapter 11. Many companies also hedge against price increases in key inputs, such as coffee beans for Starbucks or jet fuel for airlines, so don't assume that a change in input prices will immediately have an impact. For example, airlines that didn't hedge their jet fuel costs benefited more than those that did when oil prices plummeted in 2014 and 2015.

When you look at margins for different companies in the same industry, if you find one has a much higher margin, you need to understand why and how it is going to maintain those margins. Unusually high margins attract competition and tend to get pushed down over time to be more in line with the rest of the industry, unless there is something particularly special about that company that protects those margins. In Qualcomm's case discussed in Question #3, it was the high margin licensing business that was responsible for the majority of the company's overall profits, not the semiconductor chip business.

10. Is the Company Financially Healthy?

Up until now, most of the answers to these questions can be found in and around the company's income statement. But we also want to examine its balance sheet. There are a number of line items on a balance sheet, but the ones we are immediately drawn to center on cash and debt positions. If a company doesn't have a decent amount of cash on hand to pay its bills and a cushion for emergencies, that is a big red flag for investors; after all, "Cash is king."

How much cash does it have on its balance sheet? Is the cash position growing? Is it higher than it was in the prior quarter? Is the company's cash position larger than it was a year ago? A shrinking level of cash relative to revenue is always a cause for concern.

The same questions apply to a company's debt level, but we have to introduce some math to determine if the company's business can handle the amount of debt it has. The first thing we look at is its debt ratio. To do so, we use the following:

Total debt-to-capital ratio

$$= \frac{(\text{Short-term debt} + \text{Long-term debt})}{(\text{Short-term debt} + \text{Long-term debt} + \text{Shareholders' equity})}$$

When confronted with formulas like the preceding one, we find it best to use a quick example to remove any math-related fear. After all, it's basically some simple addition and division.

Let's look at consumer product company Procter & Gamble (PG). Perusing the company's balance sheet for the March 2015 quarter, we find it had $15.075 billion in short-term debt, $17.364 billion in long-term debt, and shareholders' equity of $63.38 billion. Let's calculate:

Total debt-to-capital ratio

$$= \frac{(\$15.075 \text{ billion} + \$17.364 \text{ billion})}{(\$15.075 \text{ billion} + \$17.364 \text{ billion} + \$63.38 \text{ billion})}$$

$$\text{Total debt-to-capital ratio} = \frac{\$32.439}{\$95.819}$$

$$\text{Total debt-to-capital ratio} = 33.85\%$$

Generally speaking, the lower the total debt-to-capital ratio, the better. But we have to remember that dynamics differ from industry to industry. That means acceptable total debt-to-capital ratios for a consumer products company will be very different than a defense contractor, which is very different from a young biotechnology company that barely has any revenue. We like to compare a company's total debt-to-capital ratio with those of its competitors and peers, which we identified in the first five questions. If you find one that is substantially higher than the rest, it could be a red flag.

On the other hand, don't be alarmed if you see companies without any debt on their balance sheets. Even after the explosion in debt-fueled corporate share buyback programs that resulted from the low- to no-interest rate environment post-financial crisis, there still were companies that were debt free.

Here are a few things to consider once you've looked at both the cash and debt levels: First, what is the net cash position per share, and how does it compare to the company's stock price? Let's break that down a bit, shall we?

$$\text{Net cash per share} = \frac{(\text{Total cash} - \text{Total debt})}{\text{Shares outstanding}}$$

In its March 2015 quarterly financial statements, Procter & Gamble had $13.16 billion in cash, total debt of $32.439 billion on its balance sheet, and 2.88 billion shares outstanding. Using those figures, at the end of that quarter:

$$\text{PG's net cash per share} = \frac{(\$13.16 \text{ billion} - \$32.439 \text{ billion})}{2.88 \text{ billion}}$$

$$\text{PG's net cash per share} = \frac{-19.279 \text{ billion}}{2.88 \text{ billion}}$$

$$\text{PG's net cash per share} = -\$6.69$$

It's important to point out that if a company has more debt than cash on its balance sheet, and companies like Procter & Gamble and hundreds of others fall into this category, you will see a negative net-cash-per-share figure. All that means is they have more debt than cash.

Depending on the business and its cash generation, higher debt than cash levels could be nothing major or it could be something that could cause you to strike the company from your stock shopping list.

Think of a person who has racked up so much debt—possibly from credit cards—that at the end of each month there is no money left over once the bills are paid, including the interest on all that credit card debt. If this person can't meet those minimum monthly payments—and we've all run into a person or two in our lives who has fallen into this situation—in Wall Street–speak, that person lacks proper debt coverage. That is, after all the monthly expenses (rent, utilities, car payment, and so on) and the interest payment on debt (those credit cards), there are very little funds for anything else, or insufficient funds to pay the interest. It is not a fun place to be at all.

On the other hand, most people who have a mortgage on their home have less cash in their checking accounts than they owe on their mortgage. In this instance the total debt-to-cash ratio isn't necessarily a problem. What you would be interested in is the ability to comfortably make the monthly mortgage payments on top of normal living expenses. It is the same thing with a company and is commonly referred to as the company's ability to service (make the interest payments on) its debt in investor-speak.

When we look at a company's balance sheet, we want to determine how comfortably it can pay all its obligations and how much will be left over to possibly return cash to shareholders and/or reinvest in its future growth. We look at its required interest payments (interest expense on the income statement) relative to the free cash flow from operations. We then look at what is left over from those payments to invest in its business (capital spending, research & development) so it can continue to grow (new products, new markets, geographic expansion, and so on). We like to see that management is cognizant of the need for a cash safety net as well, particularly during more challenging economic times such as the financial crisis that began near the end of 2007 and spanned until early 2010 when, for a period of time, it was almost impossible for companies to borrow any money.

The quick way to determine how easily a company's business can handle its interest payments is to examine what we call its *interest coverage ratio*. It means doing more math, but it's necessary to avoid a company that could fall into trouble down the line.

We determine a company's interest coverage ratio by using some information on its quarterly income statement as follows:

$$\text{Interest coverage ratio} = \frac{\text{Operating profit}}{\text{Interest expense}}$$

The higher the coverage ratio, the more easily a company can handle its interest expense payments—the company has got it covered. As you look at different companies and perform this quick calculation, a good rule of thumb is to steer clear of those companies with an interest coverage ratio of 1.5 or lower because they could be hard pressed to meet interest expense payments if things get a little difficult (economic slowdown or a recession). Should you encounter a company that has an interest coverage ratio near or below 1.0, our recommendation is to avoid it like the iceberg that hit the *Titanic*. In other words, steer clear as fast as possible—there simply are too many other companies out there that offer better prospects.

Let's take another look at Procter & Gamble. In that same March 2015 quarter, the company's operating profit clocked in at $3.45 billion and its interest expense for the period was $149 million, which means it will likely pay nearly $600 million in interest expense for the year (4 × $149 million = $596 million). Applying our interest coverage ratio formula:

$$\text{Interest coverage ratio} = \frac{\$3.45 \text{ billion}}{\$596 \text{ billion}}$$

$$\text{Interest coverage ratio} = 5.78$$

Procter & Gamble has more than sufficient interest expense coverage alone in that particular quarter, given its $3.45 billion in operating profit, which you might have suspected given how we have to replace all of its products, which typically are consumables, every few weeks or every few months.

Another metric related to interest coverage is total receivables. This measures how much the company has sold, but for which it has not yet received payment. If this number is rising faster than revenues, it may mean that the company is having trouble collecting payments from its customers and could be headed for a cash-crunch that would require it to borrow money to plug the gap between sales and receiving payments and/or it may need to write off some of those receivables as uncollectable, which is obviously never a good thing.

As you can see, a company's balance sheet offers a fair amount of insight into the financial health of a company. Don't be scared off because of words like *debt, leverage,* and *coverage,* because at the end of the day all that's required is some pretty basic math. In the Resources section of our website, www.CocktailInvesting.com, you will find a breakdown of key metrics you can use to assess a company's balance sheet as well as its income statement. Although we all like to talk about revenue and earnings per share, the balance sheet is not to be ignored.

11. What's the Catalyst for Growth or Improved Profitability?

One of the more frustrating things we have heard during the last 20-plus years when it comes to looking at stocks is, "It's trading below X times earnings. That's cheap!" Always remember that stocks tend to be cheap for a reason; just like a deal that sounds too good to be true, there's probably a good reason that stock is trading at a price that looks so cheap. Once you know why, it may not look like such a bargain!

Flipping this around, it means you should have a reason for buying a particular stock at a certain time. If not, well, you're pretty much just throwing darts.

Wall Street lingo borrows a term you may remember from your high school chemistry days—the *catalyst.* A catalyst, in simple chemistry terms, is a substance that increases the rate of a chemical reaction.

The same concept holds for investing in stocks as well. In some of the earlier questions, we identified potential catalysts—new products, new product categories, and so on—that are expected to drive top- and bottom-line growth (top line means revenues and bottom line means earnings). Other catalysts include accelerating, if not favorable, economic or psychographic (the *where* and the *how* companies and consumers are spending) data. Here are several examples of catalysts:

- The introduction of Apple's iPhone 6 smartphone models in September 2014 drove big shipment volumes for Apple and boosted the shares from $99 in early September 2014 to just over $129 in late February 2015. Adoption of those newer smartphone models benefited key Apple suppliers like Skyworks Solutions (SWKS), which saw its share price climb to $102 in March 2015 from $55 in September 2014.

- Similarly, the sharp drop in coffee prices that began in 2011 and lasted into early 2014 occurred at a time when Starbucks (SBUX) was rapidly expanding internationally and overhauling, as well as improving, its food offerings. During that time, the company's earnings grew from $0.76 per share in 2011 to $1.33 in 2014, and its share price climbed to a high of $40.73 in late 2013 from $16 in early 2011. Figure 10.2 shows data from the World Bank on changes in coffee prices from October 2005 to October 2015. Keep in mind that Starbucks has a history of hedging against coffee bean prices and coffee accounts for only around 10% of Starbucks overall costs, so be wary of overestimating the impact of a catalyst. In this case, this is a catalyst of limited importance, although the chart alone could lead you to believe otherwise.

- Shares of the Hershey Company (HSY) benefited in 2011, 2012, and 2013 due to the sharp drop in cocoa bean prices, as is shown in Figure 10.3 using data from the International Cocoa Organization.

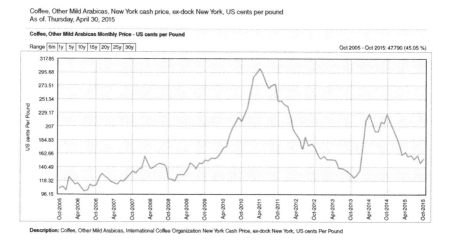

Figure 10.2 Monthly price of coffee (other mild Arabicas) in U.S. cents per pound from October 2005 to October 2015
SOURCE: International Coffee Organization

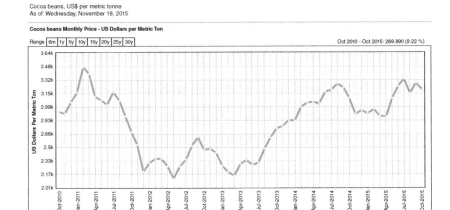

Cocoa beans, US$ per metric tonne
As of: Wednesday, November 18, 2015

Figure 10.3 Monthly price of cocoa beans in U.S. dollars per metric ton from October 2010 to October 2015
SOURCE: International Cocoa Organization

- The growing adoption of streaming video through Netflix (NFLX), Amazon (AMZN) Instant Video, Hulu, and similar services has boosted demand for Internet infrastructure equipment from the likes of Cisco Systems (CSCO).
- The continued shift toward online shopping has done wonders for Amazon shares, but the purchased items still need to get to you or the intended recipient. Beneficiaries of that pickup in shipping have included United Parcel Service (UPS) and FedEx (FDX).
- When oil prices fell in the latter half of 2014 and early 2015, so too did jet fuel prices (as is illustrated in Figure 10.4 with data from the U.S. Energy Information Administration), which are a key cost component for airlines. The Cocktail Investor would take another step deeper and would discover that the fall in prices would not affect all airlines similarly because some, such as United Airlines, Delta, and Southwest, hedge against future increases in fuel prices. Falling prices ended up actually costing these airlines dearly versus a company like American Airlines, which doesn't hedge, thus was able to benefit disproportionately from the decline. For example, hedging was expected to cost Delta Airlines approximately $1.2 billion in 2015.[13]

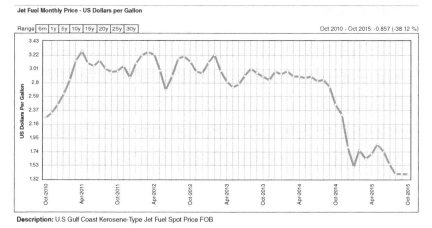

U.S. Gulf Coast Kerosene-Type Jet Fuel Spot Price FOB, US$ per gallon
As of: Monday, November 16, 2015
Source: US Energy Information Administration

Description: U.S Gulf Coast Kerosene-Type Jet Fuel Spot Price FOB

Figure 10.4 U.S. jet fuel spot prices from U.S. Energy Information Administration

As you see in the previous examples, catalysts often have a ripple effect that allows for multiple investment opportunities along the supply chain—for example, Apple's impact on Skyworks, or pain points like the growth in streaming that led to Internet bottlenecks that you probably experienced as sporadic Internet speeds, which drives us all crazy. The obvious catalyst isn't always the one that will generate the greatest returns. While Apple's shares quickly climbed in response to iPhone 6 excitement, Skyworks shares offered an even better return. Why is that? Because with each new version of the iPhone, Apple needed more and more of Skyworks' radio frequency (RF) semiconductors, as did competing smartphones from Samsung, LG, HTC, and others. This meant that for each additional iPhone purchase, Skyworks sold more chips to Apple than in the prior model. This meant that Skyworks' revenue grew faster than smartphone industry shipments. To put it in Wall Street lingo, the company enjoyed rising dollar content per device, which had a multiplier effect on its revenue compared to overall smartphone shipments. Sometimes, it pays to take a step back and look at the bigger picture.

In chemistry, the opposite of a catalyst is something called an *inhibitor*. A formal definition reads something like this: A reaction inhibitor is a substance that decreases the rate of, or prevents, a chemical reaction. To us, an inhibitor is a lot like a headwind that slows down the speed of a plane, while a catalyst is more like a tailwind that pushes the plane along, often resulting in a shorter flight time.

One of the best examples of an inhibitor or a headwind that led to a near-death spiral for one company in particular was the evolution of the smartphone. That explosion, which only grew as Apple and Google (GOOGL) entered the race with their software platforms, transformed the landscape and laid waste to early market share leaders BlackBerry and Palm.

Sometimes a catalyst for some companies can be an inhibitor for others. Take the current bout of falling oil prices. It's good for airlines and likely good for consumers, but not good for oil-producing companies, which had already cut capital spending and announced layoffs due to the initial fall in oil prices. These price drops also were likely to curb demand for alternative energy solutions like solar and wind, which made falling oil prices an inhibitor, or headwind, for companies like First Solar (FSLR), SolarCity (SCTY), and SunPower Corp. (SPWR). The Cocktail Investor again takes a step further and would think about those secondary industries that would be affected by the fall in oil prices, such as those firms that provide equipment used in the discovery and extraction of oil, like Caterpillar, which saw its shares get pummeled as its revenues fell dramatically along with the price of oil and other natural resources.[14]

The bottom line is that even if shares of a company's stock are cheap, if you can't identify a catalyst—or if you uncover an inhibitor—you probably should move along and look at another stock instead.

12. Is Today's Price Right?

This last question is one of the most important and moves us from thinking about the business of the company we're thinking of investing in to the shares.

If you buy shares too late in a cycle, you may be paying too much and will have missed most, if not all, of the upside to be had. While it's a bit trite, the old Wall Street adage of "Buy low, sell high" does ring true—but how do you know what is "low"?

All of this speaks to one of the most important toolkits an investor, either individual or professional, must have. With a variety of valuation tools at your disposal, you can be prepared like Batman confronting one of his various villains: The Dark Knight has to know which tool to grab from his utility belt to thwart whatever mayhem is before him. The same goes for us (granted, we're not facing off against the Joker, Penguin, or Catwoman, but you get the idea).

There is no shortage of valuation tools, and odds are, you're rather familiar with some of the more common ones, like the price-to-earnings (P/E) ratio or dividend yield covered in Chapter 9. However, you might not be familiar with some of the variations. Just as you can exercise with variations of the standard push-up (the basic P/E ratio), we can scrutinize these P/Es on a historical basis, compare them to the industry peers that we identified with Question 6 (peer valuation), and even compare them against multiples for the S&P 500 index (better known as the relative P/E), which tells us relative to the market at large if a stock is priced more richly or at a discount. The same tweaks hold true for using dividend yields.

Of course, not all companies pay dividends, and there are more than a few that do not generate earnings. In situations like these, we turn to other valuation metrics, such as enterprise value (EV) to revenue or EV to earnings before interest, tax, depreciation, and amortization (EBITDA) and price-to-book value. As with P/E ratios and dividend yields, these metrics can be scrutinized on a historical, peer, and relative basis, as well. In the interest of preserving your sanity, we are going to stick to the primary metrics we use to value a company in the upcoming examples. For more on enterprise value (EV) and its associated metrics, please look in the Resource Guide on our website (www.CocktailInvesting.com), where we will give you a quick run through it and other valuation metrics as well as point you toward good resources for those who want to dive deeper.

While not overly difficult, it can be taxing to pull all of the various pieces of information together, but we find doing so really helps us understand the company and how it stacks up against its competitors. As you start to roll up your sleeves and do your homework on both the company and the stock, our recommendation is to build a valuation framework that includes some combination of historical, forward-looking, peer, and relative metrics mentioned above.

We prefer to triangulate the upside by using several valuation tools to home in on a price target. If three metrics zero in on the same price, or thereabouts, we have a lot of confidence in that target. If, however, those tools kick out three different and varying price targets, then we have far less confidence in any one of those figures.

Most investors, we have found, focus on the upside, while too few consider the downside, which is how low the shares can go. We look at that to assess what the net upside (upside less the downside) is likely to be. To get interested in a stock, we generally like to see at least a net upside of 20 percent. That could take the form of up 30 percent with 10 percent downside, up 25 percent with 5 percent downside, or a different permutation. In our experience, this has been a highly beneficial rule of thumb from which we waver only on the rare occasion when there are extraordinary extenuating circumstances.

Case Study: Starbucks Corp.

After falling nearly 14 percent in just a couple of weeks amid the 2015 late summer market pullback, were Starbucks shares priced at an attractive entry point?

While enjoying some benefit due to falling wholesale coffee bean costs, remember that Starbucks hedges its coffee costs so this impact is limited; more importantly, Starbucks began improving its food menu during the prior year and was beginning to pick up the pace of its wine and beer offerings. The company was in the process of adding alcohol sales to 24 locations. Granted, that was a small number compared to Starbucks' total base of stores, but keep in mind that the chain's La Boulange menu rolled out in a rather disciplined fashion as well.

According to a *USA Today* article from the summer of 2015,[15] Starbucks had in the previous months submitted liquor license applications for "several hundred more locations throughout the country," which told us that the company was as serious about adding alcohol as it was when it expanded its food menu in a big way. (If you hadn't noticed, Starbucks now offers a full line of sandwiches, salads, and other items that have taken a bite out of sales at McDonald's.)[16]

Pairing food with coffee, tea, and other beverages was pretty much a no-brainer for the chain. But getting people to see Starbucks as a place to go for alcoholic drinks could be a little more daunting nationally than it was at Washington's Dulles International Airport, one of the initial locations where Starbucks offered adult beverages.

Given the title of this book, naturally we rather enjoy the idea of enjoying a glass beer or wine at Starbucks, but at the time it was not yet clear that the "If You Build It, They Will Come" idea would work in this case. In addition, while there likely would be several common-alities between the company's alcohol initiative and its food-expansion one, both occurred during a period of falling coffee prices, which was ongoing at the time.

During the summer of 2015, Starbucks shares fell from a high of $59 to a bottom of $43 when the Dow Jones Industrial Average opened down 1,000 points on Monday August 24, 2015, before finally closing at $51.09 on August 25. At that price, shares were trading at 27× expected 2016 earnings of $1.87 per share ($51.09/1.87 = 27.3$). That's a bit higher than average multiple of 24.0 for the price lows from 2011 to mid-2015, but a 21 percent discount to the average price-to-earnings multiple of 34.2 at which the shares peaked during the 2011 to 2015 time frame.

So was $51.09 a good price at which to buy shares of Starbucks? The way to answer that is to assess the upside potential versus downside risk at a given price.

Upside Potential versus Downside Risk

In order to determine the potential price range for Starbucks in the next year, we will use three metrics:

1. The range between the highest and lowest P/E ratio over the past five years
2. The range between the highest and lowest dividend yield over the past five years
3. The P/E ratio for the current price versus future EPS compared to the same metric for competitors over the past five years

Price-to-earnings (P/E) and Dividend Yield Ratio Range

Here you'll see just how useful the P/E ratio is when determining a good purchase price for a stock. From 2011 to August 25, 2015, Starbucks shares ranged from a P/E ratio (using the current market price and estimated annual EPS for 2015) of 20.7 to 37.3 as is shown in Figure 10.5. If we multiply the expected earnings per share (EPS) for 2016 of $1.87 by the low end of the minimum P/E ratio (20.7) and by the high of the average P/E ratio (34.2), we get an upside price target of $63.94 (top row under "Implied 2016 Values") and a downside price target of $38.64 (bottom row under "Implied 2016 Values"). In the example we've marked the numbers to which we refer in a larger font.

We use the high end of the average and the low end of the minimum for the range in order to be more conservative. If we underestimate how high the price may go, the biggest risk is that we don't buy the shares and end up missing the opportunity. Not ideal, but that is a better outcome than buying because we've overestimated the potential and ended up losing money. We use the low end of the minimum so that we don't underestimate just how far the price could fall. Putting those two, average upside and maximum downside, together gives a better net upside assessment. Refer to Figure 10.5 as we walk you through the analysis.

The data in Figure 10.5 were compiled by finding the lowest and highest closing price for each year along with the actual earnings-per-share (EPS) estimated for 2015 and dividends paid each year. The P/E ratio was calculated by dividing the low and high share price for each year by each year's EPS. The dividend yield was calculated by dividing the annual dividend for each year by the low and high share price.

This information can be obtained from a variety of sources such as Yahoo! Finance, Google, Schwab, Fidelity, Bloomberg, YCharts, Value Line (available at most libraries or at ValueLine.com), Zacks Investment Research, MarketWatch, Nasdaq.com, Dividend.com, and DivData .com, as well as company annual reports.

When pulling the data together, we suggest double-checking with at least one other source to make sure there isn't an error in the data. Also be aware of the impact of stock splits or reverse stock splits and make sure they have been accounted for correctly such that all data are consistent. This means that, for example, in 2015 Starbucks had a 2-for-1 stock split, so for every one share investors owned, they were given two. To be sure to be comparing years accurately, the stock prices going backward

Starbucks Corp. (SBUX) – Risk-to-Reward Analysis

	Earnings per Share	Closing Share Price High	Closing Share Price Low	P/E Ratio High	P/E Ratio Low	Annual Dividend	Dividend Yield High	Dividend Yield Low	Dividend Growth
2011	$0.76	$23.23	$15.77	30.4	20.7	$0.30	1.29%	1.90%	NA
2012	$0.89	$30.84	$21.58	34.6	24.2	$0.38	1.23%	1.76%	27%
2013	$1.10	$41.00	$26.61	37.3	24.2	$0.46	1.12%	1.73%	21%
2014	$1.34	$41.90	$34.37	31.3	25.7	$0.55	1.31%	1.60%	20%
2015E	$1.58	$59.01	$39.62	37.3	25.0	$0.64	1.08%	1.62%	16%

	P/E Ratio High	P/E Ratio Low		Dividend Yield High	Dividend Yield Low
Average	**34.2**	24.0		**1.24%**	1.75%
Maximum	37.3	25.7		1.31%	**1.90%**
Minimum	30.4	**20.7**		1.12%	1.60%

Implied 2016 Values

	Est EPS	P/E Ratio Derived High	P/E Ratio Derived Low	Estimated Dividend	Dividend Yield Derived High	Dividend Yield Derived Low
Average	$1.87	**$63.94**	$44.81	$0.72	**$57.82**	$41.00
Maximum	$1.87	$69.82	$47.99	$0.72	$54.61	**$37.67**
Minimum	$1.87	$56.92	**$38.64**	$0.72	$63.88	$44.79

SBUX Share Price	Current Price $51.09	Target Price $45.00	Current Price $51.09	Target Price $45.00
Upside from Average High P/E	25.2%	42.1%	13.2%	28.5%
Downside from Minimum Min P/E	−24.4%	−14.1%	−26.3%	−16.3%
Net Upside	**0.8%**	**28.0%**	**−13.1%**	**12.2%**

Note: Share price for 2015 is from Jan 1st to August 25th

Figure 10.5 Starbucks Corp. valuation analysis, 2011–2015

SOURCE: Company reports, Bloomberg, and YCharts. SBUX share prices as of August 25, 2015.

need to have been divided by two, as will the earnings-per-share and dividends-per-share.

When you look at changes in earnings-per-share over time, keep in mind the impact of share-buyback programs, which have become particularly prevalent in recent years. When a company buys back its own shares, it reduces the number of shares outstanding, which can significantly impact earnings-per-share because it is calculated by dividing earnings (net income) by the total number of shares outstanding, as is illustrated in Figure 10.6. Here we see that for the same net income of $100, with 100 shares outstanding, EPS is $1.00 while for 90 shares outstanding EPS is $1.11, which means that a 10 percent reduction in shares outstanding created the appearance of an 11 percent increase in EPS, yet the company's net income remained the same. In other words, despite the favorable optics as a result of shrinking the number of shares outstanding, the company didn't make any more money!

Returning to the Starbucks valuation, look at the numbers under the title "Current" below the "P/E Ratio" heading. At a closing price of $51.09 there would be 25.2 percent in potential upside (using the high end of the average at $63.94) versus potential downside of −24.4 percent (using the low end of the minimum at $38.64), or 0.8 percent net upside. If we also add in the company's current dividend yield of 1.2 percent, it equates to 2 percent net upside over the coming quarters.

But that's using just one valuation metric, and we mentioned earlier you can have much more confidence in your upside and downside price targets if you triangulate them using more than one valuation metric. In this case, let's look at Starbucks' dividend yield. Over the same time frame, Starbucks' share price peaked at a dividend yield of 1.08 percent in 2015, and bottomed out at 1.9 percent in 2011.

Remember that if the stock price rises while the dividend paid remains the same, the dividend yield will fall; a $1 dividend generates a 10 percent yield when the stock price is $10, but only a 6.67 percent when the stock price is $15.

Net Income (Earnings)	$100	
Shares Outstanding	100	90
Earnings per share (EPS)	$1.00	$1.11

Figure 10.6   Share buyback impact on EPS

Although the Starbucks' dividend yield is rather small, at less than 1.5 percent, it has been increasing its dividends every year since it paid its first quarterly dividend of $0.05 per share in 2010, which is meaningful. For the last several years prior to September 2015, it had raised that quarterly payment to $0.16 per share. Dividends increased 27 percent from 2011 to 2012, and rose 21 percent and 20 percent in the following years with a 16 percent increase from 2014 to 2015.

Keep in mind that *dividends can also be indicators of strong growth potential,* which surprises many as conventional wisdom believes that companies that reinvest their earnings are more likely to experience strong growth than those that give some of their earnings back to investors through dividends. Being big fans of data over beliefs, we dug into the data and found a fantastic report[17] by Robert Arnott and Cliff Asness, which we highly recommend as a quick and informative read. Their research will improve your ability to identify those companies and management teams that are most likely to generate superior shareholder value over the long run.

Could we know that Starbucks would increase its dividend in 2016? Not really, but for valuation purposes, as well as the company's shared intention to return capital to shareholders, it would be reasonable to assume a 12 percent dividend increase in 2016 to $0.72 per share. Even if we're too conservative on our 2016 dividend increase, it still looks like net upside of more than 20 percent would exist if the shares dipped closer to $45.

With the P/E ratio we used the high for the average P/E ratio and the low for the minimum to create the price range (34.2 and 20.7 in Figure 10.5). To calculate a price range using the dividend yield we use the high of the average, just like with the P/E ratio, but the low of the maximum dividend yield. This is because the higher the dividend yield for any given dividend, the lower the price. A $1 dividend represents a 1% dividend yield with a $100 stock price, but a 10% dividend with a $10 stock price. Since we want to identify the lowest price possible, we use the highest dividend yield, which in this case would be 10%.

Applying the high for the average and the low for the maximum dividend yields (1.24 percent and 1.90 percent from Figure 10.5) to our forecasted 2016 dividend yield implies potential upside to $57.82, ($1.87 divided by 1.24 percent) and potential downside to roughly

$37.67 ($1.87 divided by 1.90 percent). From a percentage basis versus the August 25 closing price, that is up 13.2 percent and down −26.3 percent, which means when using this metric, the upside is less than the downside.

Let's adjust our question, shifting our perspective in the process, which we find can be rather helpful and tends to uncover items that we have overlooked previously.

Rather than determining if a particular price is a good price, how about calculating at which price we would want to buy the stock?

As we stated earlier, we like to see at least a 20 percent net upside when looking at dividend yield analysis and P/E analysis. At around $45 per share, we have a dividend yield net upside of 12.2 percent and a P/E ratio net upside of around 28 percent. We'd prefer to see a higher net upside on the dividend yield side, but we are comfortable with the P/E ratio side. Given how relatively insignificant the dividend is at less than 2%, we typically wouldn't consider that analysis to be as important. We'll give you more on why as we move through look at Starbucks' peers.

Not only should you look at pricing relative to a company's historical norms, but also relative to its peer group, which ideally consists primarily of competitors that are of similar size and product offering. However, defining a peer group is usually not all that straightforward, even in the case of a Starbucks. We looked at Starbucks against two different types of peer groups; the first was food-and-drink chains (Dunkin' Brands, McDonald's, Panera Bread, Wendy's) while the second we dubbed the "guilty pleasures" group (Altira Group, Las Vegas Sands, Mondelez International, Philip Morris International, the Hershey Company, Wynn Resorts). This investment theme refers to those little treats and would-be harmless vices that we as consumers like or need to have from time to time, even though there may be a form of guilt associated with indulging. Chocolate, beer, wine, spirits, cigarettes, junk and fast food, gambling, and more are typical products from these companies, which tend to have inelastic demand for their products, good cash flow generation, and meaningful dividend income on average. We suggest when defining peer groups for a company you think a bit creatively about just what it is that the company offers its customers, such as the guilty pleasures group.

Refer to Figure 10.7 as we walk you through this comparative valuation analysis.

Starbucks Corp. (SBUX) – Risk-to-Reward Analysis

	Earnings per Share	Closing Share Price High	Closing Share Price Low	P/E Ratio High	P/E Ratio Low	Annual Dividend	Dividend Yield High	Dividend Yield Low	Dividend Growth
2011	$0.76	$23.23	$15.77	30.4	20.7	$0.30	1.29%	1.90%	NA
2012	$0.89	$30.84	$21.58	34.6	24.2	$0.38	1.23%	1.76%	27%
2013	$1.10	$41.00	$26.61	37.3	24.2	$0.46	1.12%	1.73%	21%
2014	$1.34	$41.90	$34.37	31.3	25.7	$0.55	1.31%	1.60%	20%
2015E	$1.58	$59.01	$39.62	37.3	25.0	$0.64	1.08%	1.62%	16%

	P/E Ratio High	P/E Ratio Low		Estimated Dividend	Dividend High	Yield Derived Low	Dividend Growth
Average	34.2	24.0	1.24%	1.75%	$0.72	$57.82	$41.00	12%
Maximum	37.3	25.7	1.31%	1.90%	$0.72	$54.61	$37.67	12%
Minimum	30.4	20.7	1.12%	1.60%	$0.72	$63.88	$44.79	12%

Implied 2016 Values	Est EPS	P/E Ratio Derived High	P/E Ratio Derived Low
Average	$1.87	$63.94	$44.81
Maximum	$1.87	$69.82	$47.99
Minimum	$1.87	$56.92	$38.64

	Current	Target		Current	Target
SBUX Share Price	$51.09	$45.00		$51.09	$45.00
Upside from Average High P/E	25.2%	42%		13.2%	28.5%
Downside from Minimum Min P/E	−24%	−14.1%		−19.8%	−8.9%
Net Upside	0.8%	28.0%		−6.6%	19.6%

Note: Share price for 2015 is from Jan 1st to August 25th

Figure 10.7 Starbucks Corp. comparative valuations

SOURCE: Company reports, Bloomberg and YCharts. SBUX share prices as of August 25, 2015.

There are a couple of trends we want to look at to understand how Starbucks is being priced relative to its peer group over time. The first thing we want to look at is how earnings-per-share (EPS) has evolved. In this example, we look at EPS growth over the five years from 2011 to 2016, with the latter half of 2015 and 2016 being forecasted consensus estimates. Those last three words—*forecasted consensus estimates*—refer to the figures (revenue, profits, earnings) published by Wall Street analysts that are averaged to form a "consensus" view of what a company (in this case Starbucks) will deliver in a particular quarter or year. We've also looked at just the later years, 2013 to 2016, which allows us to look at the long-term trend and compare it to the nearer-term trend.

If we look at the EPS growth trends for Starbucks, we see that the near-term growth is quite consistent with the longer-term growth. That gives us more confidence to predict that same level of growth going forward, based on the findings to the prior 11 questions. Out of the group, Starbucks has had the most stable, positive EPS growth with the exception of Altria, which has enjoyed an average of 8.5 percent growth for the entire period. A negative EPS growth number, as in the case of McDonald's, means that earnings-per-share are actually declining.

Comparing Starbucks EPS to its peer group, we see that not only does the company have the highest (more recent) EPS growth rate, but also it is more consistent than the peer group. We can also see that Panera's earnings have struggled in recent years, with average growth from 2011 to 2016 of 7.6 percent dropping to basically a flat 0.1 percent for the 2013 to 2016 time frame. Looking at Panera's EPS from 2013 to 2016, we confirm that it's been essentially stagnant over that time frame.

Next we will look at the P/E over the years for the peer group and see how Starbucks has been priced relative to the group. To calculate the P/E for 2014, we used the average price for the last quarter of 2013 against the EPS for 2014 and similarly calculated 2015. For 2016, we took the latest price we had, the August 25, 2015, price, against 2016 earnings. Why do that? Because investors pay for future earnings, so the price you pay today is based on what you think the company will earn per share in the future. We don't want any particularly unusual or far out P/Es from the assembled peer group to skew the data, so we averaged the P/E ratios for each peer group.

We then compared the P/E ratios for the peer group to Starbucks and found that with the exception of Wynn Resorts for 2015E, Starbucks has always priced at a premium. This is time for a bit of a gut check. Does this premium make sense? We just discussed that Starbucks' EPS growth was the highest and one of the two most stable, which makes it reasonable that investors would be willing to pay more for each dollar of earnings.

Looking at the trends in the level of premium investors have been willing to pay for Starbucks versus the peer group, we can see that the August 25, 2015, price, which is still above our target buy price of $45, is at the lower end of the historical norm for Starbucks' premium, which tells us that Starbucks is less expensive relative to its peers on this date than it has typically been in the past. This gives us additional comfort that there is decent upside potential in the stock at a price of $45.

Another way we like to look at Starbucks relative to its peers is using P/E relative to EPS growth, or the PEG ratio. This looks at what investors are willing to pay for each dollar of earnings relative to the growth of those earnings. A good rule of thumb is that a PEG ratio of less than 1 indicates stock price is low relative to its earnings growth while a PEG ratio of more than 1 indicates that the stock price may be too expensive relative to earnings. However, PEG ratios vary widely across industries. In this analysis, we used the P/E ratio for the given year, 2014, 2015E, and 2016E against the 2013 to 2016E EPS growth. We used the more current growth rates, as that is more impactful on current stock price. *Investors don't pay today for the growth of the past; they pay for future growth.*

Dunkin' Donuts has experienced a declining PEG ratio, which makes sense with its slowing growth. McDonald's PEG really doesn't give us much help in pricing Starbucks since it is negative, which again makes sense because its earnings keep falling and have been falling at an increasing rate—a really bad sign! Panera Bread is a major outlier that really jumps off the page. What's going on here? Remember the nearly nonexistent growth? Here it is rearing its ugly head. Dividing by 0.1 percent is going to give you a very big—really freaking big—number! This indicates a stock that you usually want to avoid like crazy, as it is wildly overpriced.

Looking across the PEG ratios for the entire peer group, we can see that there is a very wide range that runs from −7.8 to +208. What does that tell us about how Starbucks shares should trade?

Unfortunately, not a darn thing!

Sometimes the analysis doesn't give us much to go on because the companies within a peer group vary just too widely, as is the case here. But that doesn't mean that PEG ratios are pointless—far from it. It just means that in this case, we won't use this metric to assess Starbucks versus its peers. However, we do learn something from looking at Starbucks' PEG ratio. It has fallen over time, which tells us that it is less overpriced today than it has been in the past, although it is still a bit richly priced since the ratio is above 1, but keep in mind that some industries tend to remain well above a PEG of 1 for extended periods of time. Investors always need to do the research for a particular stock and industry. At $45, Starbucks' PEG would be 1.24, getting closer to 1, which is generally viewed as a "fair" price.

Finally, we look at dividend yield, which is the total dividend for the current year divided by the current share price. A quick look across the peer group shows us that here as well, there is a wide range, and, as we shared previously, Starbucks doesn't have a dividend yield that gives investors much to get excited about at 1.3 percent. At our buy target price of $45, the yield increases a bit to 1.4 percent, but is still not a serious income generator for an investor, yet investors are still paying more for Starbucks' earnings that any other company in its peer group, which tells us that investors don't buy Starbucks for its yield. This tells us that like the PEG ratio, comparing Starbucks' dividend yield to its peer group isn't very helpful in determining a good purchase price.

Not all metrics are going to give you an "*Ah-ha!*"

Here we've seen that while a pullback in a stock may be tempting, it may not be a large enough pullback to give you the sufficient risk-to-reward trade-off needed to warrant adding the shares to your portfolio. Keep in mind, though, that *there are no guarantees in investing. We can only deal in probabilities.* This analysis will help you identify a price at which you are more likely to enjoy positive returns over time, but that doesn't mean that the price couldn't drop well below our target price of $45. It doesn't guarantee that the price couldn't drop to a point where the P/E is lower than it has been since 2011, but it does tell us that is highly unlikely. In Chapter 11 we talk about keeping a list of stocks you would like to add to your portfolio, but are waiting for a more attractive price.

This is why it is important to always keep an eye on the markets as a whole. For example, during the financial crisis, stock prices and the related P/E ratios dropped to historically exceptionally low levels in late 2008 and 2009. In hindsight that was a great time to buy following a a painful ride down! That being said, stocks never stay for long at P/E ratios that are well below their historical norms, as over time they tend to reflect future growth prospects, so sit tight and know that time will be your friend.

The bottom line is that after answering all of the 12 questions, it is possible that you will not buy the shares of whichever company you've put all this work into. That's okay, because when you're done, you will have a much better understanding of the company, its business, how it trades, what will move the stock, and at what levels buying it offers a better-than-favorable risk-to-reward trade-off. Always be disciplined, and don't fall in love with a company's shares just because you happen to enjoy the company's product rather immensely. That's another big mistake we've seen investors make—becoming emotional over the shares they own.

By following these 12 questions, you will sleep better at night as you invest. But when do you sell? How far down do you go with a stock that you've purchased whose share price is falling? We will get to that in Chapter 11, where we'll discuss how to maintain your portfolio over time.

Before we move onto funds, we thought we would share some insight from an expert in her field, Emmy Sobieski. Our Cocktail Conversation focused on what she considers key data sources and the various ways she collects, views, and analyzes data.

As of the fall of 2015, Emmy Sobieski was the senior research analyst for Nicholas Investment Partners. Her prior investment experiences include serving as vice president and senior director of Oppenheimer Funds, where she provided research coverage for $6 billion in technology holdings for several of their strategies, including mid-cap and convertibles. She also served as co-manager of the Nicholas-Applegate Global Technology Fund, which was up a whopping 494 percent in 1999!

Lessons from an Expert Technology Sector Analyst

Lenore Hawkins: What do you think are the most important data sources?

Emmy Sobieski: Data can come from almost anywhere. I use Yahoo Finance and Reuters and different professors who are subject matter experts in the area in which I'm searching.

I recommend reading the company's 10-K cover to cover and including all the notes. I particularly focus on what the management team thinks their business is. I also like to look at the risks they've itemized in the 10-K. The risks are put in descending order of importance to the management team. I focus primarily on understanding the first couple of risks listed. After that, they are often the more boilerplate-type that you see in most 10-Ks.

I also like to look at the long-term charts to see where most people have purchased the stock to get an idea of long-term support levels.

LH: What about the mainstream media outlets, like the *Wall Street Journal*, *Financial Times*, or *Barron's*?

ES: If you've done your work on your industry and your company, then things that come out in the *Wall Street Journal*, etc., should not be a surprise to you. This should just be for confirmation.

LH: What do you look at to see where the market is? Is it overvalued? Is it bottoming out like it did in March 2009?

ES: Normally market shifts are about valuations correcting in either direction, but March 2009 was more about the reversal of the need for the banks to mark-to-market on accounting, so that catalyst bottomed the market. I'll keep an eye for changes like that, but in terms of valuations, I look at market cap as a percent of GDP, but I only look at that in terms of extremes, not in terms of direction.

In terms of direction of the market, I look at leadership of the market. What type of industries are leading, those that are viewed as being aggressive or those that are viewed as defensive? If the defensive ones are leading, that tells me people are nervous. I also pay attention to the change in leadership. If utilities were performing well, but all of a sudden energy and technology (which are more aggressive) start performing well, that can tell you where you are in terms of economic cycle and it can also tell you how risk-averse or risk-seeking investors are.

I also look at breadth. Is it just four large-cap stocks leading or is it broad-based, and then again in terms of broad-based industry trends, which ones are strong on a broad-based level versus having a few very large ones pulling the sector performance up?

For instance, if you have the Dow Jones Industrial Average doing really well and the Russell 2000 and NASDAQ doing poorly, that tells you that the aggressive, growth-oriented names aren't doing well and you have poor internals and poor breadth, which means investors are not risk seeking.

Then there is valuation. I look at price-to-sales rather than price-to-earnings because earnings can be so easily manipulated. Sales are also less cyclical than earnings. So I look at price-to-sales a little, but just like with market capitalization as a percent of GDP, I just look to see where we are with respect to the extremes. Are we at the higher or lower end, otherwise, I don't think they are particularly helpful.

LH: You've specialized in technology throughout your career. Where do you look to spot new trends? How can you see the "next big thing" before it hits the headlines? How do you recognize that a particular area within technology is getting too risky or overpriced?

ES: I'm not that tech savvy as a consumer, so when I adopt something it is on the verge of mass appeal. I also look at what the teenagers are doing because they lead all the trends. In 2014, the average megapixel for a front-facing camera on a cell phone, the one that you would use for a selfie, was just over 1 megapixel. The back-facing camera is 15 megapixel, 10 megapixel, 8 megapixel, which is just silly when you think about how popular selfies have become. So when I was a CES, there were a lot of announcements about high-megapixel front-facing cameras from phone manufacturers. So then I looked at what companies would have the most exposure to this but that also doesn't have a lot of other things that would dilute its exposure to this so they can get the biggest bang for the buck. So I found one company that only sells chips for cameras. Increasing the megapixels for the front-facing camera meant they'd be selling more chips per camera.

I also look at what is everyone doing, what do they wish they were doing, and what is the enabling tech. You have your smart watch or your watch with a GPS and you wish it were a smaller watch, or thinner, or you wish it could track certain things, so then I look at companies capable of doing that. Effectively, it is what is the choke point and which company could make the breakthrough.

I think of all these trends and I talk to either people in the industry or analysts or friends and then I go not to investment conferences but to the actual industry conferences. This is a great way to learn about the industry and speak with others in the industry.

LH: What do you think are the most critical metrics to look at when assessing a stock?

ES: There are several:

- Always, always read the 10-K and analyze the stock as if you were buying the entire company.
- Look at Michael Porter's Five Forces[18] for the company.
- Is the management talented? Have they been successful in their previous positions? What's the educational background? Did they attend highly competitive schools? Do they have a track record of being highly competitive, outperforming people?

> • Is the company in a good position within the industry, and is the industry in a good position? You essentially want to be moving with a fast-flowing current, the industry, and then in the fastest boat, the company.

As we were finishing up our delicious steak dinner over a phenomenal bottle of red wine, Emmy commented that throughout her career she has been asked over and over how it is that she's been able to do what she does so successfully. When she tells them, essentially, what we had just discussed, they respond that there is no way that can work because it is too simple. But it has worked for her!

This fits well with our investing rules of thumb: If we can't explain it on a cocktail napkin with a crayon, we have no business being in it. Keep this in mind as we look at funds next.

Individual Stocks versus Funds

Now that we've walked you through what is necessary to successfully select stocks for your portfolio and identify target prices at which you will be comfortable buying them, you might be feeling a bit overwhelmed by the amount of time required. We understand! That's why for most people it makes sense to have a combination of stocks and funds, given the realities of our busy lives and just how few hours there are in the day.

The process for selecting a fund versus a company will be the same as for stocks up to the point where you pick an individual company. Rather than picking a company, you'll look for a fund that invests in the area in which you are interested, which is getting easier over the years as more and more specialized, highly focused funds are appearing. We've already discussed the difference between a mutual fund and an exchange-traded fund (ETF) in Chapter 9.

When assessing a fund, investors should immediately look at the following:

- *Inception date:* If the fund doesn't have much of a track record, it is difficult to understand how it will perform under different market conditions, unless the fund manager has a track record under a different fund that followed the same strategy as the one you are evaluating. Rule of thumb is that if it is less than three years old, wait for it to age a bit. If it is under five years, be careful of putting more than 3 percent of your portfolio into it. The exception is an index fund, as you can look up the performance of the index rather than the fund. In this case, just verify the stability of the company offering the fund.
- *Assets under management (AUM):* Our rule of thumb is that a fund with AUM under $100 million is a red flag, unless of course the fund is new. In that case, what we said regarding the inception date applies. Also be careful of exceptionally large funds, as an enormous size can hinder performance. If, for example, the strategy is an active one that requires finding mispriced small-cap companies, that is possible with $200 million, but it gets much more challenging when the fund has to put $2 billion to work! Make sure the fund isn't too big to be able to execute on its own strategy. For a passive index fund, having a large number of assets under management does not impact performance.
- *Exchange-traded fund (ETF):* For this type of fund, you'll want to look at the average daily trading volume, just to get an idea of how much it trades. The liquidity, which is really all about the ability to get out of it quickly and easily, as well as the difference between the price the seller wants and what the buyer is willing to pay, is better the more the shares trade. For an ETF, the liquidity is really about the liquidity of the underlying securities, so an ETF that holds a bunch of rarely traded bonds is going to be highly illiquid and should be avoided, unless you are very confident that you understand the risks. In general, the average number of shares traded multiplied by the ETF's share price should be at least $20 million (this number is referred to as the average dollar volume).

- *Expense ratio:* This is what the fund manager charges for managing the fund. The higher the expense ratio, the greater the fee. You'll want to make sure that the level of fees is in line with that type of fund. Index funds should have the lowest fees, because they cost relatively little to run. For example, you can easily find an S&P 500 index fund with an expense ratio of less than 0.2 percent. For mutual funds that invest in large U.S. companies, look for an expense ratio of no more than 1 percent. For funds that invest in small or international companies, which typically require more research, look for an expense ratio of no more than 1.25 percent.

- *Fees:* These only apply to mutual funds, and although sales of these types are on the decline, there are still funds with "front-end" loads as well as "back-end" loads, typically referred to as redemption fees. These fees are mostly designed to stop traders from moving in and out of the fund attempting to make a quick speculation profit. They often decline over time and may go to zero after a few months or years. If the fund you are contemplating has such fees, look around to see if you might be able to avoid them by buying through a company such as Charles Schwab. There are also 12-b1 fees that you may need to pay if you purchase your mutual fund through a retail broker. These can be around 0.25 percent and are a recurring annual fee. We don't think there is any compelling reason to ever buy a fund through a broker when you can simply pick up the phone and call Schwab or Fidelity or go online with them and do it for free.

- *Minimum investment:* This only applies to mutual funds. ETFs trade like a stock, which means you can buy just one share of the ETF. Before you proceed any further, verify that the minimum investment is at or below the minimum amount you are considering investing. Also note that many funds have a different minimum for IRAs than for after-tax brokerage accounts.

Those items should help you quickly eliminate inappropriate funds so that you waste as little time on them as possible. Now we'll dive a bit deeper into how the fund's strategy should relate to various metrics.

The first thing you need to do with those funds that have made the cut so far is read all material on the fund provided by the fund manager, which can typically be found online. For example, to research the ETF with ticker symbol HACK, just type ETF HACK into your search engine and you'll see the website for the fund. Read the Fact Sheet, Prospectus, and Statement of Additional Information, as well as the most recent annual and quarterly or monthly, if available, reports. You should also search online for ETF rankings as well as other people's reviews on the fund to help you develop your own opinion. Like everything else in life, be judiciously skeptical of what you read and consider the source, but the Internet does provide a wealth of information at your fingertips that should not be ignored.

Strategy and Management. Make sure you understand the fund's strategy and that it truly fits with what you are trying to accomplish. If you are looking at an actively managed fund, look at who is running it and how long they've been doing it. Make sure you are comfortable with the experience and background of those running the fund and with their track record, which may be reflected in other funds they managed previously. Understand how much of the fund's performance is attributable to the current management. You don't want to get excited about a fund with a great track record if the current management team has only been in place for three months! Look over the performance of the fund relative to the markets as a whole and within the particular sector. Understand how the fund in the past performed during particularly challenging times (downside risk) and during strongly favorable market conditions (upside potential).

For example, Lenore had a colleague come to her all excited about a fund with phenomenal annual returns, or at least phenomenal at first glance. She quickly glanced at the fund's strategy and saw it focused on biotechnology companies. She immediately pulled up the iShares Nasdaq biotechnology exchange traded fund (IBB), which tracks the investment results of an index composed of biotechnology and pharmaceutical equities listed on the NASDAQ and saw that the fund that had so excited her colleague had generated roughly the same returns as this passively managed exchange-traded fund, but charged much higher fees. We can't stress enough to always assess the performance of a fund, or a stock for that matter, on a relative basis.

Number of Fund Holdings. Most mutual funds may hold 60, 70, or more positions in different equities or bonds. Some funds may have over 100 different holdings, but here's the problem with funds that hold a lot of securities. For example, if you were to create a portfolio, made exclusively of 50 randomly chosen stocks out of the S&P 500, statistics tell us that the returns on that portfolio would, over time, track the S&P 500 within a very close range of typically 3 to 5 percent. This means that for a fund manager to outperform an index like the S&P 500, or a particular benchmark, she or he either must hold fewer positions or be radically overweight in a few particular stocks or in a sector, like the financials or technology. Investors need to look at a particular fund and then at its sector weightings. If the fund has more than 50 holdings and its sector weights are very close to those in the index it measures itself against, such as a small-cap fund compared to the Russell 2000 index, then this fund is unlikely to outperform a simple index. A fund that looks like this is basically mimicking the very index it is trying to beat. While we like funds for the diversification they provide, there can be too much of a good thing.

Top Ten Holdings. Understand just how concentrated the fund is. Do the top 10 holdings account for 40 percent or 10 percent of all assets? Does one particular holding have a relatively significant ownership position in the fund? For example, in November 2015, Amazon shares accounted for 10.8 percent of the assets in the Consumer Discretionary Select Sector SPDR Fund (XLY) even though that fund held 90 positons at the time.[19] When we see situations in which individual stocks each account for more than 5 percent of a fund's assets, we tend to keep close tabs on them because more often than not, they drive the direction—good or bad—of the fund. Keep in mind that very specific funds, such as Pure Funds Cyber Security ETF (HACK), will have a much higher concentration than a fund that seeks to cover a broad spectrum. Understand the major holdings for the fund and make sure they sync with your reasons for wanting to own the fund.

Turnover. A fund's turnover rate, meaning the rate at which it buys and then sells holdings, needs to be consistent with its strategy. Many actively managed funds turn over 80 percent, 100 percent, or even more of the portfolios annually. This makes for a lot more short-term gains than occur in index funds, which increases costs and also increases costs through trading fees, all of which lower your potential returns.

Cash on Hand. Funds have to keep some portion of the fund assets in cash for normal course of business redemptions or for buying opportunities as market dips inevitably occur. The cash amount typically ranges from as low as 3 percent to as high as 7 or even 10 percent. This is dead money, earning no return. So for every $100 invested, at any given time, maybe only $95 is working for you. If a fund has a notably large level of cash, make sure you know why, and that the reason makes sense to you. For example, if the fund is actively managed, versus a passive index, and the manager thinks that it is going to have much better buying opportunities in the coming months, a higher balance would make sense. During a serious bear market (defined as a downturn of 20% or more across several broad market indices, like the S&P 500 and the Dow Jones Industrial Average, over at least a two-month period), it isn't uncommon for actively managed funds to have unusually high cash balances relative to normal market conditions, but make sure you understand what the level of cash is for the fund and why.

Performance. Finally, compare the fund versus the fund manager's stated benchmark, or in the case of a passively managed fund, its underlying index. These should be spelled out in the fund's prospectus. You should also compare its performance over the longer term with an appropriate market index to understand its relative performance. For example, you would want to compare the Pure Funds Cyber Security ETF to the NASDAQ, given it is a technology-based fund. Look over the fund's past performance and decide if you can stomach its level of volatility.

Cocktail Investing Bottom Line

Investing in an individual stock requires a greater time commitment than a fund. If you cannot put in the time, we recommend focusing on funds. Thankfully, today there are all kinds of highly focused funds that can let you invest in a particular thematic while minimizing stock-specific risks. Funds may also be a better choice in an emerging technology sector, where it is extremely difficult for anyone who is not an expert in that particular field to determine which companies are more likely to succeed. Given the realities of our busy lives, most investors will be best served with a portfolio made up of both stocks and funds.

- While it may be tempting to buy a "hot" stock on a tip from a friend or because you heard it on TV, you need to understand the company and its business before considering buying its shares.
- Our 12 questions provide a framework for not only understanding a company and its business but also helping you uncover the key drivers of the business and the competitive landscape, as well as its opportunities and risks.
- Financial filings, press releases, annual reports, and other sources of industry or company "intelligence" are your friend. The more you familiarize yourself with them, and the math used to understand their meaning, the more comfortable you will become.
- Even after using the first 11 questions to scrutinize a company, you still need to determine if there is sufficient net upside from the current share price to warrant buying the shares.
- There is no "silver bullet" or one "golden calculation," and we prefer to use a series of valuation tools to determine the potential upside as well as the downside risk to focus in on our net upside requirement of at least 20 percent.

Endnotes

1. Shara Tipken, "Apple's iPhone Sales, Weak Forecast Rock Investor Confidence," cNet (July 21, 2015), www.cnet.com/news/apples-iphone-sales-weak-forecast-rock-investor-confidence/.

2. Ibid.

3. "Apple Inc. Q3 2015 Unaudited Summary Data," images.apple.com/pr/pdf/q3fy15datasum_2.pdf.

4. Qualcomm Inc. Annual Report, www.sec.gov/Archives/edgar/data/804328/000123445215000271/qcom10-k2015.htm#s213a4ff9ed694807b300585555 ba7870.

5. Ibid.

6. Matt Egan, "Apple's iPhone Suppliers Are Getting Crushed," CNN Money (July 22, 2015), money.cnn.com/2015/07/22/investing/apple-iphone-supplier-stocks/.

7. Paul Ziobro and Marie Ng, "Walmart Rachets Up Pressure on Suppliers to Cut Prices," *Wall Street Journal* (March 31, 2015), www.wsj.com/articles/walmart-ratchets-up-pressure-on-suppliers-to-cut-prices-1427845404?alg=y.

8. "Iron ore," en.wikipedia.org/wiki/Iron_ore.

9. Sarmistha Acharya, "Samsung Leads Global Smartphone Market with Strong Sales in Third Quarter," *International Business Times* (November 22, 2015), www.ibtimes.co.uk/samsung-continues-lead-global-smartphone-market-highest-sales-third-quarter-1529905.

10. Securities and Exchange Commission, "Forms 3, 4, 5," www.sec.gov/answers/form345.htm.

11. Noam Noked, "Rule 10b5-1 Plans: What You Need to Know," *Harvard Law School Forum on Corporate Governance and Financial Regulation* (February 5, 2013), corpgov.law.harvard.edu/2013/02/05/rule-10b5-1-plans-what-you-need-to-know/.

12. "Apple Inc. Q3 2015 Unaudited Summary Data."

13. N. B., "Gambles that Haven't Paid Off," *The Economist* (January 19, 2015), www.economist.com/blogs/gulliver/2015/01/fuel-hedging-and-airlines.

14. Zack's Equity Research, "Caterpillar October Sales Drop of 16% Worst in 5 Years," Zacks (November 20, 2015), www.zacks.com/stock/news/198695/caterpillars-october-sales-drop-of-16-worst-in-5-years.

15. Aadmar Madhani, "'Evenings' at Starbucks: Coffee Shop to Sell Wine, Craft Beer, Small Plates," *USA Today* (August 18, 2015), www.usatoday.com/story/money/2015/08/14/evenings-starbucks-coffee-shop-sell-wine-craft-beer-small-plates/31713183/.

16. Brad Tuttle, "Triumph of Starbucks & Fast Casual over McDonald's and Fast Food," *Money* (January 23, 2015), time.com/money/3680474/starbucks-fast-casual-mcdonalds-fast-food/.

17. Robert D. Arnott and Clifford S. Asness, "Surprise! Higher Dividends = Higher Earnings Growth," Copyright 2003, CFA Institute. Reproduced and republished from *Financial Analysts Journal* with permission from CFA Institue. All rights reserved. www.researchaffiliates.com/Production%20content%20library/FAJ_Jan_Feb_2003_Surprise_Higher_Dividends_Higher_Earnings_Growth.pdf.

18. "Porter's Five Forces," Quick MBA, www.quickmba.com/strategy/porter.shtml.

19. "Consumer Directory Select Sector SPDR Fund," www.etfchannel.com/symbol/xly/.

Chapter 11

Building the Portfolio

The signal is the truth. The noise is what distracts us from the truth.
— Nate Silver

We cannot solve our problems with the same level of thinking that created them.
— Albert Einstein

The key to investing is not assessing how much an industry is going to affect society, or how much it will grow, but rather determining the competitive advantage of any given company and, above all, the durability of that advantage.
— Warren Buffett

C ongrats! After working your way through the preceding chapters and building your set of answers to the 12 questions we shared with you in Chapter 10, you've successfully assembled your target investment portfolio. It's not easy, and odds are, it took more work and time than you thought it would. Let's remember, however, that if it was easy, then everyone would do it, and we all know that simply isn't the case.

While you let out a sigh of relief, we're reminded of what former Intel CEO Andy Grove once said, "Only the paranoid survive." Now we admit that's a bit harsh, but the gist of what Grove was getting at is now you need to be on guard for mishaps, shortfalls, and other things that can derail the reasons why you added a company's stock to your holdings in the first place.

This gets us back to one of the key points we made early on in our conversations with Bob, Sophia, Reilly, and Tyler—investing is *not* a snapshot in time. It's not cooking in a crockpot that you can "fix and forget" for a prolonged period of time. If you invested in the S&P 500 on January 2, 1998, then took a long Rip van Winkle-esque nap and woke up on July 29, 2009, you'd find the S&P 500 was pretty much exactly where it was when you went to sleep.

It's that kind of "falling asleep at the switch" that undoes all the hard work that Reilly and Tyler did in building their portfolio and sabotages your investment returns. If you fall into that trap, the same could happen to you, and we don't want that for you.

As we mentioned to Bob, Sophia, Tyler, and Reilly before, investing is much like exercise—you may be out of shape at first, but as you read up on companies, their industries, and dig into new products and technologies, before too long your ability to piece together the investing puzzle will get stronger. To build your investing muscles you need to work at it, and while we'd all like to exercise regularly, we know there are times when life can get the best of us. The good news is that you have the Cocktail Investing tools to get back on the investing workout plan, but be wary of any Rip van Winkle-type naps, short or long.

While the investing markets and the economy aren't always aligned, as we discussed in Chapter 3, you will need to keep an eye on what is happening in both the domestic and the global economy, as we discussed in Chapter 4. Between January 1998 and July 2009 (that 11-year period during which the S&P 500 generated nonexistent returns) we had two recessions, including the Great Recession. The economy is very much a living thing that can be strong, can stumble, and can even catch a cold and contract. Generally speaking, as the economy strengthens, companies make more money, they expand, jobs are created, wages improve, and consumers spend more. As the economy slows, which is also a natural part of the business cycle, companies and consumers may slow their

spending, but in a recession corporations tend to cut back more dramatically and shed jobs, while consumers slash their spending. Having
an accurate read on the economy is key to being a successful investor.
That's why we spend so much time tracking economic data points from
a variety of sources.

You'll want to make sure you are aware of changes in the political
world, namely with regulations, legislation, and taxation, that can affect
your investments, as we discussed in Chapter 5. A change in the tax code
could affect a particular type of company in which you are invested, or
perhaps changes to the treatment of mutual funds could make those more
or less advantageous. Regulations that affect what a company can sell,
to whom it can sell, where it can buy raw materials, or what it has to
pay employees, such as changes to minimum wage law or benefits like
the Affordable Care Act, may change the fundamentals for a company
in which you've invested. There's also the regulatory mandate that pulls
forward demand, only to watch it crash once the mandate date has been
passed. We've seen this time and again in the auto and truck industry,
particularly with regard to engine emissions.

In Chapter 6, we talked about disruptive technologies that can
create new opportunities for companies—think of Apple and the
game-changing iPhone that completely changed Apple's business—or
challenges for others. That same iPhone helped destroy not only the
pre-smartphone mobile phone business but also early smartphone
entrants BlackBerry and Palm. One day, something new will likely
come along that will do to the iPhone what it did to the BlackBerry.
Just one example among many that can be found at the intersection of
computing power, increasingly fast broadband speeds, and the Internet.

On that January 2, 1998, that we mentioned a few paragraphs above,
there was no such thing as Facebook, Netflix, and smartphones let
alone tablets, voice interfaces, mobile payments, and the "appification"
of things from software to TV. By 2015 we had the "podification" of
coffee and at-home soda systems like SodaStream, as well as a new
detergent pod delivery system developed by Procter & Gamble. Each of
these examples has altered the competitive playing field. If we don't pay
attention to industry and company innovations and developments, we
run the risk of staying with a company that could see its competitive
advantage become a disadvantage, like BlackBerry did with its keyboard,

or Hewlett Packard and its PC market share that totally missed the mobile revolution with smartphones and tablets. Something similar can be said for Microsoft and the desktop computer. You get the idea.

Are pain points like the ones we identified in Chapter 7 easing up, or are they getting worse? Has there been any slowdown in the frequency of cyberattacks and identity theft? Did a company or group of companies bring a new super-duper solution to market that outsmarted the hacking culture? Has there been a sustained change in the California drought situation that started back in January 2013? Has a new technology or product been developed that can more efficiently desalinize ocean water to help alleviate the water problem? Has consumer preference shifted away from bottled water because of higher prices? Depending on the answers to those questions that tie to Chapter 7 or to other pain points you've identified, a change could be in the making. We'd note that pain points tend to cry out for a solution—sometimes they happen and sometimes they don't. If they do, you want to know what they are and what they mean to your investments.

Finally, when you decided to purchase a particular stock, you did so because you had identified a thematic trend that you wanted to take advantage of, then decided that the company was fundamentally strong and the stock price was at a point where the potential risk versus reward was at a level with which you were comfortable. If you are unsure of what we just said, you may want to reread Chapters 8, 9, and 10. We know it took Bob more than one read to get comfortable with what we were talking about and to understand that when thought through carefully, investing was far different from gambling.

Now this brings us full circle to the first page of this chapter—you've bought the stock, and you need to monitor all those factors uncovered in answering the 12 questions and ones like them that we raised in Chapter 10 to make sure you still want to own it, and to know when you need to sell it.

We've broken it down into three categories to monitor:

1. The thematic trend
2. The company and its business
3. The stock and its share price

Monitoring the Trend

In Chapter 8, we corralled and assembled a smorgasbord of economic, demographic, and psychographic data alongside developing technologies and regulatory mandates to formulate our thematic trends. The beauty of doing all this up-front work is you've already identified the key pieces of data and other critical items to monitor. You've also uncovered the sources for those information nuggets, and hopefully the frequency in which they are reported.

That takes a lot of the bite out of monitoring the trend, but not all of it. Aside from formal data, we also keep our eyes open for news stories, like those you may find in a variety of magazines and newspapers like *Bloomberg BusinessWeek, Economist, Wired, Fast Company, Successful Farming, Time, Money, Scientific American, Popular Science, Wall Street Journal, New York Times,* and *Investor's Business Daily.* Increasingly, there are more and more resources online, like TechCrunch, MentalFloss, DroughtMonitor, and dozens of others.

You may be tempted to drop them all into your browser bookmarks, but we'd recommend using an aggregator service like Feedly and an online storage and clipping service, like Evernote, which saves and categorizes articles and other news items for later use. These services will cost you a little bit, but from a time management and information flow perspective, we find them very worthwhile.

One other important trend tracker source comes from the companies themselves. At industry events and conferences, a key member of a company's management team may make a presentation that is filled with data that we can use to monitor a thematic trend or two. We had two such great examples that pertain to the Connected Society in September 2015.

At Apple's annual new product reveal event in September 2015, ahead of introducing the all-new Apple TV, CEO Tim Cook shared the following—"We believe the future of TV is apps." Not surprising, given the moves by Netflix, HBO, Hulu, and others to offer apps that allow customers to stream video programming on almost any connected device. Thanks to its leading position in global video streaming across multiple categories, combined with the ubiquitous iPhone and iPad (according to Adobe Digital Index[1]), Apple has some unique perspectives on the direction of video consumption and viewer habits.

A few days after Apple's presentation, Lowell McAdam, the chairman and CEO of Verizon Communications, announced at an investment conference that "40 percent of Millennials do not and have never had a TV in their home and another 20 percent have said they have got it, but they don't use it that much and they are considering cutting it. But what you see in the data volumes of our networks, which have experienced 20× growth, is they are watching it over mobile and they are watching it in digital media versus broadcast kind of media."[2]

On the one hand, these nuggets confirm the slow death of the broadcast industry at the hands of the connected society, which is not all that different than what happened to the newspaper industry, as we discussed in Chapter 7, when it ran headlong into the Internet. On the other hand, it shows the insights we can gather by listening to company or subject-matter-expert presentations. Sometimes you may walk away with a bag full of nuggets, sometimes just a few, but in our view, they are worth it.

In monitoring a thematic trend, you want to be mindful if it's accelerating, running at a pretty steady state, cooling off, or starting to fade. Some of this can be determined from the data you're tracking, but another useful trick is to keep tabs on how often it's being mentioned across the various media outlets, from other companies (as well as its customers and suppliers), among your friends, colleagues, and co-workers, and in some cases our daily language.

For example, somewhere between 2009 and 2010, the "selfie" explosion started, and by the end of 2012, *Time* magazine considered *selfie* one of the "top 10 buzzwords" of that year; although selfies had existed long before, it was in 2012 that the term "really hit the big time." That was huge for Facebook, Instagram, and other social media and photo-sharing platforms. Today, the word *selfie* is pervasive as is the act of sharing it. Think of the impact that had on mobile phones, the primary tool for the selfie, and the need for high-resolution cameras for both the front- and back-facing cameras.

If your monitoring shows the thematic trend is accelerating, generally speaking, that is a good sign. If it's tracking or hitting a bump in the road, we'd say that's good to normal, but be sure to check the long-term opportunity to make sure the thematic tailwind remains intact. If, however, signs are pointing to a pronounced slowdown in a thematic trend or signal that it may be becoming a headwind, it could be time to consider alternative investments in a different theme, assuming there are well-positioned companies that meet the net upside requirements we discussed in Chapter 10.

That offers us a nice transition to …

Monitoring the Company

Much like monitoring a thematic tailwind, the work in Chapter 10 helped you uncover most, if not all, of the key levers that drive a company's business, from key industry data points to understanding which business units or products really drive a company's overall revenue and profit stream to what are the key ingredients or cost drivers. Just like with monitoring the trend, monitoring the company means maintenance reading, which consists of reading company and competitor, and even key supplier, press releases, financial filings, and presentations that can be found on the Investor Relations section of corporate websites; industry reports; overviews (those nuggets can be very insightful!); and trade magazines and various other publications that touch on a company and its business. These are the usual suspects we outlined earlier in the chapter as well as the growing list of online media.

Don't forget those organizations that track industry data as well as forecast what they expect to happen in the coming quarters and the next few years. For example, when examining shares of firearms manufacturer Smith & Wesson (SWHC), you would be taking a hard look at firearm background check data published by the Federal Bureau of Investigation monthly. Are background checks accelerating compared to the last few months? Is the number of checks up year-over-year or not? If so, for how many months? And so on.

If we wanted to monitor how rail companies were doing, we'd look to the weekly railcar loading data published by the American Association of Railroads. To get a bead on heavy truck demand, we'd be keeping tabs on the manufacturing economy through monthly industrial production figures published by the Federal Reserve, truck tonnage data published by the American Trucking Associations, and industry order, production, and backlog data that is collected and published by ACT Research.

If you were drilling down on apparel companies, you should be checking on cotton prices and the condition of the cotton crop, which is published by the National Cotton Council of America and other organizations.

All that may sound like a lot, but once you know where to look, if you just jot down what you need to track and where to look it up, much of this can be something you do quickly and efficiently over your morning coffee or on the subway or bus during your morning commute.

Pretty much each industry and company has recurring metrics that will clue you into the tone of the business as well as its vector and velocity. This also means watching for new developments—remember, in many ways a company is like a shark that needs to swim in order to force water over its gills so it can survive. A company that rests on its laurels could fall victim to the changing landscape around it because of economic, demographic, technology, or regulatory shifts and changes. In conducting your ongoing company monitoring, here are a few questions that you should be asking; this is by no means a complete list, but more of a starter kit. As you dig deeper into the inner workings of a company, its supply chain, and competitive landscape you'll find yourself adding to these:

Has the company introduced new products and services? Is it leading the pack and breaking new ground with a new technology, or is it following behind a competitor and responding with a "me-too" product or service? Will this new product help improve the company's profitability?

As we've noted more than few times in this book, Apple has been an innovator with its iProducts (iTunes, iPod, iPhone, iPad) that have fostered much creative destruction across several industries, but these products have forced product responses from the company's smartphone competitors, like Samsung, LG, HTC, Motorola, and others. Another example is Tesla Motors, which sent Ford, General Motors, Honda, and other automotive manufacturers back to the drawing board after its Tesla Roadster and then its Model S, a fully electric luxury sedan, were hits with consumers.

Have any of a company's key suppliers developed a new technology that can be incorporated into an existing product or help the customer company bring a new one to market?

There are all sorts of examples one can think of, but again, perhaps the most recognizable is the iPhone, which thanks to the Apple supplier base introduced all sorts of breakthroughs when it announced its various iProducts. Think about how Apply Pay can impact the way consumers shop and interact with businesses.

Has the company altered its product or service portfolio in any way? Does this open up a new demographic or target audience that has never used the company's products or services before?

Seeing the growing demand for apartments by Millennials and other Cash Strapped Consumers rather than single-family homes at a time when vacancy rates were falling, traditional high-end single-family homebuilder Toll Brothers (TOL) moved into this market in 2014.

Has a competitor decided to target market share gains and introduced disruptive pricing at the expense of margins and profits in the short to medium term to succeed?

While this can be disruptive in the short-term, world-class companies with strong brands that offer products and services that consumers and other companies want tend to weather such storms. In the short run, competitor moves like this can pressure margins and profits in the short term and potentially decrease revenue if your company needs to respond.

We've seen such disruptive pricing from the likes of T-Mobile USA and Sprint, both of which have been aggressively trying to win wireless consumers from AT&T and Verizon Communications.[3]

Case Study: Starbucks Corp.

Have changes in input costs resulted in the company having to boost prices for its products and services, or have input costs fallen, which could help boost a company's profits and earnings?

In Chapter 10, we put Starbucks through the valuation wringer. We know Starbucks has been a coffee company, but increasingly it is becoming a coffee, tea, and food company. Key ingredients therefore

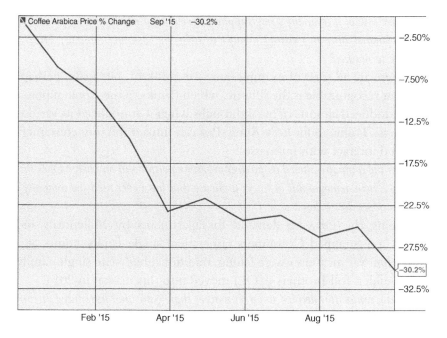

Figure 11.1 Percentage change in Arabica coffee bean prices, December 2014–September 2015
SOURCE: YCharts

include primarily coffee (Figure 11.1), but also milk (Figure 11.2), wheat (Figure 11.3), and cocoa (Figure 11.4). In the company's 10-K filing for its fiscal year ending September 2015 with the Securities and Exchange Commission, which you can find at www.sec.gov, we find that Starbucks purchases, roasts, and sells high-quality whole-bean Arabica coffee beans and related coffee products. So let's look at the price of Arabica beans.

Looking across the charts of these commodities, the prices of coffee, milk, and wheat have fallen over the past year, with both coffee and milk down over 30 percent while cocoa prices actually trended up over the year. An investor in Starbucks would need to know how changes in the prices of these commodities could affect Starbucks margins. A great way to understand what is most impactful to the company is to look at the "Risk Factors" section in the company's 10-K.

In the company's 2015 10-K, one of the main risks itemized is "Increases in the cost of high-quality Arabica coffee beans or other commodities or decreases in the availability of high-quality Arabica

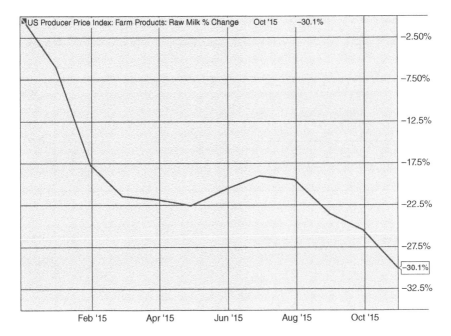

Figure 11.2 Percentage change in U.S. Producer Price Index: Raw milk, December 2014–October 2015
SOURCE: YCharts

coffee beans or other commodities could have an adverse impact on our business and financial results." The 10-K also tells us, "We also purchase significant amounts of dairy products, particularly fluid milk … "

The 10-K goes on to say, "Because of the significance of coffee beans to our operations, combined with our ability to only partially mitigate future price risk through purchasing practices and hedging activities, increases in the cost of high-quality coffee beans could have an adverse impact on our profitability." This tells us that changes in the spot price of coffee will impact the company's bottom line more than if it were to lock in purchase prices for Arabica beans well in advance.

Earlier in this chapter, we saw that coffee and milk prices had fallen over 30 percent during the prior year. If we take a further step back with coffee, we can see that by September 2015, prices had fallen about 37 percent over the prior 5 years. Milk prices, by comparison, had fallen about 9 percent over the prior 5 years, ending in October 2015. Looking

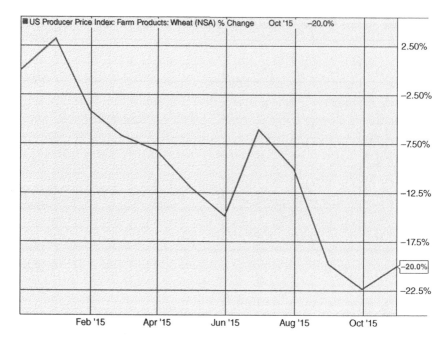

Figure 11.3   Percentage change in U.S. Producer Price Index: Wheat, November 2014–October 2015
SOURCE: YCharts

at past performance, we would expect to see Starbucks' margins benefit from these falling prices and would want to confirm that was the case. If not, further investigation would be in order to determine why that was the case.

Looking forward, we would want to look at research reports concerning where the price of coffee in particular is expected to go. Prices would be affected by weather patterns and any changes in crop plantings. Falling prices could very well mean that many farmers, over the years, would have chosen to switch from coffee to some other type of crop. Over time, this would mean a decrease in the available supply, which would then push prices up, which would hurt Starbucks' margins if they were not able to then raise prices sufficiently to cover the higher costs. This is the kind of thought process Cocktail Investing is all about.

Have there been any regulatory mandates or other changes that will impact a company's costs structure?

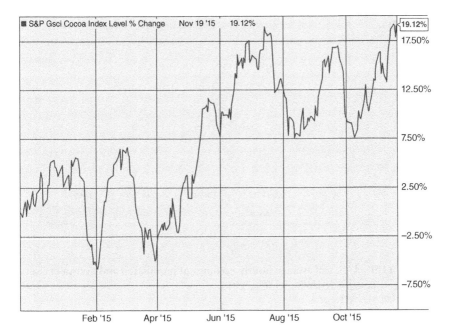

Figure 11.4 Percentage change in GSCI Cocoa Index: November 2014–November 2015
SOURCE: YCharts

Starbucks also mentions in its 10-K that its financial conditions might be adversely affected by "increases in labor costs such as increased health care costs, general market and minimum wage levels and workers' compensation insurance costs." If we look at just wage costs for the majority of Starbucks employees, the lifesaving baristas, we can see that labor costs have been steadily moving up over the five years from 2010 through 2015. See Figure 11.5.

But what about any larger future changes? As of September 2015, the federal minimum wage stood at $7.25 per hour; however, there were a growing number of states boosting their minimum wage in increments, with some like New York City and Seattle and the California cities of Oakland, Los Angeles, San Francisco, and Berkeley approving phased-in increases that would eventually take their minimum wage to $15 an hour.

To understand the impact of these changes, we looked at the city of Seattle because in June 2014, the Seattle city council passed a $15 minimum wage law to be phased in over time, with the first increase to

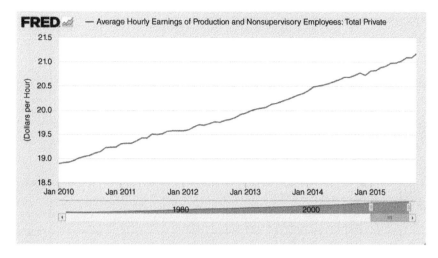

Figure 11.5 U.S. real average hourly earnings of production and nonsupervisory employees: January 2010–September 2015
SOURCE: U.S. Federal Reserve

$11 an hour starting on April 1, 2015. By the later part of 2015, evidence was already emerging that the minimum wage increases were having a negative effect on restaurant jobs in the Seattle area.

According to data assembled from the American Enterprise Institute, the Emerald City Metropolitan Statistic Area started experiencing a decline in restaurant employment around the beginning of 2015 (when the state minimum wage increased to $9.47 per hour, the highest state minimum wage in the country at that time), and the 1,300 jobs lost between January and June of 2015 represented the largest decline during that period since 2009 during the Great Recession.[4] The loss of 1,000 jobs in May 2015 following the minimum wage increase in April 2015 was the largest one-month job decline since a 1,300 drop in January 2009, again during the Great Recession.[5] Odds are high that similar results were likely to be seen as these higher minimum wages took effect in other cities and states.

Comments from the September 2015 U.S. Federal Reserve's Beige Book (a qualitative assessment of the U.S. economy, compiling findings from each of the 12 Federal Reserve districts) pointed out that concerns about upcoming minimum wage hike increases, as well as higher costs associated with the Affordable Care Act, were in fact relatively widespread.

Getting back to our Starbucks example, the line item on the company's income statement that would reflect these pending minimum wage hikes, as well as any changes in healthcare costs, would be "store operating expense." As seen in Figures 11.6 and 11.7, Starbucks had done a good job keeping its store operating expenses in check relative to revenue growth for most of 2015. Given what we suspected would be coming, this would be a line item to watch, as it could pressure profits and potentially result in the company needing to boost prices to maintain, if not add to, profits. Boosting prices can create a tricky situation, because past a certain point, it can turn a guilty pleasure, such as the pumpkin spice latte or peppermint mocha latte, into an expensive beverage that turns off consumers.

One of the final questions we ask after we've completed 90 percent of our monitoring homework is:

Have Wall Street analyst expectations changed over the last few weeks to reflect any of the answers to the above questions as well as any others that materially impact a company's business?

Before we start to answer that question, perhaps like Bob or Sophia, you've never heard the term "Wall Street analyst expectations" before. They're the consensus estimates for revenue, profits, or earnings per share that are obtained by averaging expectations from all of the investment professionals that publish their forecast for a particular company.

That's not as straightforward as it sounded inside our heads. Since we've been sticking with Starbucks, we can turn to Yahoo Finance! (or any other financial resource that publishes analyst expectations like Nasdaq.com or Bloomberg), and we find the average of the 25 analysts that publish earnings-per-share estimates for Starbucks was $0.43 for the quarter ending September 2015. You'll notice the "low estimate" and "high estimate" for that three-month time period—0.43 and 0.45, respectively—which gives us the expected earnings range for that quarter.

For the same three-month period, as Figure 11.8 shows, only 22 analysts have shared their revenue expectations and that average is $4.90 billion, up 17.1 percent year over year. Unlike the relatively narrow expected earnings range, the expected revenue range is much wider at $4.78 billion on the low side and $5.14 billion on the high side. As you can see, depending on the period of time, more or fewer analysts publish their forecasted figures.

STARBUCKS CORPORATION
CONDENSED CONSOLIDATED STATEMENTS OF EARNINGS
(in millions, except per share data)
(unaudited)

	Quarter Ended		Three Quarters Ended	
	Jun 28, 2015	Jun 29, 2014	Jun 28, 2015	Jun 29, 2014
Net revenues:				
Company-operated stores	$3,915.0	$3,290.5	$11,310.7	$9,702.3
Licensed stores	475.2	408.1	1,380.5	1,166.1
CPG, foodservice and other	491.0	455.1	1,556.7	1,398.7
Total net revenues	4,881.2	4,153.7	14,247.9	12,267.1
Cost of sales including occupancy costs	1,953.9	1,711.5	5,804.9	5,135.7
Store operating expenses	1,392.4	1,176.5	4,032.5	3,486.1
Other operating expenses	131.6	120.6	394.5	346.3
Depreciation and amortization expenses	236.5	180.1	659.6	524.2
General and administrative expenses	288.5	269.4	892.8	752.6
Litigation credit	—	—	—	(20.2)
Total operating expenses	4,002.9	3,458.1	11,784.3	10,224.7
Income from equity investees	60.3	72.9	168.0	183.9
Operating income	938.6	768.5	2,631.6	2,226.3
Gain resulting from acquisition of joint venture	—	—	390.6	—
Interest income and other, net	25.5	19.4	36.6	57.0
Interest expense	(19.1)	(16.4)	(52.3)	(47.7)
Earnings before income taxes	945.0	771.5	3,006.5	2,235.6
Income tax expense	318.5	259.0	899.7	755.4
Net earnings including noncontrolling interests	626.5	512.5	2,106.8	1,480.2
Net earnings/(loss) attributable to noncontrolling interests	(0.2)	(0.1)	1.9	(0.1)
Net earnings attributable to Starbucks	$ 626.7	$ 512.6	$2,104.9	$1,480.3
Earnings per share - basic	$ 0.42	$ 0.34	$ 1.40	$ 0.98
Earnings per share - diluted	$ 0.41	$ 0.34	$ 1.39	$ 0.97
Weighted average shares outstanding:				
Basic	1,498.5	1,503.5	1,499.3	1,507.9
Diluted	1,515.7	1,522.0	1,516.3	1,527.8
Cash dividends declared per share	$ 0.16	$ 0.13	$ 0.48	$ 0.39

Figure 11.6 Starbucks Corp. consolidated income statement, June 30, 2015
SOURCE: Starbucks Corp.

Starbucks Corporation (USD in millions)

	Quarter Ended		Three Quarters Ended	
	28-Jun-15	29-Jun-14	28-Jun-15	29-Jun-14
Company Operated Store Revenue	$3,915.0	$3,290.5	$11,310.7	$9,702.3
Increase	19.0%		16.6%	
Store Operating Expenses	$1,392.4	$1,176.5	$4,032.5	$3,486.1
Increase	18.4%		15.7%	

Source: Company reports.

Figure 11.7   Starbucks Corp. summary results, June 30, 2015
SOURCE: Starbucks Corp.

As we saw in the commodity input price charts, the cost side of the equation for a company can swing based on supply, demand, and other factors, like weather, for example, affecting coffee bean production.

What we needed to determine was if Wall Street's expectations had caught up with what had been going on in reality. In the case of Starbucks, as seen in Figure 11.8, per the EPS Trends box, there had been little change in earnings expectations for the September 2015 and December 2015 quarters as well as the year ending September 2016 [Note: Starbucks is what we call a "funny fiscal" because its fiscal year ends at the close of September, not December like the vast majority of companies].

Looking at that lack of change over the prior 90 days, and comparing it to the changes in coffee, dairy, wheat, and cocoa prices, there may be a reason to think those Wall Street expectations could be a bit conservative.

Viewing the earnings history box, however, we find that Starbucks seems to be one of those companies that tends to deliver exactly what's expected when it comes to its bottom-line earnings—note all the zeroes between EPS estimated, EPS actual, difference, and surprise percentage. This tells us that Starbucks is pretty adept at managing expectations for its revenues and earnings in upcoming quarters.

Now, why did we point all of that out?

In addition to knowing what's expected, we want to determine if there has been an upward or downward move in those expectations over the last week, month, or longer. If we see key input costs are moving in a direction that is favorable for a company—as we saw with coffee, milk,

Starbucks Corporation (SBUX) · NasdaqGS   ⊕ Add to Portfolio [f Like] ⟨1.8k⟩

57.09 ↑ 0.80(1.42%)

Analyst Estimates   Get Analyst Estimates for: [   ] [GO]

Earnings Est	Current Qtr. Sep 15	Next Qtr. Dec 15	Current Year Sep 15	Next Year Sep 16
Avg. Estimate	0.43	0.47	1.58	1.87
No. of Analysts	25.00	16.00	27.00	25.00
Low Estimate	0.43	0.46	1.57	1.80
High Estimate	0.45	0.50	1.60	1.91
Year Ago EPS	0.37	0.40	1.33	1.58

Revenue Est	Current Qtr. Sep 15	Next Qtr. Dec 15	Current Year Sep 15	Next Year Sep 16
Avg. Estimate	4.90B	5.39B	19.15B	21.40B
No. of Analysts	22	13	27	27
Low Estimate	4.78B	5.27B	19.03B	20.77B
High Estimate	5.14B	5.55B	19.38B	21.94B
Year Ago Sales	4.18B	4.80B	16.45B	19.15B
Sales Growth (year/est)	17.10%	12.30%	16.40%	11.80%

Earnings History	Sep 14	Dec 14	Mar 15	Jun 15
EPS Est	0.37	0.40	0.33	0.41
EPS Actual	0.37	0.40	0.33	0.42
Difference	0.00	0.00	0.00	0.01
Surprise %	0.00%	0.00%	0.00%	2.40%

EPS Trends	Current Qtr. Sep 15	Next Qtr. Dec 15	Current Year Sep 15	Next Year Sep 16
Current Estimate	0.43	0.47	1.58	1.87
7 Days Ago	0.43	0.48	1.58	1.87
30 Days Ago	0.43	0.47	1.58	1.87
60 Days Ago	0.43	0.47	1.57	1.86
90 Days Ago	0.43	0.47	1.57	1.86

Figure 11.8   Starbucks analyst estimates from Yahoo! Finance
SOURCE: Yahoo!

and wheat prices for Starbucks—or signs that revenues may be picking up because industry demand is improving or better yet both, but we don't see revenue or earnings expectations being changed to reflect those moves, it could be mean the group of analysts following the company are asleep at the switch. This could spell opportunity, as upside surprises tend to lead to pops in stock prices, particularly if the company issues a rosier than expected outlook.

Similarly, if costs are moving in the wrong direction and/or revenue looks to be hitting a serious headwind, and the analyst group hasn't updated its expectations to account for this, it could signal that a revenue or earnings shortfall could be had.

A few final thoughts on what it means to monitor a company and its business ...

Aside from all the data you're collecting, we encourage you to note your own observations as you move around in your day-to-day life. Are you seeing more of one product than another? What stores are experiencing long lines? Is there a new service that your friends are talking about, or one their kids can't stop using? Are once-busy stores now far less occupied with customers? All good fodder to track in your investing notebook!

When you see things like this, *always*, ask yourself, "What does that mean?" The answer will help cut to what is really going on. The last thing you want to do is get all excited about a long line in front of a new fast-food restaurant only to find out it's because there was a fire in the kitchen and customers are stacked up waiting for their orders.

Between those kickstarter questions, examples, and answers that was quite a bit to chew on. Here's a quick recap:

By looking at the developments in and around the companies that are at the heart of your investments ("We buy companies, not pieces of paper called stock certificates"), you can put noise into context and wind up with either confirming or warnings signals. You have to pay attention to the continuum of companies that surround the one you've invested in as well as any new ones that may enter the industry (Tesla and automobiles, for example).

Announcements such as better than expected revenues and new product instructions from customers could be bullish for your company, but if a competitor announces a new customer win or new product offering that ups the ante for your company, it could spell trouble. As you collect all of these data points—industry, company, supplier, competitor, and customer—the big question is, how does all of this impact the business of the company you've invested in? Asked another way (as we said, shifting one's perspective is helpful and insightful!), is the data tracking as expected, falling short, or stronger than anticipated?

Depending on the answer, it could mean that expectations for a company's revenues, profits, and bottom-line earnings need to be updated. If such adjustments are called for, that could mean the shares need to be revalued, so you will want to take another look at the numbers you came up with using the tools in Chapter 10's Question 12. This could alter the upside versus downside potential to be had, which may change your opinion on whether to continue to own the shares.

All of this ties to the final section, which is ...

Monitoring the Stock Price

This is where the rubber hits the road.

If you've never owned any stocks before, you might think that opening up your monthly brokerage statement and quickly reviewing your holdings is what we mean when we talk about monitoring a stock. To the almost 52 percent of Americans who do not own stocks, according to the most recent 2013 Survey of Consumer Finance published by the Federal Reserve[6] in 2014, this probably sounds rather logical.

Unfortunately, there's more to it than that. While reviewing your monthly statements should be *part* of your overall financial review, just like shoring up your checking and savings accounts, when we talk about monitoring a stock's price we have something else in mind.

Monitoring a stock's price centers not only on the movement of the actual share price—up, down, or essentially flat—from where you bought it, but also on how the valuation figures you put together toward the end of Chapter 10 have changed in response to the move in the share price and updated Wall Street expectations for your company's revenues, profits, and earnings per share. Don't get us wrong: We like to jump up and down when a stock that we own soars higher and get seriously frustrated when one drops more than expected, but to us it's primarily all about today's price relative to future revenues, profits, earnings, and cash generation that could fuel future dividend increases that drive tomorrow's price.

Think of the historical valuations you put together as you answered Question 12 in Chapter 10 as the historical framework, or what we like to call *bumper guards,* for the stock price. These bumpers help you understand the valuation multiples where your stock has peaked and bottomed in the past.

As a stock moves higher, we want to keep in mind the distance to its upper valuation bumper. As it climbs, the distance between the current valuation and that upper valuation bumper will shrink. In Wall Street speak, this means the valuation multiple is rising and the shares are more expensive relative to the company's earnings than they were before.

For example, let's say you bought shares in Company PDQ at $10 and it was expected to generate $1 in earnings per share over the coming 12 months. Pretty simply, PDQ shares would be trading at 10× those expected earnings. Based on your historical valuation work, you know that PDQ shares have peaked at 14× expected earnings and bottomed at 8× expected earnings, which gives rise to your net upside target of 20 percent in the shares —40 percent up to $14 (14 × $1.00) and down 20 percent to $8 (8 × $1.00). Don't you love how all of this from the last few chapters comes together?

Now after a few months, PDQ shares have climbed to $13, which means you are up 30 percent from your $10 purchase price. This means PDQ shares are trading at 13× the expected $1 per share in earnings, which is far closer to the upper bumper of 14×, and in Wall Street speak they are more expensive than the 10× earnings you paid for the shares a few months prior. At the $13 mark, you have upside of just under 8 percent to your $14 price target and potential downside of 38.5 percent to that lower bumper of $8. To us, situations like that, which have a negative net upside (+7.7% − 38.5% = −30.8%), do not have a desirable risk-to-reward trade-off.

What to do, what to do?

The good news is you have some options:

A. You could certainly continue to hold the shares if you were so inclined.
B. You could sell all of your PDQ shares, book a nice win, and use the returned capital and profits to buy another promising-looking contender, park the cash in your account until another well-priced opportunity came along, or you could do something fun with your gains.
C. A third option would be to sell a portion of your PDQ position, ringing the register and locking in profits on your sold shares while keeping some of the PDG position intact to potentially capture further upside. In Wall Street lingo, this is known as "taking some chips off the table" or "trimming the position."

In this case, of those three options, we would opt for option B for the following reasons:

- The shares have climbed 30 percent in a few months, which is a fantastic return considering the average annual return for the S&P 500 since its inception in 1928 through 2014 was approximately 10 percent.[7]
- The incredibly unfavorable risk-to-reward trade-off is −30.8 percent. Need we say more?

Generally speaking, we are fans of "taking some chips off the table" after the first 20 percent upside move. In the PDQ case, at the $13 level there was simply far more potential downside than upside to be had for our liking. Instead, we would recommend more risk-averse investors trim back their PDQ position after the shares hit $12, a 20 percent return from the initial $10 purchase price, by selling half their shares while keeping the rest in play. Even after booking that 20 percent profit, you would still have "skin in the game," meaning you have to continue your active monitoring duty.

Now what if during your initial monitoring activity of PDQ shares, earnings expectations for the company were revised higher to $1.20 per share from the $1.00 at the time you purchased your PDQ shares? It would mean you would adjust your upward price bumpers to $16.80 (14 × $1.20) and the lower bumper to $9.60 (8 × 1.20).

Of course, we would want to double-check that these P/E ratio derived bumpers still mesh with the other valuation metric bumpers you calculated back when you first were contemplating buying PDQ shares. If this sounds a bit fuzzy to you, review Question 12, "Is today's price right?" in Chapter 10. Should those other updated metrics confirm the revised bumper levels, your confidence level in them should be much higher. If, however, those other metrics do not confirm the revised bumper levels, then your confidence and comfort level should be low.

Even though we would still be inclined to trim PDQ shares back once they were up 20 percent from the initial purchase price (our rule of thumb!), the increased earnings expectation points to more potential upside to be had for the remaining portion of the shares you would continue to own if you only trimmed back half your original position.

At that $12 level with expected earnings now sitting at $1.20 per share, PDQ shares have potential upside of 40 percent (from $12 to $16) and potential downside of 20 percent (from $12 to $9.60), or net upside of 20 percent. Because you continue to own those remaining PDQ shares, they are part of your regular stock monitoring efforts.

As we hinted at above, upward earnings revisions are "fun" because more often than not, they drive stock prices higher. Negative revisions, also known as "cutting earnings" or "slashing the outlook," as you can imagine, have quite the opposite effect on stock prices—they tend to drive stock prices lower. In some cases, they go much lower. Under some market conditions, even a small miss for reported earnings versus the consensus expectations has led to sharp drops—in the range of 10 to 20 percent—for a company's stock price.

Case Study: DSW Inc.

Let's take a look at what happened with footwear and accessory vendor DSW Inc. (DSW), which on August 25, 2015, reported quarterly earnings of $0.42, missing the Thomson Reuters consensus estimate of $0.43 by $0.01 per share. DSW generated revenue of $627 million during the quarter, missing the consensus estimate of $636.86 million. That's a miss on the revenue line and the earnings line—in other words, a double ouch, which often generates a serious stock spanking from investors. DSW reiterated its guidance for fiscal 2015 net profit between $1.80 and $1.90 per share, up from $1.69 per share in 2014.

The combination of those two shortfalls saw DSW shares drop more than 11 percent in trading on August 25 to $27.28 from the closing price of $30.87 the day before. That is just one example, but there are more to be had with each quarterly reporting cycle.

If you were a DSW shareholder and you "bought and slept"—that is, did not do your proactive stock monitoring—you may not have picked up on the signs that DSW was in for a rough earnings patch. Some of the signs you could have seen were weak monthly Retail Sales reports published by the Commerce Department in the first half of 2015, the lack of wage growth materially above the rate of inflation in data released by the Department of Labor in 2014 and 2015, the huge increase in average credit card debt reported by CardHub for the second quarter of

2015, or the wide miss by Macy's (M) relative to expectations and the cut to its full-year outlook on August 12, some 13 days before DSW reported its quarterly results.

After that drop in DSW shares, the question an existing shareholder should have asked was, "Do I see enough net upside in the shares to warrant holding onto them?" The answer hinges on what you turn up when you've input the revised revenue, profit, and earnings expectations in your valuation work. We think that when a company misses by 2.3 percent on the quarterly figure ($0.01/$0.43), which is less than 1 percent on the annual figure and that sits at the midpoint of the $1.80 to $1.90 per share company guidance, an 11 percent drop in the shares could be appealing to new investors that are willing to roll up their sleeves. Investors could start buying here if they decide that the overall tone of the business is one that can support the company's outlook AND they are comfortable that there is enough net upside in the shares to meet their requirements. Again, we like to see at least a net upside of 20 percent.

Would we have been buyers of DSW shares on that pullback?

We wouldn't have been because even though DSW fits with our thematic view of the cash-strapped consumer, the economic signposts as of September 2015 would have had us rather concerned about consumer spending prospects and what that meant for traditional retailers, such as DSW. The company also faced a growing threat from the convenience of online shopping, most notably from Zappos, which lets customers return items free of charge. Talk about convenience that is hard to beat. Both of us will cop to buying several sizes of shoes via Zappos only to return all but the one that fit. Is it any wonder consumers continue to shift more and more of their shopping online?

In terms of DSW shares, even after that 11 percent pullback they were trading at a 1.6 PEG ratio (the September 18, 2015, price of $28.19 divided by $1.85 per share in earnings = 15.2x). We divided 15.2 by 9.5, which was the company's earnings growth rate for 2015 that we arrived at by dividing expected 2015 earnings of $1.85 per share by the $1.69 per share in earnings delivered the year before, which was significantly higher than the PEG dividing line of 1 that we talked about in Chapter 10.

Where would we have found DSW shares to be appealing? It would have depended on a couple of things.

To us, if we could have gotten comfortable with the company's ability to fend off threats from the growing competition while offering compelling products at attractive prices and were confident it could hit the 2016 EPS expectations of $2.08 per share, we would have put DSW shares on our watch list if either:

A. The shares dropped to somewhere between $20 and $25 versus the current share price of $28.19. Between that $20 and $25, the shares would have had a PEG ratio of roughly 1.0 based on the expected 2016 figure of $2.08 per share. We must reiterate that we would need to be comfortable with the company's business and ability to hit that figure; or

B. Signs emerged that DSW's earnings in the coming quarters were going to be stronger than expected—if signs emerged that the consumer were spending more than we expected, if we saw evidence that DSW was a recipient of that greater spending, and it increasingly looked like the company would deliver earnings closer to $1.95 per share in 2015 instead of the forecasted $1.85 per share, which would mean a PEG ratio just below 1.0 (vs. the PEG of 1.6 we mentioned above). We must reiterate that we would have to be comfortable with the company's business and ability to hit that figure.

After all these examples, there is still one nagging question: How do you know when to sell a stock?

Sell or Buy More?

This is one of the most common questions we get from both individual and seasoned investors and is almost as important as when to buy. As you've come to appreciate through the above examples, there is no hard-and-fast rule. There are rules of thumb to follow for sure, but because all of this is unfolding (just like a movie plot!), it requires the constant monitoring that we've been yammering on about in this chapter.

As we mentioned earlier, we like to trim back a position (meaning, sell some portion) after the shares climb 20 percent above our purchase price, provided the theme as well as data and company monitoring turn up reaffirming signals. If the signals are mixed, we may wait for some additional data to get a clearer picture. If the signals are turning negative, we may sell all the shares. As we do this, we are mindful of our upper and lower valuation bumpers, making sure to update them as new data and expectations—good or bad—become available, so that we always know where today's price fits in.

After trimming the position and making any adjustments to our valuation bumpers, we not only continue to monitor the trend and the company, we also continue to track the distance between current valuations and the valuation bumpers. As the distance between those two narrows, we are more inclined to trim back more of the stock position.

Let's get back to the PDQ share example from a few pages ago. Remember, in that example, you bought shares at $10 and the share climbed to $12 and based on revised expectations you boosted your price target to $16. If the shares continued to climb, reaching $13 and then $14, we would recalculate our net upside, and in doing so, we would find at $14 that there was now 14 percent upside to $16, but more than 28 percent downside to our lower price bumper near $10. Seeing this, we would complete another round of monitoring for PDQ, revising our valuation bumper calculations along the way. If the upper valuation bumper did not move higher and the net upside remained at −14 percent (+14% − 28%), we would likely close out our PDQ position, meaning sell all the shares, at $14.

What's the advantage to selling in that staged way?

That staged selling booked an initial 20 percent profit when we trimmed back at $12 and also freed up capital that we could have invested in another well-positioned stock at the right price, assuming there was one. By holding onto the remaining shares and exiting them at $14, we booked an additional 17 percent profit ($14/$12) on those PDQ shares. Averaging those two sell orders, our average return on PDQ shares was 30 percent, as shown in Figure 11.9.

There's nothing like making money along the way as a stock moves higher, but what about when a stock falls, like with the DSW shares? It depends.

Transaction Summary

Action	Company	Ticker	Price	Shares	Value
Buy	PDQ Inc.	PDQ	$10	100	$1,000
Sold	PDQ Inc.	PDQ	$12	50	$600
Sold	PDQ Inc.	PDQ	$14	50	$700
					$1,300
			Return on PDQ shares		**30%**

Figure 11.9   Trimming PDQ shares

What was the reason for the drop in the shares? How does it match up against any revisions to your upper and lower bumpers based on new data for the theme or the company? What was happening in the overall stock market that day or last few? What about the company's sector? What's happening with the stock prices of its competitors? Did a major competitor come out with some news that surprised the markets? Did a supplier hint to the markets that the company might have reduced its orders, indicating slowing sales? You need to look around to see what is driving the moves in the share price.

The answers to these types of questions as well as the magnitude of the pullback will dictate whether you should sell the shares, or use the pullback to buy more. Buying additional shares when the price falls to scale into or maintain your target portfolio weighting is a time-tested strategy that reduces your average cost as you build out your position size in a particular stock or ETF.

Figure 11.10 is an example of how scaling into a position works. You decide that you want to have 2 percent of your $100,000 portfolio invested in PDQ, but rather than buying it all at once, you decide to stage it in two steps. This is often a wise decision, as there is no way to know that in a week, shares won't be priced lower than today. We often scale into a position in three or more steps, unless there is a compelling reason to think the shares are likely to have bottomed out for a particular set of reasons. We are showing just two steps here, for the sake of brevity.

You purchase the first half, $1,000 at $10.00, which translates to 100 shares. After a few weeks, the share price falls to $8.89 and you decide to purchase the remaining portion. However, at this point your initial PDQ investment is no longer worth $1,000; it is now worth $889.

| Total Portfolio | | $100,000 |
| Target Allocation | 2% | $2,000 |

Transaction Summary

Action	Company	Ticker	Price	Shares	Amount Invested
Buy	PDQ Inc.	PDQ	$10.00	100	$1,000
Buy	PDQ Inc.	PDQ	$8.89	125	$1,111
			$9.38	225	$2,111
Sold	PDQ Inc.	PDQ	$12.00	225	$2,700
			Return on PDQ shares		**28%**

Figure 11.10   Scaling into PDQ shares

Other investments in your portfolio have actually gone up in value, so your total portfolio today is still $100,000. Today, to have 2 percent of your portfolio allocated to PDQ you need to purchase $2,000 – $889 = $1,111 worth of shares, which at $8.89 is about 125 shares. The total you have invested in the shares is the original $1,000 plus the second purchase of $1,111. Notice how you've purchased even more shares at the lower price, which helps lower your average cost on the shares to $9.38. When you sell all the shares at $12 per share, your total return will be 28 percent.

If the share price continued to fall further, but you were still convinced of the fundamentals of the business, you could purchase even more shares to maintain a 2 percent position in PDQ in your portfolio. This would only be reasonable, however, if you have good reason to believe that the market is simply mispricing the shares.

For more risk-averse investors, there are trading tools like stop-loss orders and stop-limit orders that can help minimize your losses. Much has been written on them and their differences, which you can read more about at Investopedia. Our rule of thumb for using those tools kicks in only after we have built out our entire stock position over the course of several buys, generally between two and four transactions. We tend not to go "all in" on a stock in one fell swoop, but instead prefer to use pullbacks in share price to build out the position at lower prices. Once we've reached a targeted position size relative to our overall portfolio, then we may utilize a stop-loss or stop-limit order on that position. As this particular stock climbs higher, we would revisit those stop-loss and stop-limit orders, boosting them as needed; we see that as part of our regular stock-monitoring program.

We must give you a word of caution here on stop-loss or stop-limit orders, as they do have their dangers. If you set a stop-loss at say 10 percent below today's price and in a week the stock drops 10.2 percent, the order will be triggered and your shares will automatically be sold. The problem is, the stock could have just experienced a wacky quick dip (technical term) to that level for mere minutes and within a week be up higher than where it was when you set the stop-loss. This is the challenge with using an automated trigger. Then again, if you are on vacation and shares of the stock go on a rapid descent, a trigger could be a lifesaver. Automatic triggers can be particularly dangerous during periods of heightened market volatility, when everything is moving up and down more dramatically, so carefully consider the pros and cons.

A happy medium for some may be to set up alerts that send you an email or a text if the stock price drops by, say, 8 percent if you think you might want to sell after a 10 percent decline. This way you'll know you need to pay very close attention and figure out what is causing the stock price decline, so if it does fall 10 percent, you'll have determined if you want to trim back or sell the entire position, use the drop to build your position size at more attractive prices, or do nothing and keep your position size intact as is. Most online brokerage services have this alert capability.

We also like to decide ahead of time just how much we are willing to let the price fall before we sell completely out of the stock or fund. Stock prices can occasionally fall despite the fundamentals remaining strong—for example, when there is a major market correction after a prolonged bull run. When that happens, it is better to just get out as quickly as possible and then buy back in at a lower price once things have settled down and you've had time to double-check your other indicators and key data to make sure the fundamentals are still intact. The challenge is that we only know after the fact that it was a major correction.

During such a time, many will argue, "Today, it is all going to turn around," and sometimes they are right. As a general rule of thumb, we don't like to let a position drop much more than 15 percent before we get out, unless there is some compelling reason to stay in. Occasionally, if we are dealing with something that we know will be unusually volatile, we'll expand that to 15 to 20 percent. It is important to have these rules set up beforehand so that if/when the time comes, we don't find ourselves double-thinking and getting all tied up in emotional knots about not wanting to give up.

In our view, it is far better to take the emotion out of the equation as much as possible. Establish the price at which you will get all out and stick with it. As the price of a stock moves up, we typically also move our "floor" price up. One of the best ways to make money over the long run is to minimize how much money you lose. That sounds pretty obvious, but it is really easy to follow a company's shares further and further down, every day thinking, "Tomorrow it'll turn around, I just know it!" Any seasoned investor will tell you that mentally wishing a stock higher rarely works.

Here are some helpful reminder questions to summarize what we've been talking about:

- Are the valuation metrics you looked at in Question 12 in Chapter 10 getting too high relative to your company's peer and/or historic multiples? This means the stock price may be getting to a point where you consider selling at least some.
- Have you uncovered something in the theme or in your company monitoring that has either raised or lowered revenue, profit, and/or earnings expectations? Is it a short-term blip or has something fundamentally changed?
- Are the shares trading at even more attractive valuation multiples than before? If you are still convinced of the fundamentals, you could consider adding more to maintain your target allocation for your portfolio (e.g., a stock that has fallen in price now represents 2 percent or your portfolio instead of your initial target of 3 percent).
- Has the upside-to-downside trade-off shifted enough to warrant buying the shares, or despite the changes to the valuation metrics, the potential upside-to-downside trade-off remains the same? If the metrics have not improved, you'd likely not want to purchase even more.
- Have expectations been revised higher by the Wall Street community over the last few days or weeks, or have they moved lower? How does this affect your "bumper" price points?

Just like with exercise, the more you do this, the easier it will become. Along the way, you'll put pieces together quicker, draw conclusions easier, and be more comfortable in "all the math" that comes with valuing and revaluing a stock.

What will help you get in fighting shape is the fact that you need to do all of this monitoring for each individual company stock that you own. So, the more stocks you own, the more time you should be spending on monitoring. That's why we recommended you think about how much time you can regularly devote to this kind of recurring "homework" because you'll also want to update your portfolio contender list along the way as well. If you own 10 stocks, we think you should have somewhere between 3 and 5 on the bench.

Taking stock, pun intended, of the answers to these questions and the others we've shown you along the way is all part of the regular maintenance you need to perform on your investments. To us, it's a lot like taking care of your car. Once you buy a new car, or a used car as we're seeing more and more with the cash-strapped consumer, you drive it home, and before too long you've racked up a few thousand miles. At that point, you have some regular maintenance on the vehicle—changing the oil, brake pads, tires—all the things that will keep it humming for you. From time to time, there could be damage, maybe from an accident, a rock putting a crack in your windshield, or something else unforeseen that is beyond repair and forces you to get a new car. If you forget to change the oil, past a certain point it will start to affect performance of your vehicle; forget too long, and it could lead to even bigger problems.

Where this comparison breaks down is that most people have one or maybe two cars, but in a portfolio you may have several stocks to as many as two dozen. There is no simple rule that says if you spend X minutes a week per stock then you will be fine. There may be some weeks when you spend a lot of time reading up on one particular company, and because of the frequency of the data and other information you should be tracking, others may take only a fraction of that.

We can tell you first hand that the first few weeks of quarterly corporate earning season (January, April, July, and October) can be more time-consuming as hundreds and hundreds of companies issue press releases, hold conference calls, and submit filings to the SEC.

During this time, it helps to stay focused on just those companies you want to track, and luckily websites such as Seeking Alpha and several others furnish transcripts of corporate earnings conference calls. In our experience, reading several of them side-by-side can prove far more insightful than listening in real time to just one. If you plan ahead and stay focused, it need not be overwhelming. You can do this!

Cocktail Investing Bottom Line

Just as you take care of your health with regular medical and dental checkups, mixed with eating right and regular exercise, so, too, does your investment portfolio need regular care and monitoring. Conditions in the global economy change over time, as does the political landscape and the prevailing narrative, particularly if a new disruptive or enabling technology is poised to unleash creative destruction on a particular industry or three. Just keep paying attention the way we've discussed throughout this book and you'll find it all becomes like riding a bike.

- In addition to monitoring government supplied data, to stay up to date and informed, be sure to track other indicators such as customer, supplier, and competitor press releases, financial filings, and other commentary such as conference presentations to help you put all the investing puzzle pieces together to determine if a Cocktail Investing trend is heating up or cooling off.
- Be diligent in your reading of various business periodicals, financial news websites, and industry trade publications to stay abreast of the prevailing narrative, all the while looking for confirmation as well as potential changes in the vector and velocity for both your Cocktail Investing Thematic and your corresponding investment(s).
- Monitor movements in your investments against the Cocktail Investing Thematic data points you are tracking (obesity levels, average household income levels etc.) as well as the valuation framework to determine if you should be holding steady, scaling into the security position, or trimming back.
- When monitoring your investments, do not fall in love with them, as emotional attachments to stocks tend to hinder investment returns rather than help.

Cocktail Investing Final Thoughts

- You will make mistakes. Even the greatest investors in the world experience surprise losses. It happens and you should treat them as learning experiences, rather than beating yourself up over them and fearing trying again. Figure out what you did that didn't work, know that the best of the pros have had whopping mistakes as well, and move on.
- Not all your investment decisions will work out the way you think. Investing is all about probabilities. There are no guarantees. Know when to cut your losses and move on.
- Do not fall in love with your holdings. We have seen this happen time and time again, with people hoping, believing, and in some cases trying to wish their stocks higher. Stick to what the data tell you.
- Do not buy your entire stock position at once. Ease into it and build it out across two to three transactions, depending on the net upside to be had. We like to use pullbacks to scale into or build out our position size because it helps improve our average cost basis.
- Do not put all your eggs in one basket. For every thematic tailwind, there are a few ways to invest in it; you just might have to wait for the right net upside to emerge.
- Try to focus on areas that really draw your interest, and don't forget to have fun along the way. Investing can be frustrating when you are searching for data that you think are available but can't locate. The more interested you are in the particular investing theme, the less annoyed you'll be by the bumps along the way. That's why we recommend you begin with one of the Cocktail Investing Themes you find most interesting.
- Visit us for more tips and information at CocktailInvesting.com!

Cheers, and here's to a successful investing life!

Endnotes

1. Giselle Abramovich, "Apple Leads Streaming Video Battle: ADI," CMO by Adobe (June 4, 2015), www.cmo.com/articles/2015/6/3/apple-leads-streaming-video-battle-adi.html.
2. Brett Feldman, "Verizon Communications' (VZ) CEO Lowell McAdam Presents at Goldman Sachs Communacopia Brokers Conference (Transcript),"

Seeking Alpha (September 17, 2015), seekingalpha.com/article/3517776-verizon-communications-vz-ceo-lowell-mcadam-presents-at-goldman-sachs-communacopia-brokers-conference-transcript?part=single.

3. Ryan Knutson, "Sprint Escalates Wireless Price War with Half-Off Bills," *Wall Street Journal* (December 2, 2014), www.wsj.com/articles/sprint-escalates-wireless-price-war-with-half-off-bills-1417533378.

4. Mark J. Perry, "Minimum Wage Effect? From Jan. to Sept. Seattle MSA Restaurant Jobs Fell −700 vs. +5800 Food Jobs in Rest of States," *AEIdeas* (October 21, 2015), www.aei.org/publication/minimum-wage-effect-from-jan-to-sept-seattle-msa-restaurant-jobs-fell-700-vs-5800-food-jobs-in-rest-of-state/.

5. Ibid.

6. "2013 Survey of Consumer Finances," www.federalreserve.gov/econresdata/scf/scfindex.htm.

7. J.B. Maverick, "What's the Average Annual Return for the S&P 500?" Investopedia, www.investopedia.com/ask/answers/042415/what-average-annual-return-sp-500.asp.

Appendix: Definitions, Metrics, and Resources

An investment in knowledge pays the best interest.

— *Benjamin Franklin*

More important than the will to win is the will to prepare.

— *Charlie Munger*

W e've presented you with a lot to absorb, and in a few places we referred you to the Appendix. The first half of this Appendix follows up on several topics from Chapter 2 (investment services, online brokerage services, and more), and offers a deeper dive on bonds, the yield curve, and more from Chapter 9 (Designing Your Portfolio). Finally, because we are all about data—collecting and using data to put the investing puzzle pieces together—we've shared several of our go-to resources to help get you going. We're always looking for new resources and repositories of information, which is why we recommend you check with our more in-depth and regularly updated resource list at www.CocktailInvesting.com.

Chapter 2

There are a lot of investment services out there, so we've just listed a few that we've personally used and/or thought useful. For a more complete and more up-to-date list, please visit the website for this book at www .CocktailInvesting.com.

Newsletter Services

- MarketWatch List of Ten Newsletters to Read: www.marketwatch .com/story/10-investment-newsletters-to-read-besides-buffetts-2015-03-02.
- Various publications and subscription options are at TheStreet.com (Full Disclosure: At the time of publication, Chris Versace and Lenore Hawkins were responsible for a subscription-only, investing newsletter service at The Street).
- Morningstar.com provides a variety of subscription newsletter services for ETFs, mutual funds, and individual stocks. Morningstar .com also provides extensive research on all of the above through premium subscriptions to its site.
- Company Notes Digest from Avondale Asset Management is a free weekly collection of quotes about the economy and industry derived from transcripts of earnings calls and presentations during the week, available at avondaleam.com.
- Gluskin Sheff's Breakfast with Dave is a subscription-only, daily newsletter written by David Rosenberg at www.research .gluskinsheff.com/epaper/viewer.aspx.
- Hussman Funds Free Weekly Market Commentary by John Hussman, Ph.D. is at www.hussmanfunds.com/weeklyMarketComment .html.
- Mauldin Economics, a collection of free and subscription newsletters, is available at www.mauldineconomics.com.
- Things That Make You Go Hmmm, by Grant Williams, is a subscription newsletter at www.ttmygh.com.
- Forbes Investing Newsletters, a selection of subscription newsletters from a range of authors, is at www.forbes.com/newsletters/all/.

Online Brokerage Services

- Nerd Wallet has a good tool for comparing options given the amount you expect to hold in your account and an estimate of the number of trades you may execute per month—www.nerdwallet.com/investing/best-online-broker#

  Additional opinions can be found at:

- Barron's—www.barrons.com/articles/SB51367578116875004693704580502703510707706?alg=y
- Investor Guide—www.investorguide.com/article/online-broker-comparison-guide/
- The Street—www.thestreet.com/online-trading/compare-best-online-brokers.html

Questions for a Potential Investment Advisor or Broker

- Forbes 10 Questions to Ask a Financial Advisor, www.forbes.com/pictures/el45gejei/10-questions-to-ask-a-financial-advisor/
- CNBC 10 Tough Questions to Ask a Financial Advisor, www.cnbc.com/2014/10/15/10-tough-questions-you-need-to-ask-your-financial-advisor.html
- MarketWatch 25 Questions for a Financial Advisor, www.marketwatch.com/story/25-questions-for-a-potential-financial-adviser-2014-06-19
- Kiplinger What to Ask a Financial Advisor, www.kiplinger.com/article/investing/T023-C000-S001-what-to-ask-a-financial-adviser.html

Most importantly, make sure you fully understand every way in which the broker or advisor is compensated! And don't be afraid to say, "What does that mean?" so you have a clear understanding of the services, products, and fees an investment advisor is proposing to you.

Chapter 9

To many, bonds are a lot more straightforward to understand than stocks because all you are really dealing with is (1) yield and (2) default risk.

Here is a basic primer on bonds. For more information, you can visit this book's website at www.CocktailInvesting.com.

A Brief Tour of Bonds

Traditionally, bonds have been used to provide relatively stable income streams, coupled with reduced risk of losing any part of the initial investment, referred to as the *principal*. Thanks to actions taken by the Federal Reserve and other central banks around the world, interest rates as of the writing of this book are so low that the income streams from most sovereign and corporate bonds are so low that many investors have chosen to forgo them completely in their portfolios. Historically, very low interest rates also introduce additional risk, as a bond purchased today will be worth less tomorrow if interest rates rise materially. When interest rates are rising, bond prices are falling, and vice versa. This is called an *inverse* relationship because the two move in opposite directions. This makes intuitive sense—if you buy a bond that pays 3 percent interest when the prevailing interest rate is 3 percent, after rates rise to 8 percent, the bond would obviously be worth a lot less.

Individual bonds are often also more difficult to buy and sell than stocks. For example, Charles Schwab clients can simply log on to their online account and buy or sell a stock using the stock's ticker symbol but can only trade bonds by calling Schwab and speaking with a fixed-income specialist. A fund, mutual, or ETF that invests in bonds, however, is no more difficult to buy and sell than a fund that invests in stocks. One example is the iShares 20+ Year Treasury Bond ETF that trades under the ticker symbol "TLT." As the name of this ETF suggests, it tracks U.S. Treasury bonds with remaining maturities greater than 20 years. It's far simpler to buy such an ETF than it would be for an individual investor to buy those bonds directly. For most investors, the most cost-efficient and lower-risk way to invest in bonds will be through funds.

Some bonds, such as U.S. Treasury bonds and municipal bonds, may be tax exempt, meaning that income and capital gains realized on the bonds are not subject to state and/or federal taxes, which is appealing to many investors. This feature, however, is not useful in a tax-deferred account such as an IRA or 401(k). Since investors do not have to pay taxes on these bonds, they typically offer lower yields, which makes sense for taxable investment accounts, but again is not helpful in a tax-deferred account.

Unlike stocks, bonds for the same company can vary widely based on the terms of the bond indenture, which describes the legal characteristics of the bond. Since each bond is different, it is important that you understand the precise terms before investing. If you are interested in purchasing specific bonds, first make sure to *read the bond's prospectus*. With bonds you need to make sure you understand these three things:

- Maturity
- Risk
- Yield

Maturity. The maturity date is the date that the bond investor will have the principal, also called par, returned and all interest payments cease. For example, an investor purchases a 10-year bond on January 1, 2015, for $1,000 with a $1,000 face value, yielding 5 percent, with a maturity date of December 1, 2025. The bond makes its coupon payments twice a year, on June 1 and on December 1. The investor would receive 5 percent a year, paid half in June and half in December, until December 1, 2025, when they would receive the final interest payment and the $1,000 principal. Generally speaking, a short-term corporate bond has a maturity of less than five years, while an "intermediate" bond matures in 5 to 12 years and long-term matures in more than 12 years.

Risk. Risk refers to the probability that the bondholder (the investor) will not be paid according to the terms of the bond through to the bond's maturity date. The bond's risk can be assessed by knowing if the bond is secured, the bond's liquidation preference, the callability of the bond, the credit risk of the bond issuer, and interest rate risk.

A *secured* bond is backed by specified assets of the company, which can be used to repay bondholders in case the company cannot honor the bond. A bond's *liquidation preference* refers to the order in which the bondholders stand in line if the company were to go bankrupt. When a company goes bankrupt, it pays its creditors and investors in a particular order. The most senior debt is paid first; then more junior debt with common stock shareholders is paid last. The *callability* of a bond refers to a feature of some bonds called a *call provision,* which allows the bond issuer to pay off the bond before its maturity date. If you purchased a bond with an attractive yield and the company called the bond early, you would then have to find another investment to replace it, which could be difficult or impossible, making you worse off.

Next, *credit risk* refers to the likelihood that the issuer will be able to honor all the terms of the bond. In the case of a corporate bond, it refers to the likelihood that the company will be in sufficient financial health to continue to pay through to maturity. Credit rating agencies such as Standard & Poor's, Moody's, and Fitch rate bonds based on the likelihood the issuer will be able to honor them. Ratings go from AAA or Aaa, which is the best credit, to D, which is already in default. Bonds rated BBB to Baa or above are considered "investment grade." Most bonds with C ratings or lower carry a higher risk of default, and in order to compensate for this potential risk, yields tend to be very high compared to investment-grade bonds. These higher-risk, higher-yielding bonds are referred to as *high-yield* bonds.

Many mutual or exchange-traded funds will not allow for investments in any bonds that are not investment grade. Many pension funds exclude high-yield bonds as well, which gives an additional level of risks to these bonds as the universe of potential purchasers is much smaller than for investment-grade bonds. That is something to consider if you are interested in buying less than investment-grade bonds—you could have a tougher time selling them.

Finally, you need to consider *interest rate risk*. If interest rates fall, the bond will be worth more, but if rates increase, the bond will be worth less. This means you should consider where we are in the economic cycle and corresponding monetary policy moves by the Federal Reserve when contemplating buying bonds. Swings in a bond's value also depend on the bond's yield and maturity, which we will discuss next.

Yield. While bonds sound to many like something rather exotic, the secret truth is that a bond's price may be even easier to understand than a stock's. In her career as an investment advisor, Lenore has met with countless bond fund managers who have confessed after a cocktail or two that they'd never leave the bond world, as equity pricing just baffles them!

We are going to get a little bit into the math here, but after a couple of examples you'll get the hang of it. Most bonds sold in public markets have a "face value" of $1,000 and pay interest twice a year; these are called coupons—think of grandma religiously clipping her coupons twice a year. The face value means that at the end of the life of the bond, the owner will receive $1,000.

The interest rate quoted with the bond is an annual rate; thus, a 5-year, 6 percent bond would pay ($1,000 × 6 percent / 2) = $30 twice a year for five years. If you owned this bond until it matured in five years, you would receive $30 twice a year for five years, for a total of $300 in interest payments. The best way to think of a bond is to compare it to an interest-only mortgage, but in this case you are the bank. Twice a year, you receive mortgage payments, and at the end of the mortgage term, in this case the bond's maturity date, you will receive the full "face value" of the mortgage, which as we said is typically $1,000 for an individual bond. In this example, the total return over the five-year period would be the $300 in interest payments, plus the $1,000 face value at maturity, or $1,300.

Zero-coupon bonds pay no annual interest. Thus, a zero-coupon bond will simply pay the owner $1,000 at the end of the life of the bond. The interest is in effect paid in a lump sum when the owner buys the bond for less than $1,000. That is, buying a $1,000 bond with one year to maturity for $900, gives the owner an 11 percent return: ($1000 − $900) / $900 = 11 percent.

One other thing to keep in mind is that when people talk about bonds, they rarely use the term *interest rate* and instead use the term *yield*. For example, investors will say "Company XYZ's 10-year bonds are yielding 5 percent" instead of "the interest rate paid out on Company XYZ's 10-year bonds is 5 percent."

That's the basics, so let's get into the real-life application, because although a bond may have a face value of $1,000 and pay a 4 percent interest rate, which is referred to as the *nominal yield* (or the interest rate (to par value) that the bond issuer promises to pay bond purchasers), you aren't necessarily going to buy it for $1,000. It could be priced exactly at its face value of $1,000, or at a premium (which means more than $1,000) or at a discount (which mean less than $1,000).

The *effective interest rate* you receive, which is referred to as current yield, is going to be different depending on whether you buy it at, below, or above par. A bond with a 4 percent nominal yield pays 4 percent of $1,000, which is $40. If you buy this bond for $900, your current yield on it would be greater than 4 percent. It would be

$$\$40/\$900 = 4.44 \text{ percent}$$

This makes intuitive sense since you paid less than $1,000 for it; the current yield should be greater than the nominal yield.

Now the tricky bit here is that when people talk about how bonds are priced, they don't talk about the actual amount you would pay to purchase the bond. Instead, they talk about the current yield. So you'll hear things like, "The U.S. 10-year Treasury bond is currently priced at 1.9 percent." That tells you that you'll get a 1.9 percent return over the remaining life of the bond, regardless of what the nominal yield may be for the bond.

So let's figure out what you would have to pay to buy a bond. Let's assume that we have a normal $1,000 face value bond with five years left "priced" at a 3 percent current yield, but with a 4 percent nominal yield. How much would you pay for it? The amount you would pay is simply the present value of all the future cash flows—namely, $40 every year until year 5, when you would receive the $1,000 face value in addition to the $40 coupon.

If you really want to understand present value versus future values, just hang out with a kid. They understand this concept quite intuitively. Do you want a piece of candy now or in an hour after you finish your homework? There isn't a sane kid on the planet that would prefer the same amount of candy an hour later. The only way any sane kid would opt for candy an hour from now rather than right now is if you offer them more if they wait. The interest rate (yield) is how much more candy they require to wait an hour. The higher the interest rate (yield), the more they prefer now versus later.

Present value $= $ (Cash received at time t)/(1 + Current yield)t

The coupons are $40 ($1,000 face value × 4 percent and to keep it simple in this example the bond just pays 4 percent once a year).

So the present value of the first year's coupon of $40 is

$$(\$40/(1 + 0.03)1 = \$38.83$$

The present value of the second year's coupon of $40 is

$$(\$40/(1 + 0.03)2 = \$37.70$$

The present value of the third year's coupon of $40 is

$$(\$40/(1 + 0.03)3 = \$36.61$$

Notice that as the payments get further away from today, they decline in value. You may also hear of this process being referred to as the discounted cash flow, because future cash is discounted relative to today's cash. The 3 percent yield is also the discount rate in Table A.1.

Thus, at a 3 percent yield, the price for a 5-year, 4 percent bond with one payment a year is $1,045.80. Notice that a bond that pays 4 percent costs more than its face value of $1,000, when the yield is 3 percent. Bonds priced above face value are said to be priced at a *premium*.

What if the yield were 5 percent, higher than the rate on the bond? How would this affect price? Table A.2 shows how a higher yield affects the price.

When yields are higher than the coupon rate the bond pays, the bond price is below the face value of $1,000. Bonds priced below the face value are said to be priced at a *discount*. Why is this?

In order to get a 5 percent yield, meaning for an investor to get a 5 percent return on a bond that is only paying 4 percent, the price of

Table A.1 Present Value of the Cash Flows for All Five Years

Year	Cash Flow	PV of Cash Flow
1	40.00	38.83
2	40.00	37.70
3	40.00	36.61
4	40.00	35.54
5	1,040.00	877.11
TOTAL (Price)		$1,045.80

Table A.2   Present Value of Cash Flows with a
Higher Yield

Year	Cash Flow	PV of Cash Flow
1	40.00	38.10
2	40.00	36.28
3	40.00	34.55
4	40.00	32.91
5	1,040.00	814.87
TOTAL (Price)		$956.71

the bond needs to be less than the face value of $1,000. For an investor to receive a 3 percent return on a bond that pays 4 percent, the investor would have to pay more than the face value of $1,000.

Please also note that bonds are priced using a basis of 100; thus, a bond with a face value of $1,000 that is priced at $956.71 would be referred to at a price of 95.671. In this way, bonds with face values of $1,000, $5,000, or $10,000 can be easily compared by simply dividing their respective prices by either 10, 50, or 100 to get them all to an equal base of 100. For example, a bond with a face value of $5,000 that is priced at $4,890 would be quoted at $4,890 / 50 = 97.80. A bond with a face value of $10,000 and priced at $11,310 would be quoted at $11,310 / 100 = 113.10. This makes it easier to compare the $5,000 bond to the $10,000 bond.

So what about the impact of inflation on bond prices?

Interest rates reflect the cost of borrowing money. That cost is affected by the rate of inflation. When inflation is low, interest rates tend to be lower than when inflation is high. When inflation is higher, the purchasing power of the original amount loaned declines significantly; thus, the lender must increase the interest rate charged to make up for that loss of purchasing power. For example, with no inflation, a lender charges you 5 percent to borrow $100 for one year. If inflation is known to be 2 percent for the next year, the lender would charge you at least 7 percent (5 percent for the cost of borrowing + 2 percent to take into account the loss of purchasing power due to inflation). Thus, in inflationary periods, interest rates are higher.

Now you might be wondering how a bond you buy today would be affected by changes in interest rates in the future. What if interest rates were to suddenly rise? How can you evaluate the impact that could have on various bonds you are considering buying?

As of the writing of this book, we were experiencing interest rates that were phenomenally low by historical standards. The low rates could continue for a while, but eventually rates should normalize, and that would have an impact on the price of the bonds. Investors can estimate what will happen to the prices of bonds when interest rates change using something called *duration*.

Bond duration can be thought of as the weighted average term to maturity of a bond's cash flows. How awful is that description?

What that means is that *duration* is a measure of the sensitivity of the price of a bond to a change in interest rates. For those familiar with the Capital Asset Pricing Model (CAPM), duration is analogous to the way beta is a measure of stock's sensitivity to fluctuations in the market. Duration allows us to evaluate the impact of changes in interest rates on bonds with differing maturities and coupon payments by taking into account both the interim and the final coupon payments, weighting earlier cash flows as being more valuable than later ones. With that in mind, it is fairly intuitive to think that those that give more payments or bigger payments to you sooner are less sensitive than those that give you more of the payments later.

The quick answer is that the price of a bond with a higher duration will fluctuate more with changes in interest rates than a bond with a lower duration. We can also see that duration is related to the bond's maturity.

When all else is held constant, the longer the term to maturity, the higher is the bond's duration. The higher the bond's duration, the more sensitive the bond's price is to changes in interest rates. This means that an eight-year bond will be more sensitive to changes in interest rates than a two-year bond.

When all else is held constant, the higher the yield, the less sensitive the bond's price is to changes in interest rates. This means that the price of a 5-year bond with a 6 percent yield is less sensitive to changes in interest rates than the price of a 5-year bond with a 3 percent yield. If you want details on how to calculate a bond's duration, please visit this book's website at www.CocktailInvesting.com.

Yield Curve. The other aspect of bonds yields that is important because it is a meaningful metric for both the bond market and the economy is the yield curve. We briefly touched on this in Chapter 5 (The Impact of Politics and Regulation on Investing), when we discussed how the U.S. Treasury affects interest rates. The yield curve is defined as *a line that plots the interest rates, at a set point in time, of bonds having equal credit quality, but differing maturity dates.* Translation: When people talk about the yield curve, they are typically referring to the different rates paid by U.S. Treasuries at different maturities (meaning for different lengths of time such as six months, one year, five years, etc.). As we run through the business cycle, the yield curve typically starts off with an upward slope, with short-term rates lower than long-term rates as is shown in Figure A.1, which is referred to as a normal yield curve. This makes intuitive sense as lending someone money for six months is less risky than lending it to them for 10 years. A lot can happen in 10 years that can change the borrower's ability to repay the loan. A lot can happen that might make you wish you hadn't lent them the money by, say, year three. In order to compensate for the greater risks of lending for a longer period of time, the interest you get paid on that loan must be higher, the longer you lend.

When investors expect that interest rates are not going to change over time, the yield curve flattens, as shown in Figure A.2, so that short-term rates are the same as long-term rates, giving investors little incentive to lend for longer periods of time. The consequence to this is that borrowers tend to have shorter-term loans than they would like.

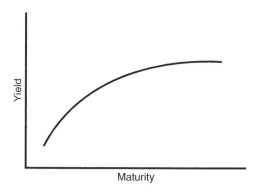

Figure A.1   Normal yield curve

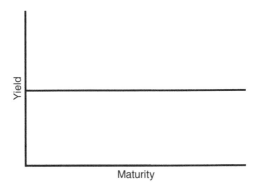

Figure A.2   Flat yield curve

For example, say you are building a factory and need to borrow a portion of the funds needed to build the factory. Given that it will take some time to build it and have the factory generating enough money to start paying off the loan, you would like to get a long-term loan. If investors are not interested in lending long-term thanks to a flat yield curve, you will need to either forgo the project or take the risk of borrowing on a shorter time frame than you would like. What's the risk there? Say you are only able to borrow the funds you need for three years. This means you need to either pay back the entire amount or get a new loan after three years, but the factory isn't expected to be built and fully functional to the degree that it will generate sufficient cash to even pay the interest on the loan for four years. This factory is expected to generate an 8 percent return. Today you borrow at 3 percent, which means you make 5 percent net with this factory. You decide to risk it, but at the end of the third year, interest rates have unexpectedly tripled to 9 percent. With this new cost of borrowing, the factory no longer makes financial sense because it actually loses money (generates 8 percent but borrowing costs 9 percent so you lose 1 percent). No bank is going to lend you the funds you need at this point, so you default on your loan and now the lenders own a partially constructed factory that in the current climate never should have been built. Everyone gets hurt.

Sometimes the flat yield curve is an intermediary step to an inverted-yield curve, shown at right. This is when short-term rates are actually higher than longer-term rates as shown in Figure A.3. This is

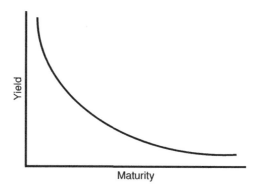

Figure A.3   Inverted yield curve

the rarest form and is often the precursor to a recession. The yield curve inverted in 2000 and again in 2006/2007, prior to the financial crisis.

When short-term interest rates exceed long-term rates, market sentiment suggests that the long-term outlook is poor and that the yields offered by long-term fixed income will continue to fall. An inverted yield curve also has an impact on homebuyers financing their properties with adjustable-rate mortgages (ARMs). These types of mortgages have interest-rate schedules that are periodically updated based on short-term interest rates; thus, when short-term rates are higher than long-term rates, payments on ARMs tend to rise. When this occurs, fixed-rate loans may be more attractive than adjustable-rate loans. For investors, an inverted yield curve allows for better returns with short-term investments.

When the yield curve becomes inverted, profit margins for companies such as community banks, which borrow cash at short-term rates (from depositors) and lend at long-term rates (loans such as mortgages), shrink. Many investment managers who oversee large funds are often forced to take on increased risk in order to achieve their desired level of returns when rates are pushed extremely low, which increases the overall level of risk being taken in the markets, which naturally makes markets more volatile.

We covered quite a bit of ground rather quickly, and for those who look to learn more on bonds, check www.CocktailInvesting.com for more resources.

REITS

REITs (real estate investment trusts) can be useful income-generating investments. When looking at REITS, investors should assess the company using much of the same 12 questions we discussed in Chapter 10 (Choosing Your Investments). REITs are different, though, in that they are required to pay out their income to shareholders. There is a wide range of strategies employed by REITs, from those that invest in mortgages to those that invest in retail space, office space, or even data storage facilities. There are some excellent online resources for learning more about the specifics of REITs, a few of which we list here:

> www.reit.com
> www.kiplinger.com/article/investing/T044-C000-S002-practical-
> investing-why-you-need-reits.html
> www.bankrate.com/finance/investing/investing-in-reits.aspx

Master Limited Partnerships (MLPs)

Master limited partnerships, or MLPs, are also potentially useful income-generating investments that operate largely in the energy sector. There are some excellent online resources for learning more about the specifics of MLPs, a few of which we list here:

> www.investopedia.com/terms/m/mlp.asp
> www.fidelity.com/viewpoints/investing-ideas/mlp-interest-growing
> personal.vanguard.com/pdf/ISGPMLP.pdf

Economic Indicators and Data Sources

If we were to list all of the various data sources that we have tracked or currently do track, we would probably have several dozen pages to add to the Appendix and odds are your eyes would either glaze over somewhere in the middle or you would think we are far more nuts than you do now. What can we say—we love data! But not all data is the same, and as we've said more than times than we can count in *Cocktail Investing* and elsewhere, you must investigate below the headlines and crosscheck data from multiple sources to confirm what you are reading, hearing, or seeing.

Over the coming pages are what we consider to be a "starter set of data." Much like that first kit of Tupperware that has several pieces to get you going, you will probably want more, as what you have in front of you becomes familiar. Before we share that starter set with you, however, we wanted to offer a few rules of thumb:

- Whether it's online or not, read newspapers (the *Wall Street Journal*, the *New York Times, Barron's,* and so on) as well as online news sources (CNBC.com, Reuters, MarketWatch, and the like), magazine articles, newsletters, and even investment blogs, all the while noting the data they are presenting as well as its source. You'd be surprised how you can build your own resource guide by proactively noticing such items. One particularly easy way to do this is to note sourcing information for data presented in tables and charts.
- As best you can, try to read the above publications from a different geography, which could mean reading the *LA Times* if you live on the East Coast as well as scanning *The Guardian, BBC News,* or other international publications. We do this on a regular basis, taking note of the various data sources as well as other confirming data points for our investing themes.
- The government and its various branches are a treasure trove of information, ranging from economic data to reports and other statistics. Is the data perfect? No, but it is what most economists and investors use, so to us it offers a good starting point that we build on. The same can be said with the U.S. Federal Reserve as well as the various Federal Reserve banks that publish regional economic data and related findings. Spend some time poking around these resources, and be mindful of getting too focused on esoteric details that, while interesting, may not be beneficial to you and your investing journey.
- Keep an investment journal to collect these data points and sources so you can crosscheck them much like we mentioned above. It's far easier to compare if you have the data easily accessible. We will both cop to being notebook carriers, with Chris having one for each company back in his equity research days, but in addition we also use services like Feedly and Evernote, as well as web browser bookmarks to collect and access information from almost any device, including our iPhones. We are also both fans of the Texture app, which brings

dozens of magazines to our fingertips for far less than subscribing to each one individually.

- When digging into a particular company, note the data the management team discusses in its press releases, financial filings (especially the 10-K), quarterly conference calls, and investor presentations, which all can be found on the Investor Relations section of the company's website. We'd recommend going one step further and doing the same for that company's key customers and suppliers as well as competitors so you have as complete a picture as possible when it comes to your data needs and resources.

General Economy

- American Institute for Economic Research
- Baltic Dry Index
- Briefing.com—Economic Calendar
- Bureau of Economic Analysis
- Federal Reserve Bank of Chicago—National Activity Index
- Federal Reserve Bank of Philadelphia—Business Outlook Survey
- Federal Reserve Bank of St. Louis—FRED® Economic and Financial Database
- The Economic Statistics Briefing Room
- U.S. Census Bureau—Economic Indicators
- U.S. Federal Reserve—Economic Research and Data

Consumer

- Bureau of Economic Analysis—Personal Income & Spending
- Cardhub.com
- Consumer Credit Report
- Consumer Insights
- Michigan Consumer Sentiment Index
- National Restaurant Association
- National Retail Federation
- Nerdwallet—American Household Credit Card Debt Statistics
- The Conference Board—Consumer Confidence
- U.S. Census Bureau—Retail Sales
- World Food Situation Report

Commodities

- CME Group
- Energy Information Administration
- IndexMundi.com
- The Plastics Exchange
- U.S. Department of Agriculture

Demographic Data

- Centers for Disease Control and Prevention
- Employee Benefit Research Institute
- National Institute on Aging
- National Institute on Retirement
- Statistical Abstract of the United States
- U.S. Census Bureau

Employment and Jobs

- ADP Employment Report
- Challenger, Gray, and Christmas Job Cut Report
- Daily Job Cuts
- Employee Cost Index
- Gallup—Payroll to Population
- Job Openings and Labor Turnover Survey
- U.S. Bureau of Labor Statistics—Monthly Employment Report

Financial Industry

- Center for Capital Markets Competiveness
- Investment Company Institute
- MergerMarket
- Moody's
- Morningstar
- Pensions & Investments
- Standard & Poor's
- U.S. Department of the Treasury
- U.S. Federal Reserve

Housing and Construction

- American Highway Users Alliance
- U.S. Census Bureau—Housing Starts and Building Permits, New Home Sales, Housing Vacancies and Homeownership, and Construction Data
- FHFA Housing Price Index
- Mortgage Bankers Association
- National Association of Homebuilders
- National Association of Realtors—Existing Home Sales
- The Standard & Poor's/Case-Shiller Index

Industrial and Manufacturing

- Advance Report on Durable Goods
- American Association of Railroads
- American Trucking Association
- Cass Freight Index
- U.S. Census Bureau—Factory Orders
- Copper Prices
- U.S. Federal Reserve—Industrial Production and Capacity Utilization
- Institute for Supply Management
- Markit Economics U.S. and Global PMI Indices
- National Fluid Power Association
- Regional Federal Reserve Bank Manufacturing Surveys

International and Trade

- ADR.com
- Bank for International Settlements
- Central Intelligence Agency—The World Factbook
- ChinaDaily.com
- Euromoney
- Eurostat
- International Monetary Fund
- Markit Economics
- National Bureau of Statistics of China

- Organization for Economic Cooperation and Development
- U.S. International Trade in Goods and Services
- U.S. International Transactions
- United Nations
- World Bank

Inflation

- Bacon Cheeseburger Index
- U.S. Bureau of Labor Statistics—Consumer Price Index (CPI), Producer Price Index (PPI), Productivity and Unit Labor Cost, and Average Hourly Wages

Regulatory and Political

- Code of Federal Regulations
- Competitive Enterprise Institute
- Govtrack.us
- Politico
- The Washington Post
- U.S. Debt Clock

Technology

- Cisco Visual Networking Index
- Consumer Electronics Association
- CTIA—The Wireless Association
- Global Semiconductor Alliance
- GSM Association
- IC Insights
- Juniper Research
- National Cable & Telecommunications Association
- Semi.org
- Semiconductor Industry Association

Magazines, Newspapers, and Other Publications*

- Barron's
- BBC News

---

* We've excluded the obvious list of news sources that would include the *Wall Street Journal*, the *New York Times*, the *Financial Times, Money, Forbes, Fortune,* and similar publications.

- Bloomberg BusinessWeek
- El Mundo
- Investor's Business Daily
- La Republica
- Le Monde
- MarketWatch
- Reuters
- TechCrunch
- The Daily Mail
- The Economist
- TheStreet.com
- Yahoo! Finance
- Zacks.com

Other Research and Information Sources

- 24/7 Wall Street
- ABI Research
- EY Insights
- Gallup
- GE Capital Insights
- Investopedia
- Nielsen
- NPD Group
- PNC Bank Economics
- StockCharts
- Wall St. Pit
- WikiInvest
- YCharts

Again, for more resources, check www.CocktailInvesting.com, and by all means, if you have a particularly favorite resource that you think we need to know about, head to the website and let us know about it. We're always on the hunt for new ones.

About the Authors

Lenore Elle Hawkins is an investor, a perpetual student of economics, a great lover of fine wines, and an exuberant dancer, particularly while cooking. She possesses an excessive adoration of dogs, an overabundance of stilettos, and an endless desire to find the humor in life.

Lenore is a founding partner at Meritas Advisors, where she serves as the firm's chief investment strategist, with over 20 years of experience in finance, strategic planning, risk management, and asset valuation; her focus is primarily on macroeconomic influences and long-term trends. In addition to her duties for Meritas clients in the United States, she also provides consulting services for ultra-high-net-worth families in Europe. She is also the co-manager of the Growth Seeker portfolio for TheStreet along with Chris Versace, her co-author for this investing tome, and is the author of the blog EllesEconomy.com.

Lenore is a regular guest on a variety of national and international radio and television shows. She appears frequently with Neil Cavuto, on both of his Fox Business Network and Fox News Channel program, along with Maria Bartiromo and Stuart Varney on the Fox Business Network. She has often appeared on One America's News Network, RT and America's Morning News as well as having been featured multiple times on Real Vision Television. She is also a regular speaker at international investing conferences.

Lenore previously served as the vice president of corporate development for a boutique wealth management firm, which provided coordinated financial planning, investment management, tax, insurance and estate planning services to its high-net-worth clients. Before that, she served as the vice president of strategic planning and corporate development for National Mobile Television, the largest mobile broadcasting company in the United States, where she was responsible for evaluation of investment opportunities and the design and implementation of complex corporate financial and operational structures. Lenore has also worked with JP Morgan in the Private Client Services practice. She began her career with Accenture, where she led consulting teams advising financial services clients, such as the Capital Group (a group of investment management companies including the American Funds, Capital Bank and Trust, and Capital International Funds), Industrial Indemnity, and Charles Schwab.

Lenore is a member of the Mont Pelerin Society, whose members include Nobel Prize recipients, economic and financial experts, high government officials, and legal scholars from all over the world. She is also on the board of directors for The Dreyfuss Initiative, founded by Richard Dreyfuss, whose objective is to provide America's youth and society at large with the tools necessary to be effective stewards of a representative democracy. She has an undergraduate degree in mathematics and economics from Harvey Mudd and Claremont McKenna and an MBA from the Anderson School at UCLA.

Lenore enjoys two bases for her work, one in sunny San Diego, California, and the other in the beautiful town of Genoa, Italy, which lies south of Milan, between Portofino and Monte Carlo on the Mediterranean Sea. While logging entirely too many frequent-flier miles every year for any sane person, the dual continental life seems to suit her, as she believes that nothing beats Genovese pesto and a rich Barolo, except perhaps dinner on the Pacific Ocean in Del Mar with a big bowl of guacamole, fish tacos, and a spicy marguerita on the rocks with salt.

On the opposite side of the ledger is **Chris Versace**, better known as The Thematic Investor and otherwise referred to as the seat-stealer, a self-proclaimed nerd who has been analyzing industries, companies, and stocks for more than 20 years. While many were sweating the thought of what job they were going to find out of college, Chris, ever the contrarian, was busy planning a backpack tour through Europe. After his return, he spent the next two years teaching high school, then landed a career in equity research that has spanned several bulge bracket investment banks and more miles hopping the globe than he cares to remember. From industrial equipment and machinery to homebuilders and building products to technology and more, he's covered them all.

After several years of near-constant travel across the United States, Europe, and Asia, during which time he met with both big and small corporate management teams to bend their ears and hit them with a barrage of questions designed to improve his understanding of their business and where it was headed, he was burned out. After taking some time off, he started creating portfolios for others and worked with some boutique investment banks on several transactions before returning to the research world with his own product—*The Thematic Investor* newsletter. Aimed at institutional and individual investors, *Thematic* looked at the intersection of economics, demographics, psychographics, technology, regulatory mandates, and more to ferret out those companies and their respective shares that were best positioned to ride major tailwinds of change. Ultimately, *Thematic* morphed into Tematica Research, a firm that serves up thematic insights to seasoned investors as well as professional investors and corporate clients. Tematica is home to the investment newsletter *Tematica Investing* and *The Monday Morning Kickoff* as well as related trading services. Along the way, he has written a weekly column for the *Washington Times,* become a contributor to Real Money Pro at TheStreet and FoxBusiness.com, and become a professor at the New Jersey City University (NJCU) School of Business. He also co-manages the Growth Seeker and Trifecta portfolios for The Street.

Chris is a frequent guest on radio and TV programs, including Making Money with Charles Payne and Cavuto on the Fox Business Network, TheStreet TV, One American News Network, America's Morning News, The Chris Salcedo Show, The Sam Sorbo Show, The Edward Woodson Show, and several others. He is a frequent speaker and panel facilitator at The Money Show, Freedom Fest, and the American Association of Individual Investors.

Chris has also hosted PowerTalk, a weekly podcast that looked at key issues across a range of industries with guests such as Steve Forbes, former Secretary of Defense Donald Rumsfeld, Dr. John Lott, Lou

Dobbs, Niall Ferguson, Stephen Moore, Charlie Gasparino, Douglas Holtz-Eakin, former Secretary of Commerce Carlos Gutierrez, and Peter Schiff. On the program, he also conducted long-format interviews with executives from General Motors, Visa, Qualcomm, InterDigital, IBM, Cisco Systems, Skyworks Solutions, Slingbox, KEYW Holding, Domino's Pizza, Panera Bread, Smith & Wesson, Staples, and others, as well as discussed industry-shaping events with key members at the Consumer Electronics Association, the National Association of Development Companies, and the Truckload Carriers Association. Talking with people in the know and to companies is a great way to connect the dots and put things into perspective, and Chris is noodling a return to podcasting. Stay tuned.

Like Lenore, Chris is a voracious reader, a collector of data points, and a firm believer that simply trusting in headline reporting to understand what is truly happening in the world, in an industry or with a company, is likely going to get you into trouble. He dons his Sherlock Holmes–style investing cap, digs deep into the data, and wades through all sorts of reports, financial filings, and third-party surveys and studies to put the pieces together.

Chris's indulgences run the gamut from dark chocolate and red wine to attending more than 35 Bruce Springsteen concerts. For Chris, Springsteen is all about the intensity. Even in his 60s, the man can rock the house, spending up to four hours on stage, tracing his rich back-catalog of songs or trotting out a cover tune that brings the house down. As comedian John Stewart said of Springsteen, "He empties the tank," and that's what Chris does when looking at the palate of industries, companies, stocks, and exchange-traded funds (ETFs).

Together, Chris and Lenore, using many of the strategies discussed inside *Cocktail Investing,* co-manage the Growth Seeker model portfolio at TheStreet. We put small and mid-cap companies through their paces, looking at the shifting landscape of economics, demographics, psychographics, technology, policy, and more to identify those companies best positioned to capitalize on thematic tailwinds. At the same time, we look to sidestep those that will be left behind, like the guy who has one too many celebratory cocktails.

Index

Page references followed by f indicate an illustrated figure; followed by t indicate a table.

Printed and bound by CPI Group (UK) Ltd, Croydon, CR0 4YY

13/04/2025

14656499-0002